Politics and
Government
in California

THOMAS Y. CROWELL COMPANY

NEW YORK · ESTABLISHED 1834

NINTH EDITION

Politics and Government in California

Bernard L. Hyink
California State University
Fullerton

Seyom Brown
The Brookings Institution

Ernest W. Thacker
Los Angeles Valley College

79428

California is worth fighting for.

HIRAM JOHNSON

Third Printing

Copyright © 1975, 1973, 1971, 1969, 1967, 1965, 1963, 1961, 1959
by Thomas Y. Crowell Company, Inc.

Library of Congress Cataloging in Publication Data

Hyink, Bernard L
    Politics and government in California.

    Includes bibliographies.
    1. California--Politics and government--1951-
I. Brown, Seyom, joint author. II. Thacker, Ernest W.,
joint author. III. Title.
JK8725 1975.H9   320.4'794   75-8928
ISBN 0-690-00809-0

Thomas Y. Crowell Company
666 Fifth Avenue
New York, New York 10019

Cover design by Incentra International Inc.

Manufactured in the United States of America

Contents

Preface to the
Ninth Edition

The present political scene in California bears a remarkable
resemblance to the situation that sixteen years ago stimulated the writing of the first edition of this book. Then as
now, Californians appeared to be dissatisfied with the handling of the complicated task of governing their complex
state. The voters had just elected Democrat Edmund G.
Brown governor after Republicans had occupied the statehouse for several terms. The Democrats also captured every
state executive position except one, and were elected com-
manding majorities in both houses of the legislature.

The year 1975 is hardly a replica of 1959, however,
and the new chief executive, Edmund G. (Jerry) Brown, Jr.,
is anything but a carbon copy of his father "Pat." The
younger Brown takes office with a larger legislative majority
for his party, but with fewer solid ties to the party organization; the expectation is that he will have fewer sources
of leverage in Sacramento than did his father.

In the late 1950s, the state's two major political parties
were influential in California life and highly respected;
grass-roots movements were attracting many political ama-
teurs to become active in the Democratic club movement

and the Republican Assembly. Today, in the wake of Watergate, politics and politicians are viewed more suspiciously than ever, as reflected in the unprecedented low voter turnout in the 1974 elections.

At the time of the first edition, California's population was growing exponentially. Now it appears to have reached a plateau. What used to be the major challenges to the state government—securing more water and building more highways and schools to accommodate the burgeoning population—have been supplanted by a new set of challenges: caring for the quality of the environment, eliminating social injustices, countering the energy crisis, and dealing simultaneously with inflation and high unemployment.

Appropriately, the ninth edition is the most thorough revision since the book first appeared. A new chapter has been added on political campaigning, party organizations, pressure groups, and lobbying; and other chapters have been substantially rewritten. Special attention is given to the newly adopted revisions of the California constitution, the recent changes in rules for the Democratic presidential primary, the controversy over Governor Reagan's tax initiative, the significant changes brought about by Proposition Nine (passed in June 1974), and the effects of the new plan for legislative sessions. Also featured are a streamlined outline of the present state administrative structure and an analysis of the present financial status of the state government. The final chapter consists mainly of new material on emerging issues in the fields of social justice, the welfare system, public order, energy, transportation, and ecology.

In the preparation of this edition we were helped by interviews with numerous Californians active in the state's political process, particularly Diane Brooks of the Los Angeles County Chamber of Commerce, Joseph R. Cerrell and Harvey Englander of Cerrell Associates, Evon Gottlieb of the Los Angeles League of Women Voters, José Gomez of the United Farm Workers, Frank Harding of the Hugh Flournoy campaign, Toni Kimmel of the California Democratic Council, Joyce and Ed Koupal of the People's Lobby, William Schward and James Wood of the AFL–CIO (COPE), Bonnie Parks and George Sawyer of the California Chamber of Commerce, Lee Sanders, Ken Smith, and Rob

Smith of Common Cause, Lou Warner of Jerry Brown's office, and Kirk West of the state controller's office.

We wish to express our special appreciation to Steven Darrow Brown for his assistance in research and analysis and for conducting interviews.

The California Phenomenon

lmost everything about California is phenomenal. Its favorable climate and abundant resources generated such an overwhelming population boom, from 100,000 in 1850 to twenty-one million in 1970, that one could imagine the continent tilting toward the Pacific Ocean. But this tremendous influx so strained the Golden State's carrying capacity—degrading its climate, depleting its resources, polluting its waters, jamming its highways—that the inmigration rate has been declining in recent years. Once considered the national leader in the politics of growth, California is now challenged to show the way in the new politics of resource conservation, environmental care, land use, and coastal zone management.

Following the reapportionment of 1971, California outranked every other state in political power; it now has the largest representation in Congress and the most electoral votes. The 1970 census provided the basis for the congressional reapportionment giving California forty-three seats in the House of Representatives, compared to the thirty-eight she held after the 1961 reapportionment. As a result, her weight in selecting the president of the United

1

States increased from forty to forty-five electoral votes. And New York was displaced from the number one position she had long held in Congress, the electoral college, and the national nominating conventions. California has become the most influential and powerful state in national politics. In 1960, 1968, and 1972 the Republican party nominated a Californian for president of the United States and in three previous national conventions chose a Californian as vice-presidential nominee (one of whom became chief justice of the United States Supreme Court). Richard M. Nixon, a Californian, was elected president in 1968 and 1972. From 1953 through 1968, the Republican floor leader or whip in the United States Senate came from the Golden State. And any California governor, by virtue of his office alone, is automatically considered by his party as a possible presidential or vice-presidential nominee.

Because of its size, its political clout, and its reputation for firsts, both in problems and in reforms, California politics and government are evermore in the national and world spotlights.

States with the Most Electoral Votes

1951–60		1961–70		1971–80	
New York	(45)	New York	(43)	*California*	*(45)*
Pennsylvania	(32)	*California*	*(40)*	New York	(41)
California	*(32)*	Pennsylvania	(29)	Texas	(27)
Illinois	(27)	Illinois	(26)	Illinois	(26)
Ohio	(25)	Ohio	(26)	Pennsylvania	(25)
Texas	(24)	Texas	(25)	Ohio	(25)

WHEN AND WHY THEY CAME TO CALIFORNIA

From the time that the early Spanish explorers named the northwest coast of New Spain after the land of dazzling wealth portrayed in a novel by García Ordóñez de Montalvo, "California" has been a beckoning gleam on the horizon—a "great expectation" to millions of people. Some have en-

CONGRESSIONAL DISTRICTS BY COUNTIES

(Reapportioned by state supreme court effective 1974. Each congressional district had an approximate population of 464,486.)

1. Siskiyou, Modoc, Trinity, Shasta, Lassen, Tehama, Plumas, Glenn, Butte, Sierra, Yuba, Nevada, Placer
2. Del Norte, Humboldt, Mendocino, Lake, Napa, part Sonoma
3. Sacramento
4. Colusa, Solano, Sutter, Yolo
5. Marin, part San Francisco
6. San Francisco
7. Contra Costa
8. Parts Alameda, Santa Clara
9. Alameda
10. Parts Alameda, Santa Clara
11. San Mateo
12. Parts Santa Clara, San Mateo
13. Santa Clara
14. El Dorado, Amador, Alpine, Calaveras, Tuolumne, Mono, San Joaquin, part Sacramento
15. Parts Stanislaus, Fresno
16. Monterey, San Benito, Santa Cruz
17. Kings, parts Tulare, Fresno
18. Inyo, Kern, part Tulare
19. Santa Barbara, parts San Luis Obispo, Ventura
20. Parts Ventura, Los Angeles
21. Los Angeles (San Fernando Valley)
22. Los Angeles (Burbank, Glendale)
23. Los Angeles (Beverly Hills to Encino)
24. Los Angeles (Hollywood region)
25. Los Angeles (downtown, east Los Angeles)
26. Los Angeles (Alhambra, Glendora areas)
27. Los Angeles (Santa Monica, south coast)
28. Los Angeles (Inglewood, Culver City)
29. Los Angeles (Watts area)
30. Los Angeles (Monterey Park, El Monte)
31. Los Angeles (Hawthorne, Compton areas)
32. Los Angeles (San Pedro area)
33. Los Angeles (Whittier, Downey)
34. Parts Los Angeles, Orange
35. Parts Los Angeles, San Bernardino
36, 37. Parts San Bernardino, Riverside
38, 39. Orange
40. Parts Orange, San Diego
41, 42. San Diego
43. Imperial, part San Diego

visioned adventure, many have hoped to find material security, and others have dreamed of glamour and bright lights.

Each year since the American whalers and fur trappers began arriving in the early nineteenth century, there have been substantially more arrivals than departures. Thus, while the population of the United States has been increasing during the past century at an average rate of 40 percent every twenty years, California's population has nearly doubled every twenty years. But the expansion from fewer than 15,000 in 1846, when the American military authorities took California from Mexico, to more than 21 million by 1973 has not come from a *steady* flow of migrants. There have been periods when immigration was comparatively low, and some demographers predict that the 1970's will be one of these periods (see page 9). Within every twenty-year period, however, there has been at least one stimulus to a major population invasion from other parts of the country. By highlighting these major invasions and the explosive pattern of the state's growth, some of the unique political and governmental problems discussed in the following pages can be better understood.

Nineteenth-Century Invasions

THE GOLD RUSH   The news that James Marshall had struck gold on the shore of the American River in January 1848 brought a rush of adventurous young men, most of whom were between eighteen and twenty-five, almost all unmarried. Not all found gold, however; so they went into lumbering, agriculture, and business, and sent for women. By 1860 the population of California was 380,000, and residents born in other states outnumbered the natives two to one.

THE RAILROAD BOOM   When the Union Pacific Railroad, built westward from Omaha, was hooked up with the Central Pacific Railroad, built eastward from Sacramento, the trade and migration bottlenecks through the High Sierra passes were cleared. In 1869, the new capitol building was dedicated at Sacramento as if it were a new capitol of the United States. From 1870 to 1880 the resultant increasing land values and commercial expansion stimulated a population rise of nearly 55 percent. This was also the period when California acquired her large Chinese population, most of whom had been imported into the country by the railroad builders to work as coolie labor. Thousands were laid off in 1876 when the Southern Pacific completed its line down to Los Angeles, but they later became a permanent and productive part of California's work force.

Twentieth-Century Invasions

THE "BLACK GOLD" RUSH   Southern California was found to be rich in oil lands at the turn of the century when oil began to displace coal as the major source of industrial power. The state's oil output increased twelvefold from 1900 to 1910. As the geysers spurted skyward so did property values, attracting real estate developers and land speculators into the Los Angeles area by the thousands.

During this period the agricultural areas were converted from grazing lands to wheat fields, orange groves, and truck gardens requiring a large itinerant labor supply. Further Chinese immigration had been stopped by exclusion acts that grew out of the political turmoil of the latter nineteenth century (see discussion of Kearneyism in Chapter Four), so new labor sources had to be found. Farm organizations waged large publicity campaigns throughout the East, Midwest, and South. "Reduced railroad fares,

CALIFORNIA'S POPULATION

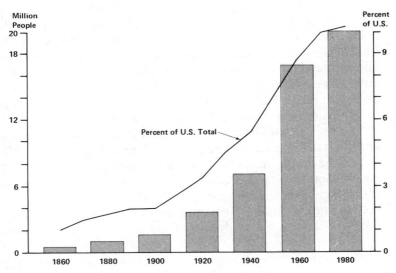

Source: 1860–1970 U.S. Bureau of the Census

gaudy pamphlets, and silver-tongued traveling salesmen were all part of the pitch to lure white laborers to the coast."[1] Not enough came to meet the demand, so the farmers and ranchers turned to Japan, Mexico, and the Philippine Islands for cheap labor.

With a developing industrial southland and a broad central farm belt feeding the thriving commercial area around San Francisco, California looked like a sure investment. Young men and women from the older states, anxious to stake out a claim in this mine of many untapped veins, boarded trains at Boston, New York, Philadelphia, and Chicago in confident mood. And the state's population jumped to 2.5 million by World War I.

THE PROSPERITY PUSH Though the population increase slowed during World War I, the prosperous twenties gave California 2 million new residents. The value of oil continued to increase. The horse and wagon were pushed to the side of the road by the new gasoline-consuming autos, buses, trucks, and airplanes. California oil producers found the Panama Canal a quick and inexpensive route for shipping oil east to sell at competitive prices. Then, in rapid succession, a series of large new fields were discovered in the Los Angeles area. The Huntington Beach strike in 1920 was followed by the Signal Hill and Santa Fe Springs strikes the next year and the Kettleman Hills bonanza in 1928. People with money to invest descended upon the southern California area. Refineries were developed to turn the crude oil into gasoline on home grounds. Improved transportation and refrigeration meanwhile sped California vegetable produce and fancy fruits to eastern markets, which in addition to enriching the growers helped to advertise California.

The most publicity, of course, came through the movies and the radio. In snow-bound Maine and Minnesota, people heard the radio announcer describe the balmy Rose Bowl weather on New Year's Day; and the local movie screens in Pittsburgh, Cleveland, and Oskaloosa were animated billboards showing palm trees and movie starlets rollicking in the surf. They used to dream of going to Florida, but now

[1] Kathleen C. Doyle, *Californians: Who, Whence, Whither* (Los Angeles: Haynes Foundation, 1956), p. 29.

California came to be regarded as the nation's playground, or a place to spend one's later years lolling in the sun living on dividends and annuities. The young people came for excitement, the middle-aged came to get in on the ground floor of a sound economic venture, the old came to retire— and all together they pushed the state's population skyward at a rate of 200,000 a year.

THE DUST BOWL EXODUS   After the crash of 1929, immigration slowed to a trickle. But in the thirties a huge migrant labor force from Oklahoma, Arkansas, and other prairie states crowded into California. When the dust blew away the topsoil from their small farms and the Depression blew away their small savings, they headed west. They heard that there was fruit rotting on the vines in California just waiting to be picked (it was not picked because it could not be sold), and they came to California with their large families because they had no place else to go. This time the state's population growth (three times as fast as the nation's) was not an indication of economic health.

THE SIEGE OF THE SERVICEMEN   World War II brought many young men to California who might otherwise never have come. Three hundred thousand servicemen who had been stationed there decided to stay after being discharged. Many others went home, talked about the climate and the oranges, and convinced their families it was worth a try. The process was repeated during the Korean War with effects yet incalculable.

THE INDUSTRIAL BOOM   World War II, in addition to bringing the servicemen to California, brought heavy industry supported by government subsidies, loans, and cost-plus contracts. The burgeoning of the aircraft industry— Douglas, Hughes, Convair, North American, Lockheed— converted placid suburbs like Santa Monica and Burbank into humming cities. Allied industries providing parts and supplies to the major aircraft producers were also given impetus. The big steel companies were encouraged by Washington to establish and expand California plants; Kaiser built a huge steel mill in the middle of Fontana's vineyard with the help of a loan from the Reconstruction

Finance Corporation. The San Francisco Bay Region experienced an industrial revival from the stimulus of wartime shipbuilding. California's oil industry particularly thrived as the state became the fuel station for tankers servicing the Pacific fleet. And new electrical supplies, chemicals, and small tools industries got their start. Civilian employment nearly tripled in manufacturing industries from 1941 to 1945, while other urban employment remained relatively constant. By the end of the war California's population approached 10 million.

Peacetime brought stimulus to California's entertainment industry, especially after television began to make use of Hollywood's talent, facilities, and know-how. Simultaneously, California's infant electronics and plastics industries became giants.

The Korean War and the cold war gave another fillip to heavy industry (for example, Kaiser's $65-million addition at Fontana) and a demand for a larger urban work force—skilled, semiskilled, and unskilled. The great migration of the 1950's was composed primarily of wage and salary workers, and civilian employment in manufacturing registered a 70 percent gain between 1950 and 1958. Manufacturing displaced the retail and wholesale trades as the top employer. California industry has grown considerably over the past twenty years. The expanded market in California and rising national freight rates brought many manufacturing plants to the state.

The 1970 census shows that the state added about 6 million persons to the 1960 population, a gain of approximately 38 percent—an average of 1645 new residents every day. In terms of the labor force, 650 workers were added each day, and the state was having more and more difficulty absorbing them. Since 1969, the state's large aerospace industry has had to lay off thousands of workers due to the decrease of governmental contracts. As a result, the unemployment rate rose to over 7 percent in 1970.

A "POSTINDUSTRIAL" SLUMP? The aggregate population growth figures for the 1960's cover over a rather dramatic decline in "net migration," that is, the difference between the number of people moving into the state and those moving out. Whereas in the early 1960's, the net migration was over 300,000 annually, by the early 1970's the rate had dropped to under 50,000 a year. Fewer people were now coming, and more were moving away than at any time since World War II. And those who came were more quickly disenchanted. "The bloom is off the rose," explained California opinion analyst Mervin D. Field, as he displayed a 1971 poll showing a drop in the percentage of Californians who thought the state was one of the best places to live (73 percent in 1967, 64 percent in 1971). The biggest complaints among the dissatisfied were, first, air pollution, then too many people, high taxes, the cost of living, and finally crime and violence in the streets.[2]

A STATE, AND A STATE OF MIND

There are as many ways of looking at California as there are people who have come here. One of them, Richard Armour, puts it this way:

I Loved You, California

California, here they come:
Doctor, lawyer, merchant, bum.
They come by car and train and plane,
Straight from Kansas, Georgia, Maine,
Massachusetts, Minnesota,
Iowa and North Dakota.
Rich folk, poor folk, young folk, codgers,
Moving westward like the Dodgers.

Here they come, and here they are,
Living, dying in a car,
Ever moving, dawn to dark,
Looking for a place to park.
Drive-in movies, drive-in cleaners,
Drive-in spas for burgers, wieners,
Drive-in banks and colosseums,
Drive-in (one-way) mausoleums.

Under and over
In Chevy or Cad,

[2] Steven V. Roberts, "Many Californians Leaving as Glamour Wanes," *New York Times*, September 12, 1971.

Some, caught in a clover-
Leaf, slowly go mad;

While some, with scant leeway,
Slow-reaction-time men,
Miss a sign on the freeway,
Aren't heard of again.

Here, superlatives abound;
"Best" and "most" are all around:
Finest roads and oldest trees,
Biggest universities,
Hottest day and highest lake,
Lowest point and hardest quake,
Most of most, no ifs or buts,
First in peaches, pears—and nuts.

Build a house upon a hill,
Or a cliff, so that you will
Get a view of row on row
Of other houses down below.
Out with trees, and don't lament;
Fill the valleys with cement.
Thus is nature redesigned
By the modern one-tract mind.

Bulldozers aren't dozing
By night or by day;
They're opening, closing
And gnawing away,
Making molehills of mountains
(The golf course now rules),
Turning lakes into fountains
And swimming pools.

So leap with joy, be blithe and gay,
Or weep, my friends, with sorrow.
What California is today,
The rest will be tomorrow.

What California then will be
Is something I'd as soon not see.[3]

[3] Richard Armour, "I Loved You, California," *Look* (September 25, 1962), p. 54. Reprinted by permission. (The last two lines did not appear in *Look* and were supplied by Mr. Armour.)

"The masked builder strikes again!"

V. Partch in the Los Angeles Times, *August 18, 1963. Reprinted by permission.*

It is a *geographical* phenomenon. Located between the 32d and 42d parallels of north latitude and angling between the 115th and 124th meridians, California stretches 1200 miles along the Pacific coast of the United States (the distance from Charleston, South Carolina, to Boston) and is 150 miles wide at its narrowest point. The state's 158,693 square miles are three-fourths rolling hills, foothills, and rugged mountain ranges, and one-fourth flat valleys and deserts that geologists say were once vast lakes. The lowest spot in the United States (Death Valley, 282 feet below sea level) is 60 miles away from one of the highest peaks (Mt. Whitney, 14,495 feet in elevation). There is snow in June in the High Sierra and outdoor swimming in January at Palm Springs, 100 inches of rainfall yearly on the northwest coast and less than 2 inches in the southeast desert. California contains the largest American county (San Bernardino, 20,131 square miles) and one of the smallest (San Francisco, 45 square miles).

It is a *demographic* phenomenon. With over 21 million people, California now contains 10 percent of the entire U.S. population. Nine out of ten Californians live in urban areas, making it the state with the largest number of cities of 100,000 or over. But during the last decade over 80 percent of the population growth has been in the suburbs, with some of the "central cities"—San Francisco, Los Angeles, Oakland, and Stockton—actually declining in population. The most populous county in the country is Los Angeles County with more than 7 million inhabitants; in contrast, mountainous Alpine County has fewer than 600 inhabitants. Of the people now living in California, over 40 percent are from other states. It continues to be a mobile population, with a third of all families moving every year.

It is a *sociological* phenomenon. California is a state of great ethnic variety. Nearly 10 percent of the people living there are foreign-born. Seven percent of the state's population is black, and 14 percent Mexican-American. More than half of all Americans of Asian ancestry live in California—approximately 500,000. California also has a native American Indian population of about 91,000. Now approximately 25 percent of the state's population, these ethnic minorities are increasing at five times the rate of the whites in the metropolitan cores, which, like Washington, D.C.,

are soon to become nonwhite majority cities. Practically
every religious group in the world has adherents who live
in California; the new Jerusalem of the "Jesus Revolution,"
California also could be considered the new Sodom—being
first or nearly first nationally in suicide, crime, drug addic-
tion, homosexuality, wife swapping, and divorce. There are
more quacks per capita there than in any other state; but
California has had its share of the world's outstanding
writers and scientists, with more than twenty-five Nobel prize
winners. It is simultaneously a stronghold of the John Birch
Society and the Black Panther party, the lyrical Watts
Towers and the ugly Watts riots. Disneyland, Esalen, the
California Institute of Technology, Jascha Heifetz, Pacific
Coast jazz, Nob Hill, the Haight-Ashbury hippies, and student "sit-ins" against the "multiversity" at Berkeley—all are
located in California, a land of contrast and paradox.

It is an *economic* phenomenon. With an annual gross
output of nearly $120 billion, California would rank seventh
in the world if it were a separate nation. California's per
capita income usually exceeds the national average by about
20 percent and almost always puts it among the top five
states. But, at the same time, the state's unemployment rate
is often considerably above the national average. Although
less than 30 percent of land area is under cultivation, California consistently leads the nation in gross income from
agricultural products. Every major crop produced in the
United States, except tobacco, is grown commercially in
California. The state produces 1.5 million bales of cotton a
year, second only to Texas. Forty percent of all the fruit
marketed in the United States is from California, including
85 percent of the grapes, and nearly every lemon and apri-
cot. Almost any American olive is a California olive, and
the same can be said for almonds, artichokes, dates, figs,
garlic, nectarines, persimmons, and pomegranates. California leads the nation in the production of forty-one crops and
livestock products, is second in fourteen, and third in six!
Only Texas exceeds California in mineral (and oil) production, and nearly all useful minerals known to man have been
found in this state. Only Oregon has more timberland and
California's wood products industry is the largest in the nation. The state is also number one in the total catch of fish.
During the last quarter century, more than 12 percent of

the nation's new construction took place in California. The state's two natural harbors (San Francisco and San Diego) and one artificial harbor (Los Angeles) make it a major participant in foreign trade. The main export is unmanufactured cotton, shipped principally to India and Japan; and its leading import is coffee from Brazil and Colombia. California tops the nation in food manufactures, is the leader in aircraft production, and is rapidly gaining on the eastern industrial states in other heavy manufactures— steel, fabricated metals, and plant machinery.

Abundant natural resources and rich croplands, supporting a heavy industrial framework, up to now have provided California with a continued structure that *should* be able to accommodate unlimited upward expansion. Potential threats to the state's "carrying capacity" are less economic than they are *ecological*. Overbuilding of houses and highways has increased the vulnerability of the land to erosion and flooding; the automobile culture (by 1980, there are likely to be as many as 20 million vehicles in California) is causing acute arterial congestion around all major urban nerve centers at morning and evening rush hours, not to speak of the continuing air pollution problems. These and related ecological issues will be returned to in the concluding chapter.[4] Here it is only necessary to note that in the 1970's, for the first time in the state's history, California, whose name has become virtually synonymous with "growth," may be reaching its limits.

SELECTED REFERENCES

BURDICK, EUGENE, "From Gold Rush to Sun Rush," *New York Times Magazine*, April 14, 1963, pp. 37–39.
———, "The Three Californias," *Holiday* 37 (October 1965): 60–74.
GENTRY, CURT, *The Last Days of the Late Great State of California*. New York: Ballantine Books, 1969.
LILLARD, RICHARD G., *Eden in Jeopardy*. New York: Alfred A. Knopf, 1966.

---

[4] A 1973 report from the U.S. Office of Emergency Preparedness shows California was subjected to more kinds of natural disasters (earthquakes, floods, fires, landslides, etc.) than any other state during the period of 1963–72.

MC WILLIAMS, CAREY, ed., *The California Revolution*. New York: Grossman, 1968.

PIERCE, NEAL R., *The Mega States of America: People, Politics, and Power in the Ten Great States*. New York: Norton, 1972, pp. 564–694.

Saturday Review, September 23, 1967 (special issue on California).

2
The Development of California's Constitutional System

Calfornia was a part of Spain while the thirteen British colonies across the continent were fighting for their independence. It became part of the new nation of Mexico when the Spanish-American colonies tore loose from their mother country in the 1820's. A victory prize in the war between the United States and Mexico in the 1840's, California became part of the United States in 1850. The legal and constitutional heritage it brought with it as it entered the Union was therefore different from that possessed by most of the thirty existing states. The only states with Spanish backgrounds that preceded California were Florida, Louisiana, and Texas. Vestiges of the Spanish and Mexican periods are prominent in California government architecture, religious shrines, county, city, and street names, and have seasoned the state's cultural life with rodeos, fritos, tacos, and enchiladas. Some of our present-day government and law can be traced back to California's Latin American era. Town governments with elected officials and the three branches of government—executive, legislative, and judicial —were established under Mexican rule. Thus, a brief trip back to the days of the conquistadores and caballeros will furnish background for a better understanding of California government.

UNDER SPANISH RULE

The west coast of what is now California was explored for Spain by Juan Rodríguez Cabrillo in 1542, but actual colonization was not attempted until two hundred years later. In 1769, fearing Russian encroachment from Alaska and English penetration from Canada, José Gálvez, the Spanish king's visitor general, dispatched a religious expedition under Fray Junípero Serra and a military force under Gaspar de Portolá to "civilize" the natives to the north. The three colonizing institutions used by the religious and military authorities were missions, military forts, and towns built for civilian settlers.

The Missions

The most important Spanish colonial institutions were the missions set up and administered by Spanish Catholic priests. The indigenous Indians were taught the religion, language, and customs necessary to make them good Spanish subjects. They were provided with food, shelter, and clothing, and in exchange were often forced to work as slaves for the missions. Soon Spanish settlements as well as Indian settlements began to grow up around these missions. The city of San Diego started in this manner. Some of the original missions still survive and continue to operate as religious centers and as museums preserving old documents and books.

The Presidios

The missions did not rely on moral force alone. Some Indian tribes were hostile to them and had to be resisted by Spanish military contingents. The earliest presidios were advance outposts protecting the missions. Eventually these military encampments attracted settlers and became little towns as the frontier expanded. The city of San Francisco started as a presidio.

The Pueblos

When the missionary and military establishments showed that civilian colonization was feasible, *pueblos* (towns) were built to attract settlers. Land, housing, and supplies were offered to those who would come, with the understanding that their surplus produce would be held in reserve to supply the military presidios. The settlers themselves were subject to military service in emergencies and were required to contribute their labor to public works projects. The municipal government that developed in most of the pueblos was headed by an *alcalde,* or mayor, appointed by the military commandant or by the governor of the entire province. The alcalde was advised by a town council, the *ayuntamiento,* which at the outset was also appointed; later however, as the Spanish settlements became more secure, the council was elected by the citizens of the pueblo. These pueblos were usually built around a central square, or *plaza*—many of which are still in evidence in modern California cities such as Los Angeles and San Jose. The pueblo-plaza arrangement is regarded as one of the earliest examples of city planning.

The Spanish Imperial System

Inhabitants of the province of California, like all other Spanish colonial subjects, lived under a rigid umbrella-shaped hierarchy with the king of Spain at the apex. All the local authorities—military, civil, and religious—were responsible to the provincial governor, and their actions could be overruled by him. The provincial governor was appointed by the king but was responsible to the viceroy for New Spain, who resided in Mexico City and was also appointed by the king. The viceroy took orders from the Council of the Indies, which sat in Madrid and translated the sovereign's wishes into administrative directives to all Spanish New World possessions. Thus, the king ruled over California indirectly—but with absolute authority, since Spanish officers at every rib of the administrative umbrella owed their positions to him.

UNDER MEXICAN RULE

In 1822, Mexico, having just achieved independence from a decaying Spanish empire, assumed control of California. Although Californians were theoretically free citizens of the young Mexican republic, the province *del norte* (to the north) continued to be regarded by Mexico as a colonial appendage. The most severe rupture from the past came with the Mexican Secularization Act of 1833. The government seized control of the missions and their lands. Mission property was to have been divided between the government and the Indians, but instability in Mexico City and the submissiveness of the Indians allowed much of the mission land to fall into the hands of local politicians. While California was under Spanish rule, control from Mexico City was tight. However, under the new republic, with its rapid succession of revolutions and regimes, laws brought by couriers from the south were often not taken seriously, and anarchy prevailed.

In 1837 the Mexican Congress enacted its most extensive body of laws for the government of California. Three branches of government—executive, legislative, and judicial—were established. The governor was appointed by the central government in Mexico City. He had little authority over policy, but was given the power to appoint all the prefects, the regional administrative officers. The prefects in turn appointed subprefects, the local administrative officers corresponding roughly to our sheriffs. The provincial legislature was a popularly elected body of seven members serving four-year terms. Although they could enact laws concerning commerce, taxes, and education, authority over all military matters remained in Mexico City. On the local level the elected ayuntamiento, as in the more developed Spanish pueblos, operated as a legislative council. But unlike the Spanish mayor, the Mexican alcalde was elected. The alcaldes, in fact, became the most important public officials in the California province. The elaborate court system (consisting on paper of a supreme court, district courts of appeal, trial courts, and courts of petty jurisdiction) could function only on the municipal or justice court level under revolt-torn Mexican rule; and the alcaldes were very often ex officio justices of the peace. If anyone wished to appeal a local court decision, he had to present his case to the governor in person.

One of the thorniest vestiges California has retained from the Mexican period is its complicated litigations over conflicting land grants. Individuals and often entire municipalities have turned up old grants by the Spanish crown or the Mexican national government whose authenticity is difficult to validate. Since the American authorities promised that they would honor all existing property rights when they assumed control of California, California courts have frequently been faced with conflicting claims of possession involving private parties and governmental jurisdictions over old mission lands and ranchos, especially where the lands contain valuable mineral deposits or water.

AMERICAN ACQUISITION

By the 1840's the American government was already taking a serious interest in California. American traders and settlers gave it increasing economic value; its continued possession by a weak Mexico made it easy prey for acquisition by a foreign power (there was good reason to believe that San Francisco Bay had more than aesthetic attraction for Britain and France), and, happily, America was in an expansive mood. It was the age for believing that we had a "manifest destiny" to impart the blessings of our civilization to less fortunate peoples. Sentiment was so high for acquisition in 1845 that President James Knox Polk sent an emissary to Mexico City with an offer to purchase California for $40 million. But the Mexicans considered it a bribe and indignantly rejected Polk's "generous" bid.

The Bear Flag Revolt

Following the example of Texas, a group of American settlers in northern California on June 10, 1846, seized a herd of horses belonging to Governor José de Castro to signal the start of a revolt for California independence. They proclaimed the "California Republic" and designed themselves a flag featuring a grizzly bear. There is no telling how successful their revolt might have been had not the Mexican-American War already started and taken the wind out of their colorful revolt. The only lasting contribution of the Bear Flaggers was their banner—the basis for the design of California's present state flag. The Pacific fleet, standing off the California coast on orders of President Polk, sailed into Monterey harbor, and Commodore Sloat debarked to begin the period of American rule.

American Military Rule

Throughout the Mexican War (1846–48), civil government in California was under the control of American military authorities. The military commanders remained in California for a year after its cession to the United States by the peace treaty of Guadalupe Hidalgo. During the war the rapidity with which these commanders were appointed and replaced made for a lack of continuing authority and much civil instability. With the coming of peace, constitutional processes almost completely broke down. Gold had been discovered at Sutter's Fort, and hundreds of Americans were entering California every day. In some areas at least a semblance of law and order was achieved through the election of American "alcaldes" with authority to adjust disputes and administer local regulations. In the mining areas vigilantes and "miner's courts" often acted in the absence of other authorities.[1]

THE CONSTITUTION OF 1849

As California came under formal control of the United States, its constitutional status had to be decided. Was it to be a territory or a state? Citizens met in various towns in the southern portion of the state to draw up a constitution that would make California a territory. Many southerners had strong Mexican ties and preferred the loosest possible arrangement with the United States. On the other hand, in the more densely populated north the predominant sentiment was for statehood; and in the spring of 1849 mass

[1] Paul Mason, "Constitutional History of California," in *Constitution of the United States and of the State of California and Other Documents* (Sacramento: State Printing Office, 1963), p. 310.

meetings calling for a constituent assembly were held in San Francisco, Monterey, Sacramento, and other cities north of the Tehachapi mountain range. The newly arrived military governor, General Bennett Riley, was a wise enough politician to know that if a convention was to meet it would be better for his prestige if he sounded the call. Riley quickly issued a proclamation for a convention to meet at Monterey on September 1. Forty-eight delegates were to be elected by geographical districts according to a numerical formula based upon a rough estimate of population. The north thus emerged in clear control of the convention, and the vote for statehood rather than territorial status passed by a three-to-one majority.

Although there were a number of heated controversies at the convention—where to locate the eastern boundary, the question of excluding free blacks, the extent of government control over corporations—the delegates took their law-drafting duties conscientiously, carefully studying existing state constitutions. Heaviest reliance was placed on the constitution of Iowa, as it was considered the most up-to-date and compact at the time.

The citizens of California ratified their first constitution on November 13 by a preponderant popular majority of 12,872 to 811.[2] On the same day, they chose their first governor, Peter H. Burnett, and other state officers, as well as members of the United States Congress (although California had not yet been admitted to the Union as a state).

Basic Provisions of the Constitution

A declaration of rights began the document, affirming that "all political power is inherent in the people . . ." but that certain rights were inalienable, "among which are those of enjoying and defending life and liberty; acquiring, possessing, and protecting property; and pursuing and obtaining safety and happiness." (How characteristically Californian to guarantee not only the pursuit but also the achievement of happiness!) The fundamental freedoms of speech, press, assembly, petition, and religion were established. The rights of habeas corpus and trial by jury and

[2] Ibid., p. 322.

prohibitions upon ex post facto laws and bills of attainder were included. Hardly any civil right of Anglo-Saxon jurisprudence was omitted, and even the right to fish was included.

Slavery was prohibited. However, the suffrage, as was common in those days, was granted only to white male citizens over twenty-one.

The constitution declared that "California is an inseparable part of the American Union, and the Constitution of the United States is the supreme law of the land."

The "separation of powers" principle was cited in establishing the three branches of government. Legislative power was located in a popularly elected two-house body. In the senate members were elected every two years and in the assembly members were elected annually; but seats in both houses were apportioned according to population. Executive power was vested in six elected officers: the governor, lieutenant governor, controller, attorney general, superintendent of public instruction, and surveyor general. The governor appointed the secretary of state and lesser officials, was given a veto over legislative measures and the right to call the legislature into special session, and accorded an unlimited pardoning power. The judicial branch was to consist of four levels of courts: a supreme court of three justices was given final appellate jurisdiction in major cases; district courts were the major trial courts; each county was provided with a county court; and the legislature was to establish justice courts within the counties as needs demanded. All judges were to be elected.

A system of state-supported public schools was created. Taxes were to be uniform throughout the state. All laws were to be published in English and in Spanish. And San Jose was made the capital.

Amendments to the state constitution required a majority vote in both houses of the legislature in two successive annual sessions, followed by ratification by a majority of the voters in a statewide election.

Major Amendments

The only significant amendments to California's first constitution were contained in a group approved by the voters in 1862. The governor's term was increased from two to four years; the position of secretary of state was made elective; the terms of senators were increased to four years and those of assemblymen to two; the legislature was made to convene every other year rather than annually; and the provisions relating to the court system were revised and made more explicit.

Criticisms

The most frequent criticism leveled against the 1849 document was that it placed no restriction upon the legislature's power to tax or spend—that it was "dumb on the subject of finance. . . ."[3] Capital had been driven from the state, it was contended, by needlessly high taxes. And later on, when the railroads and their allied industries began to dominate the state's economy, the cry that corporations were insufficiently regulated led to the convening of California's second constitutional convention in 1879. Thus, the constitution of 1849 served as the fundamental law of the state for thirty years.

STATEHOOD: ADMISSION TO THE UNION

California did not become one of the United States until September 9, 1850—nine months after the ratification of her first constitution. The delay was primarily due to the slavery issue then being debated in Congress. Although California's elected delegates to the U.S. Senate, John Frémont and William Gwinn, lobbied hard to secure rapid admission, the fact that California would enter as a free state and thus upset the existing fifteen-to-fifteen balance with the slave states stimulated a drawn-out process of political bargaining. The result was the famous Compromise of 1850: California was admitted as a free state, but the rest of the territories ceded to the United States by Mexico were organized without restrictions on slavery.

THE CONSTITUTION OF 1879

California began to feel the full impact of the nineteenth-century industrial revolution by the 1870's, when the transcontinental railroads reached the West Coast. The new economic relations that came with the new technology,

[3] Hubert H. Bancroft, *History of California,* 7 (San Francisco: History Company, 1890): 370.

the rapid urbanization of the state, and severe cyclical unemployment and agricultural depressions led to a search for remedies. The best way, it seemed, was to rewrite the whole state constitution. People did not yet look to the federal government for the control of national economic phenomena.

The Convention

Prior to 1877 four legislative proposals for a constitutional convention had been rejected by the state's voters. Sentiment for constitutional reform was successfully mobilized in that year by two groups—the Workingmen's party and the rural Grange—with one complaint in common: they disliked the railroads and contended the existing constitution allowed monopolies too much freedom.[4] The laborers were angry at the railroad's hiring of imported Chinese coolie labor at low wages, and the farmers felt they were being milked by high freight rates.

When it came to electing convention delegates in 1878, however, the Workingmen's party found itself opposed by a coalition of Republicans and Democrats that included some Grange elements. The Republican and Democratic strategy was to elect a fusion ticket of "nonpartisans." Of the 152 delegates elected, 78 identified themselves as nonpartisans, 51 as Workingmen, 11 Republicans, 10 Democrats, and 2 Independents. According to California historian Rockwell D. Hunt, "A relatively small number of men of conspicuous ability were elected as delegates: viewed as a whole the delegates would not compare very favorably with the men of '49. . . ."[5] On most convention issues the delegates divided into two basic groups—one favoring considerable state government control over the economy, the other stressing free enterprise. As a result, the final document emerged more a bundle of compromises than a reformer's magna charta.

[4] See Chapter Four for a discussion of the organization of the Workingmen's party and its impact on state politics.
[5] Rockwell D. Hunt and Nellie Van de Grift Sánchez, *A Short History of California* (New York: Thomas Y. Crowell Company, 1929), p. 547.

Major Changes from the 1849 Constitution

Rather than being completely new, the constitution of 1879 was in large part an elaboration of the 1849 document, with more specific and detailed provisions. But there were a number of important alterations.

The legislature's power was significantly circumscribed. Whereas previously there had been no restrictions on its financial powers, it was now prevented from appropriating state moneys to aid private institutions (including religious schools and hospitals), except homes for the blind, orphans, and the indigent. The governor was given the right to convene special sessions of the legislature in which only the subjects mentioned in his call could be considered. This power could be used with pointed effect when a budget bill was up for passage.

The judicial system was completely reorganized. The state supreme court was expanded to comprise a chief justice and six associate justices. County and district courts were to be replaced by superior courts created by the legislature. (For a detailed description of the present judicial structure see Chapter Nine.)

The Chinese coolie labor problem received special treatment in Article XIX—a concession to the Workingmen's party delegates. All corporations were prohibited from hiring Chinese, and their employment "except in punishment for crime" was forbidden on any state, county, or municipal project. The importation of contract coolie labor was made illegal, and the legislature was instructed to discourage any further Chinese immigration. This article was not completely repealed by the voters until 1952, although the courts had earlier found most of the clauses in violation of the United States Constitution.

There were numerous other provisions written into the 1879 constitution to protect nearly every interest represented at the convention. Thus, such details as the maximum number of acres of state-owned land to be granted one settler and whether noncultivated land was to be counted by tax assessors (properly subjects for simple legislative statutes) were included.

Ratification

The trouble with putting so many specifics into a constitution to please various convention factions arises when popular approval is sought. Almost everyone could find some provision which he considered intolerable. Among the more serious objections raised during the campaign for ratification were the arguments that the legislature was hampered by too many restrictions, that giving the railroad commission power to regulate fares and freights would leave that body an especially tempting prey for the railroad corporations, that taxing stocks and bonds of California corporations gave nonresident investors an advantage over state citizens and furthermore such taxes would discourage business expansion. The document was ratified on May 7, 1879, by a slim 10,820 majority out of 145,088 votes.[6]

Amendments

The constitution of 1879, as amended, is the fundamental law of the state today. Before the 1966 revision it had been amended more than 350 times in more than 1000 different sections, making it ten times as long as the United States Constitution and the third largest in the world, following India's and Louisiana's. California's constitution contained approximately 80,000 words, and if it were included as an appendix here, the length of this book would be nearly double! The California Bill of Rights was three times as long as the United States Bill of Rights, and the California article on local government (XI) was longer than the entire federal Constitution.

Article XVIII allows for two ways to amend and revise the California constitution. Amendments may be proposed in the senate or assembly, and if two-thirds of all the members elected to each of the two houses vote in favor, such amendments are submitted to the voters. If a majority of those voting on any amendment approve, it becomes a part of the constitution. Section 2 of this article provides for a calling of a constitutional convention. Whenever two-thirds of the members elected to each branch of the legislature deem it necessary to revise the constitution, they may rec-

---

[6] Bancroft, *History of California*, vol. 7: 399–400.

ommend to the electors that a convention be assembled for that purpose. If a majority of the voters approve such a call, a number of delegates not to exceed 120 would be selected in a special election. The delegates so elected would meet within three months after their election for the consideration of new constitutional provisions. All recommended changes would then be subject to approval of the voters.

Article XVIII itself was amended in 1962 to authorize the legislature by a vote of two-thirds of the members elected to each house to propose complete or partial "revisions" of the constitution for approval or rejection by the people. Formerly, the legislature could propose only changes specific and limited in nature. "Revisions," that is, proposals that involve broad changes in all or a substantial part of the constitution, could be proposed only by a constitutional convention. Amendments to the California constitution may also be proposed by the people through the initiative process.

The more important amendments have provided for the direct primary system (Chapter Three); the initiative, referendum, and recall (Chapter Six); changing the basis of representation in the state legislature (Chapter Seven); the executive budget (Chapter Eight); and the state civil service system.

Attempts at Revision

Although there has been constant pressure to overhaul this bulky and unwieldy document, a new constitutional convention has not been held. In 1898, 1914, 1920, and 1930 the people rejected proposals that had been voted by the legislature. The fifth time, in 1934, a bare majority of the voters approved (705,915 to 688,080), but no convention ever met!

In 1947 a joint legislative committee appointed a citizens' advisory committee to study constitutional revision. Their recommendations led to a series of amendments that were approved by the voters in 1950. These changes eliminated some 14,500 words from the constitution. Again, in 1960 the voters approved a measure that eliminated several obsolete and superseded provisions.

The California constitution spelled out in detail such

matters as a ballot form for voting for judges, use of vehicle taxes and vehicle registration taxes, and restrictions against dueling. The document also contained such items as how to finance off-street parking, the right of railroad tracks to connect at the state line to tracks in other states, and the complex procedure used by the legislature to indemnify owners for livestock slaughtered to prevent the spread of disease. Such provisions caused the California League of Women Voters to brand the constitution a "dignified repository of colorful lore."

A survey in 1961 showed a high proportion of the membership of the legislature would favor complete revision of the California constitution.[7] And in 1962 the voters approved Proposition 7, which permitted partial or complete revision through legislative action and referendum.

Commission on Constitutional Revision

In December 1963 the Joint Committee on Legislative Organization of the California legislature appointed a Citizens' Advisory Commission on Constitutional Revision to study California's eighty-five-year-old constitution and recommend changes to improve and update the document. Sixty leading citizens representing industry, agriculture, labor, education, government, and other civic groups—including the California League of Women Voters, long active in the cause of constitutional revision—served on this commission. A number of state senators and state assemblymen were also members and provided valuable liaison, as all recommendations were subject to the approval of the state legislature before submission to the electorate.

The commission first met in Sacramento in 1964 and held meetings about once a month until December 1970. The commission presented its first series of formal recommendations to the legislature based on the redrafting of Article III (separation of powers), Article IV (the legislature and initiative and referendum), Article V (the executive), and Article VI (the judiciary). With some modifications, the legislature adopted the proposed revision of the

---

[7] Bernard L. Hyink, "The California Legislature Looks at the State Constitution," *Western Political Quarterly* 15, no. 1 (March 1962): 167.

constitution by more than the required two-thirds vote of each house and presented it to the people for their approval as Proposition 1A in the November 1966 election.

Proposition 1A, 1966

Passed by approximately a three-to-one margin, Proposition 1A had the support of both Governor Edmund Brown and gubernatorial candidate Ronald Reagan. Endorsements included those of the state Chamber of Commerce, the California Labor Federation, the AFL–CIO, the League of Cities, the County Supervisors Association, the California Teachers Association, the California State Employees Association, the League of Women Voters, and many prominent newspapers including the *Los Angeles Times* and the McClatchy newspapers.

Proposition 1A dealt with about one-third of the 80,000-word constitution. The new language was modern and about 16,000 of the 22,000 words in the sections covered were deleted. The new Article IV eliminated the restrictive budget session of the legislature and provided annual sessions with no limitation on the time-length of the sessions. When the legislature finished its business, it would adjourn; it could continue in session uninhibited by an arbitrary termination date. The former constitutional limit of a $500 monthly salary was also removed, and the legislature by a two-thirds vote set its own compensation by statute. The new article also mandated the legislature to pass conflict-of-interest statutes.

Indirect initiative (rarely used) was eliminated and the percentage of signatures required for an initiative statute was reduced from 8 to 5 percent to differentiate this form of initiative from an initiative to amend the constitution, which required 8 percent of the last gubernatorial vote total to qualify a petition for submission to the voters.

The new Article V (executive) gave specific authorization for the governor to reorganize the executive branch of the government. The long line of succession to the governor's office was deleted, and it was provided that successors after the lieutenant governor be designated by statute. Relatively few substantive changes in the operation of the judicial branch were provided. Changes that were made are discussed in Chapter Nine.

Proposition 1, 1968

The 1968 state legislature approved a second group of recommendations presented by the chairman of the Constitutional Revision Commission, Judge Bruce W. Sumner. Appearing as Proposition 1 on the November 1968 ballot, this revision covered seven articles, including such subjects as education, local government, corporations and public utilities, land, state civil service, and amending and revising the constitution. An existing 14,000 words were reduced to about 2000 words.

However, Proposition 1 was defeated by the voters in 1968. There was little publicity on the issue and less campaigning than for 1A in 1966. Also, the influential *Los Angeles Times*, which had favored 1A in 1966, advised a "no" vote on Proposition 1, and this probably accounts for the heavy negative vote in southern California. The *Times* maintained that too many subjects were covered in the proposed revision and criticized the sections dealing with education and with public utilities. In an editorial, "Some flaws in Proposition 1," the *Times* objected to the fact that the legislature had revised the constitutional commission's recommendation that the state superintendent of public instruction be appointed and left the method of selection to its own determination.[8]

Revision after 1970

Despite the defeat of Proposition 1, the Constitution Revision Commission continued its work and carried on a schedule of meetings through December 1970. By that time, all of the articles had been studied and the recommendations were forwarded to the state legislature.

In the general election (November 1970), four propositions sponsored by the commission and passed by the legislature were submitted to the voters. Proposition 14, concerning the state civil service, reduced the number of persons exempt from civil service. Proposition 15 revised and amended Article XX, eliminated from the constitution

[8] *Los Angeles Times*, October 15, 1968, Part II, p. 6.

unnecessary verbiage on dueling, perpetuities, marriage contracts, rights of veterans, and absence from the state. Proposition 16 amended Article XVIII, which dealt with amending the constitution by a lengthy process involving conventions that was never used. Instead, the legislature is instructed to call a convention when a majority of the voters request it. Proposition 17 eliminated superfluous language by removing the obsolete Article XXVII from the constitution.

All four articles were approved by the electorate, thus accomplishing a good portion of the revision that had been unsuccessfully attempted in 1968. Passage of Proposition 10 on the June 1972 primary ballot revised portions of Articles X, XII, and XVII previously defeated in 1968. Propositions 6 and 7 were likewise passed in November 1972. Proposition 6 collected into a single article various provisions scattered through various articles relating to federal supremacy, state boundaries, and suits against the state. Proposition 7 created an updated Article II, revising it to bring it into conformity with recent federal legislation establishing the voting age at eighteen and the basic residency requirement in the county to thirty days.

When the Constitution Revision Committee held its last meeting in 1972, the future of further revision appeared dim. However, largely through the efforts of the chairman and a former member of the commission who had been elected to the Assembly, and with the encouragement of the League of Women Voters, four measures were passed by the legislature and placed on the November 1974 ballot.

In the general election of 1974, the voters approved four amendments to the constitution which carried out recommendations of the Constitution Revision Commission. Proposition 7 clarified the bill of rights article and Proposition 8 dealing with Article XIII on taxation deleted obsolete provisions, eliminating some 8200 words from the constitution. The section dealing with recall of elected officials was revised by Proposition 9 to allow for a time limit for gathering signatures, eliminating the grace period, and making all local officials subject to recall. Proposition 12 originally drafted by the commission eliminated 80 percent of the verbiage and clarified Article 12 of the constitution, which deals with state regulation of public utilities. All in all, about two-thirds of California's constitution has thus been substantially revised.

SELECTED REFERENCES

Book of the States. Chicago: Council of State Governments. Published biennially.

Briefs on a Long Constitution. San Francisco: League of Women Voters of California, 1964.

CAMPBELL, DENNIS, "Our Bulky Constitution—Is Pruning Season Over?" *California Journal* IV, 12 (December 1973): 404.

HYINK, BERNARD L., "The California Legislature Looks at the State Constitution," *Western Political Quarterly* 15, no. 1 (March 1962): 157–69.

————, "California Revises Its Constitution," *Western Political Quarterly* 22, no. 3 (September 1969): 637–54.

MASON, PAUL, "Constitutional History of California," *Constitution of the United States and of the State of California and Other Documents.* Sacramento: State Printing Office, 1973.

ROLLE, ANDREW F., *California: A History,* 2d ed. New York: Thomas Y. Crowell Company, 1969.

3
Voters, Nominations, and Elections

The most fundamental question of government is: *Who should rule?* Although it is generally assumed that in the United States the people rule—that is, we adhere to the principle of popular sovereignty—the federal Constitution contains no specific provision guaranteeing the citizen the right to vote or to run for office. Up to the 1950's, who could vote had been left up to the states themselves, with the exception that the right of citizens to vote should not be "denied or abridged . . . on account of race, color, or previous condition of servitude" (Fifteenth Amendment) or "on account of sex" (Nineteenth Amendment). However, state governments denied or abridged the right to vote for other reasons.[1] In seventeen states the citizen had to be literate (defined differently by the various states), and all states held to a minimum voting age requirement. Some

---

[1] The Fourteenth Amendment stipulates that the number of a state's representatives in Congress shall be reduced if the state denies the right to vote to any twenty-one-year-old citizen "except for participation in rebellion, or other crime," but this rule has not been invoked.

states allowed a person to vote after he had lived in the state only six months, while others demanded two years. And to vote on certain kinds of issues, such as approving bonds, a half-dozen states have required that the citizen be a property owner.

The provisions in the U.S. Constitution that provide for the popular election of senators and representatives go no further than to require that a state allow the same people to vote for members of Congress as it allows to vote for members of the "most numerous branch of the State legislature." If California's constitution had allowed only dog owners to vote for members of the assembly, it could have established the same requirement for voting in congressional elections.

However, in the past twenty years a far-reaching change has been taking place in the legal and constitutional basis of the suffrage. In the Civil Rights Acts of 1957, 1960, and 1964 and in the Voting Rights Acts of 1965 and 1970 the Congress has sought to guarantee the right to vote to racial and national minorities such as the blacks in the southern states and the Puerto Ricans in New York. The Twenty-fourth Amendment to the U.S. Constitution also sought to enfranchise poor blacks and whites in the South by eliminating the poll tax as a requirement for voting for federal officials. Even more revolutionary was the provision of the Voting Rights Act of 1970 that lowered the voting age to eighteen in all elections throughout the nation. All doubts about the constitutionality of this age limit were dissolved when the necessary three-fourths of the states ratified the Twenty-sixth Amendment to the federal Constitution in June 1971. The Voting Rights Act of 1970 also eliminated the literacy qualification for voting. Furthermore, the courts have declared that the long residence periods of one year or more that most states required for voting violated the Fourteenth Amendment. Consequently, we have moved very close to a uniform, national standard of voting. Technically, the states still have the power to control the requirements for the suffrage; but through constitutional amendments, acts of Congress, and court decisions, the federal government has specified such a long list of requirements that the states can *not* impose, that to practically all intents the federal government does determine who may vote.

Who may hold *national* elective office, that is, the presidency, the vice-presidency, and membership in Congress, is determined by the U.S. Constitution. The state may add no further qualifications. This was made clear in a decision of the California supreme court in the spring of 1964. Pierre Salinger sought to have his name placed on the Democratic ballot as a candidate for the U.S. Senate in the California June primary, even though he had been a legal resident of Virginia for some years past. The state supreme court upheld his right on the grounds that the only statement in the national Constitution about the residence of a senator is that he must be an "inhabitant" of the state he represents without specifying the length of his habitation in that state. So, Mr. Salinger changed his official residence from Virginia to California the very day he filed his nomination papers. He could have been elected U.S. senator without being able to vote for himself (since he did not meet the state's residence requirements for the suffrage).

However, the states do set the qualifications for the vast majority of elective offices in the American political system, that is, for everything from governor to member of a county school board.

Elections administration, too, is under the control of the states. The only operative federal check of state practices is the constitutional provision that each house of Congress shall be the judge of the elections and qualifications of its own members. The Constitution allows Congress to make or alter state election laws affecting senators or representatives; but thus far the federal legislature has chosen to regulate only campaign finances. Therefore, voting and elections in California are largely under the control of the state's citizens. They may be changed by the initiative of the people, by the legislature through constitutional amendment, and in some cases simply by statute.

WHO MAY VOTE?

In November 1972, the voters of California revised Article II of the state constitution in order to conform to the new provisions of the Twenty-sixth Amendment to the United States Constitution, the Voting Rights Act of Congress, and court decisions. The new Article II accords the right to vote in all California elections to any person who meets the following qualifications:

1. Citizenship A voter must be a citizen of the United States. If he is not a natural-born American, he must have received his naturalization papers before he registers to vote.

2. Residence The new Article II gives the legislature authority to set the residence requirements for voting. However, the California supreme court declared that, under the equal protection clause in both the U.S. and California constitutions, the state cannot require a citizen to live in the state more than thirty days before he is allowed to vote. The legislature then enacted a law that conformed to this decision. Therefore, the present legal requirement is that one must live in California, his county, and his election precinct only thirty days before the election. The state legislature may reduce this requirement even more if it sees fit.[2]

Voters away from their precincts on election day may vote in advance (in person or by mail), provided they have filed an application for an absentee ballot with the county elections official at least seven days before the election.

3. Age The minimum age for voting throughout the United States is eighteen years. There is no *maximum age*. A centenarian who can get to the polls in person or who can fill out the application for an absentee ballot can continue to vote as he has for the last eight decades.

4. Special requirements As revised in 1972 Article II of the California constitution declared that the legislature "shall provide that no severely mentally deficient person, insane person, person convicted of an infamous crime, nor person convicted of embezzlement or misappropriation of public money, shall exercise the privilege of an elector in this state." Controversy arose in the courts as to the mean-

[2] In some counties, a citizen is allowed to vote for president in the November general election even if he has been a resident of this state less than the thirty days. He must have been eligible to vote in his former state and he must appear in person at the office of the county clerk or registrar of voters at least seven days before the election. He is permitted to vote only for the office of president and he must formally register to vote in any subsequent elections.

ing of the phrase "infamous crime," which usually has been interpreted as a felony (a crime carrying a punishment of at least one year in a state or federal prison). However, a superior court in Los Angeles ruled that "infamous" implied "moral turpitude"; therefore, a resistance to the military draft on conscientious grounds might land a man in the penitentiary but since the resistance did not involve an immoral motive, he should be allowed to vote as soon as released. In 1973 the state supreme court declared that the equal protection clause of the United States Constitution required that any citizen convicted of any felony should have his right to vote restored as soon as he finished his sentence (which includes not only the time he is behind bars but also the period he is on parole thereafter). Subsequently, the United States Supreme Court ruled that the California court had misinterpreted the Constitution, leaving the issue very much in confusion. To clarify these matters, California voters in November 1974 adopted Proposition 10, which amended Article II to read: "The Legislature shall prohibit improper practices that affect elections and shall provide for the disqualification of electors while mentally incompetent or imprisoned or on parole for the conviction of a felony." So, once a convict has paid his debt to society he shall regain his right to the suffrage.

Prior to November 1972, Article II required a voter to be able to read the state constitution in the English language and to write his or her name. This was eliminated in the revised version of the Article; furthermore, the Congressional Voting Rights Act of 1970 abolished the literacy qualification throughout the country at least until 1975.

5. Registration A citizen who satisfies all of the qualifications above cannot merely walk up to the polls on election day and expect to be handed a ballot. In order to exercise his suffrage privileges he must be already registered as a qualified voter with the chief elections administrator of his county (in most counties this is a duty of the county clerk; but in the counties of Los Angeles, San Francisco, San Diego, San Bernardino, Orange, and Santa Clara the elections official is the registrar of voters). A person may register at any time except during the twenty-nine days immediately preceding any election. For example, if a prospective new voter fails to register by the end of the thirtieth

POPULATION, ELECTORATE, REGISTRANTS, VOTERS: 1964–1974

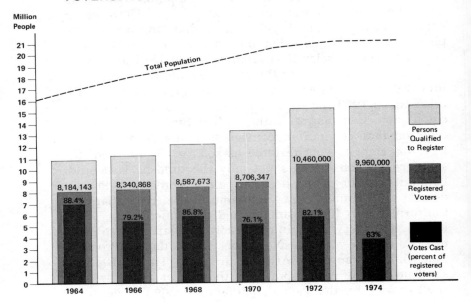

day preceding the June primary, he forfeits any chance of voting in that election and must wait until after balloting day to register for the coming November election. In most counties advance warning of the closing of registration is given by local newspapers and by deputies with the authority to process registrants, sitting at tables placed in front of post offices and supermarkets. And in 1975 the legislature passed a law allowing registration by mail.

Registration in California is "permanent"—that is, once a citizen is registered, he may continue to vote in successive elections without reregistering, providing he (a) votes in the immediate preceding general election; [3] (b) does not change legal residence; (c) does not change name;

[3] When the county registration official cancels the registration of any nonvoter in the general election, the official is required by state law to submit a double prepaid postcard to that individual informing him of the cancellation and giving him the option of remaining off the rolls (until formal reregistration) or returning the postcard indicating that he still resides at the address on his original registration affidavit, in which case the original affidavit is returned to the file of those entitled to vote.

(d) does not become ineligible because of insanity or serving a sentence for a felony; or (e) does not change party affiliation.

At the time of registration each voter is asked to indicate the party with which he chooses to be affiliated. His answer is indicated on his registration affidavit, and he becomes eligible to vote in that party's primary elections. If he "declines to state" his party preference, he may not vote in any partisan primary, and on primary election days is handed ballots only for those officers elected on a nonpartisan basis.

WHO MAY RUN FOR OFFICE?

Eligibility

The 1964 court ruling in the case of Pierre Salinger shattered the notion that a person is *in*eligible for election to any office for which he is not qualified to vote. Specific *eligibility* requirements are found in the U.S. Constitution for federal offices; in the state constitution and statutes for state senators, assemblymen, judges of the state courts, county committeemen, and officers in general law counties and cities; and in local charters for many officers in "home-rule" cities and counties.

California's elected executive officers must be voters and have resided in the state five years previous to their election. Each member of the Board of Equalization, the state's major tax agency, must in addition have resided in his district for one year. State senators and assemblymen must be voters, residents of the state for three years and of their district for one year. A ruling of the state supreme court in 1975 held that the residency requirement for candidates seeking local office be limited to a maximum of thirty days.

Getting on the Ballot

Any individual who meets the minimum legal qualification for any of the offices listed above,[4] or any one of the many other local offices, may have his name appear on the

[4] Except justices of the state supreme court and the district courts of appeal, where the only names appearing on the ballot are those of incumbents whose terms have expired or nominees of the governor in cases where the incumbent is not running for reelection.

ballot at primary election day if at least sixty days before the election he files a declaration of candidacy with the county clerk, or in municipal elections with the city clerk. The number of sponsors' signatures required varies for different offices but is nominal.

To appear on the primary election ballot of a given party as a candidate for the U.S. Senate or any state executive office, a petition bearing sixty-five signatures (of registered voters belonging to the party within the constituency of the office sought) must be filed. Aspirants for the United States House of Representatives or for the state senate or assembly are required to file a petition carrying at least forty signatures. A candidate for a party county committee needs only twenty signatures. Previously, candidates for all offices except party county committee had to pay a filing fee depending upon the position they were seeking. For example, a candidate for governor had to pay 1 percent of the annual salary of that office. However, the U.S. Supreme Court declared that such a requirement discriminated against the poor in violation of the Fourteenth Amendment to the federal Constitution. Therefore, the states must substitute some requirement other than a financial one for an impoverished candidate to get his name on the ballot. Early in 1974 the California Supreme Court ruled that in view of the failure of the California legislature to furnish such an alternative, all filing fees for that year's elections were unconstitutional. Hence, the state's Democrats had to pick their way through eighteen names to choose a nominee for governor in the June primary.

In 1975 the state supreme court declared the alphabetical listing of candidates on an election ballot unconstitutional. At the same time the court struck down the automatic listing of an incumbent's name at the head of the ballot. As a result, the names of candidates for state and local offices appeared on the basis of a randomized alphabet determined by a public drawing managed by the office of the secretary of state.

A candidate may not run as an "independent" in the partisan primaries. All contestants must themselves be registered members of a political party. Getting on the ballot in California is rather simple and relatively inexpensive; getting *elected* is something else indeed!

PRIMARY ELECTIONS

The Direct Partisan Primary

The direct primary was instituted in California and some other states to give the average voter a say in *nominating* the candidates who will represent his party in the coming general election. It is called *direct* because previously nomination had been indirect—that is, by conventions of party members led by party officials—and the man in the street had to take the candidates the party "machine" gave him.

California's direct primary is held every even-numbered year on the Tuesday after the first Monday in June —five months before the November general election. There has been some criticism of the long interim between the primary and general elections, mainly that the expense of an extended campaign narrows the field of would-be candidates.

The ballot is "longest" in gubernatorial election years (1966, 1970, 1974, etc.) when all the state executive offices are open for nomination, as well as all assembly and United States House of Representatives seats, half the state senate seats, county committeemen posts, and numerous local offices. The state executive officers serve four-year terms and are not elected in presidential election years (1968, 1972, 1976, etc.).

At a primary election, the registered Republican voter receives a different ballot from the registered Democrat. The winner in a partisan primary is the candidate who receives the *highest* number of ballots from the voters of the party.

THE CROSS-FILING SYSTEM   The Hiram Johnson Progressives (see Chapter Four) created California's highly controversial cross-filing system in 1913 with the aim of giving the voter a completely free choice in the nominating primaries. The 1909 law establishing the direct primary had allowed only supporters of a party to receive that party's nomination. The 1913 cross-filing law eliminated any such partisan requirement, permitting an individual candidate to file for the nomination of more than one party for any partisan office except county committeeman or delegate to the national nominating convention. A voter could still cast his ballot only in the primary of the party with which he was registered; but a candidate, no matter in which party he was registered, could attempt to gain the nomination of any or all parties, and his name would appear on the ballots of all parties for which he had filed a proper affidavit.

A candidate who cross-filed could win the nomination of parties in addition to his own. For example, if a registered Republican seeking nomination to Congress were to gain a plurality in both the Republican and Democratic primaries, he would become the nominee of both parties, and be listed on the November general election ballot with both "Republican" and "Democratic" after his name. His election would be almost a certainty since his name might be the only one on the ballot for Congress or since he might have to face only nominal opposition from a third-party candidate.

For four decades it was the political way of life in California for aspirants to state and national office to cross-file. And in a majority of the primary contests throughout the state one candidate would capture both major party nominations. For example, in the 1940–52 period 84 percent of the state senate races and 72 percent of the assembly races were decided in the primaries.[5] Lesser state executive officers, such as Frank M. Jordan, the secretary of state, were reelected in this manner term after term. Occasionally, a major office would be won in the primaries. Hiram Johnson gained three party nominations—Republican, Democratic, and Progressive—for reelection to the U.S. Senate in 1940. Earl Warren won both major party nominations for his second term as governor in 1946, and William Knowland was nominee of both Republicans and Democrats for reelection as U.S. Senator in 1952.

THE MOVE TO ABOLISH CROSS-FILING   Increasing criticism of the cross-filing system arose. It was argued that the practice gave an unfair advantage to certain types of candidates: (1) the incumbent who always headed the list and was usually better known than any of the other candidates,

---

[5] Joseph P. Harris, *California Politics* (Stanford: Stanford University Press, 1955), p. 42.

(2) the candidate with the most money who could mount a "blitzkrieg" campaign in the primaries and capture both party nominations before the opposition could get organized, and (3) the candidate with the most extensive newspaper support, since many voters did follow the recommendations of their local editor in voting for the state officials. Democrats insisted that cross-filing was especially favorable to Republicans because they were often incumbents and definitely had more money and press support than did their Democratic opponents. Another serious objection was that cross-filing weakened party responsibility and cohesiveness. It would be absurd for the Democratic state convention to meet after the primary, adopt a platform, and pledge all the Democratic nominees to support that platform, when as a matter of fact most of the winners of the Democratic nominations were Republicans who had successfully cross-filed. Furthermore, in every election cross-filing had produced a minority winner somewhere in the state. That is, a candidate would have won both party nominations through a plurality vote (not a majority) in each party. The majority of voters in that primary had voted against that candidate but he was to all practical intents elected.

Supported by the League of Women Voters and other groups, the California Democratic leadership waged a campaign in the 1950's to abolish cross-filing. Seeking to forestall this, the legislature, most of whose members were beneficiaries of cross-filing, proposed a change in the law which was approved by the voters in 1952. The election-law amendment required that in future primary elections the names of candidates would appear on the ballot along with the party of their affiliation. (From the 1914 through the 1952 elections there were no party labels for candidates in the primaries.) Therefore, beginning in 1954 party designations appeared on the primary ballots, usually in abbreviated form—"Rep." for Republican, "Dem." for Democrat, and "Proh" for Prohibition. (Wags suggested that "Rep." stood for Reprehensible and "Dem." for Demagogue.)

Partly as a result of this change the number of successful cross-filers diminished dramatically between 1954 and 1958. However, the drive for outright abolition was too strong to be stayed by any half-measures. Pat Brown was elected governor in 1958 on a platform that included a promise to eliminate the practice. The 1959 legislature, under strong Democratic control, changed the primary election to prohibit cross-filing. Since then, the only way a candidate can capture the nomination of any party other than his own is by a write-in campaign.

The Presidential Primary

A voter in the direct partisan primary in presidential election years is given the opportunity to select California's delegates to the national nominating convention of his party. California is among the majority of states that have taken the selection of national convention delegates away from the party committees or state party conventions.

California's convention delegates for each party, varying each convention year according to formulas set by the national parties (in 1976, there were 280 Democratic delegates and 96 Republicans—each with one vote), were selected as a group rather than individually. A Democratic voter, for example, chose between slates of Democrats seeking to be delegates.

California is in the midstream of sweeping changes in its presidential primary. Prior to 1972 each presidential candidate would designate a committee of his supporters in California. This committee would draw up a list or slate of candidates for seats in the national convention and then would circulate petitions. If enough registered voters of the party (at least 0.5 percent of the vote cast for the party's candidate in the last gubernatorial election) signed the petitions the slate would be placed on the presidential primary ballot. On primary election day in June,[6] the registrant who had indicated his party preference received a ballot containing rival slates of delegates.[7] The slate receiving the

---

[6] California has a *consolidated* presidential primary. The ballot contains not only the slates of delegates for the national convention but also the usual lists of candidates seeking congressional, state legislative, county, and judicial offices.

[7] The official ballot does not list individual members on the rival slates of delegates. The slates are merely identified by the particular presidential candidate to whom they are pledged. The voter, however, receives a list of the individuals on the rival slates by mail in the packet containing his sample ballot.

highest number of votes became California's delegation to the national convention of the party. Members of the delegation were considered to be morally bound to support the designated candidate until released by him. Hence, California has had a "winner-take-all" primary.

The McGovern-Fraser Commission of the national Democratic party ordained some significant changes in the manner in which delegates to the party's 1972 national convention were chosen. Accordingly, each Democratic presidential candidate who wished to enter the California primary called a caucus of his or her supporters in every one of the state's forty-three congressional districts. Each caucus, by secret ballot, would nominate a specified number of individuals. Then, a statewide committee representing the candidate would make up a slate of delegates from the names submitted by the district caucuses. In the June primary the Democratic voters of California chose among eight rival slates on the "winner-take-all" basis. The Republicans, meanwhile, held no district caucuses and relied on state committees to draw up the slates for the two contenders in their primary (President Nixon and Representative John Ashbrook).

Perhaps even more upsetting to California's political *status quo* was a provision adopted as a constitutional amendment in the June 1972 primary and incorporated as a part of the revised Article II in November of that year. In this measure the voters ordered the legislature to set up the "Oregon-type" presidential primary effective for the 1976 elections. Instead of the presidential candidates having to take the initiative in getting their names on the California ballot, it will now be the responsibility of California's secretary of state. He is to keep himself abreast of any political gossip and is to place on the presidential primary ballot the names of all persons whom he finds are "recognized candidates throughout the nation or throughout California for the office of President of the United States." Any candidate whom the secretary of state chooses not to recognize may still get on the ballot by circulating petitions among his supporters in California. Furthermore, a person whose name the secretary of state has chosen to put on the ballot may withdraw by filing an affidavit that he is not a candidate. The legislature must enact laws to implement this new plan, e.g., specifying the method of selecting the slates of delegates who will be pledged to the various candidates named by the secretary of state.

The Democratic party has added a further complication. Its 1972 national convention voted a prohibition against "winner-take-all" primaries. As of 1976 each presidential candidate is to receive delegates from California in proportion to his popular vote in the Democratic presidential primary, or, at least, some of the delegates are to be elected by the districts rather than the state at large. In compliance with both the California constitution and the rules of the Democratic national convention, the California legislature in the fall of 1974 enacted a law that established new procedures for the Democratic presidential primary, leaving the Republican primary unchanged. The new statute divides the Democratic presidential primary ballot in 1976 into two parts: (1) the Presidential Preference section and (2) the Delegate Selection portion. The Presidential Preference part will be set up according to the "Oregon-type" primary. The California secretary of state is to place on this ballot the names of all candidates "generally advocated for or recognized in the news media throughout the United States or California as actively seeking the nomination of the Democratic Party for President of the United States." By February 1, 1976, the secretary of state is to announce publicly the names she intends to place on the ballot. Any person named may have himself crossed off the list by submitting an affidavit that he "is not now a candidate" for president. Furthermore, any Democrat not chosen by the secretary of state may have his name added as a presidential hopeful by circulating a petition and securing the signatures of 1 percent of the registered Democratic voters in California.

On primary election day in June 1976, California Democrats will indicate their favorite among the candidates appearing on this Preference ballot. However, this phase of the primary will be only a "straw vote"; it will be purely advisory with no binding effect. The really significant choices will be made in the Delegate Selection section of the ballot. It is by this means that California's delegates who will actually vote in the Democratic National Convention will be chosen. Most of the state's delegates will be

DEMOCRATIC

FOR DELEGATES TO NATIONAL CONVENTION		Vote for One Group Only	
Candidates Pledged to GEORGE S. McGOVERN	Democratic	2 ➞	○
Candidates Pledged to EDMUND S. MUSKIE	Democratic	3 ➞	○
Candidates Pledged to SHIRLEY CHISHOLM	Democratic	4 ➞	○
Candidates Pledged to JOHN V. LINDSAY	Democratic	5 ➞	○
Candidates Pledged to HUBERT H. HUMPHREY	Democratic	6 ➞	○
Candidates Pledged to EUGENE J. McCARTHY	Democratic	7 ➞	○
Candidates Pledged to SAMUEL WILLIAM YORTY	Democratic	8 ➞	○
Candidates Pledged to HENRY M. JACKSON	Democratic	9 ➞	○

chosen by congressional districts. Each presidential candidate will have the opportunity to nominate candidates for delegates in each congressional district. The persons he has named will be pledged to support him if they are elected delegates.[8] In addition, any group of five California Democrats may, by circulating petitions, place on the ballot a slate of unpledged candidates for delegates who are not committed to any particular presidential candidate. On primary election day the Democrats in each congressional district will elect their quota of delegates. Following the primary, the elected delegates from all forty-three districts

[8] The actual pledge taken by a candidate for delegate reads: "I personally prefer _____ as nominee of the Democratic Party for President of the United States, and hereby declare to the voters of the Democratic Party in the State of California that if elected as a delegate to their national party convention, I shall support _____ as nominee of my party for President of the United States until released by him or until he fails to receive at least 15 percent of the vote on any ballot wherein his name is placed before the convention in nomination."

will meet and select additional delegates from the state at large to complete California's contingent to the Democratic National Convention.

The Nonpartisan "Primary"

One state executive officer—the superintendent of public instruction—superior, municipal, and justice court judges,[9] and county elective officers are *elected* at the June primary elections when their terms expire. They appear on the ballot without any party affiliation, and may be voted upon by *all* registered voters. The candidate who receives a majority of the votes for one of these nonpartisan offices is declared elected. If no candidate receives a majority, a run-off is held at the coming November election between the two candidates with the highest number of votes.

Many California voters do not declare their affiliation with any of the legally recognized political parties in this state; at the time of registration they either "Decline to State" their party preference or they indicate membership in one of the small, unofficial parties. None of these Californians may vote for candidates for partisan office in the June primary, but they are instead given an abbreviated ballot with only the names of candidates for nonpartisan office. Secretary of State Edmund G. Brown, Jr., in 1974 expressed concern over the fact that more than one half million Californians had declined to state their party affiliation, representing an increase of almost 75 percent in this group since 1970. Particularly disturbing was the large number of young voters, between eighteen and twenty years of age, among the "Declined to State." To Brown, this betokened a growing disenchantment with politicians and the political party system.[10]

Municipal officers are also elected on a nonpartisan basis in all general law cities on the second Tuesday in March or on the corresponding Tuesday in April. Charter cities may set their own election dates, but usually these are held in March or in April.

---

[9] The special provisions for the appointment and election of supreme court and district courts of appeal judges will be discussed under the court system in Chapter Nine.

[10] *La Habra Star*, April 17, 1974.

PRESIDENTIAL ELECTORS		Vote For One Party	
BENJAMIN SPOCK, for President JULIUS HOBSON, for Vice President	Peace and Freedom	**2** ➔	◯
GEORGE McGOVERN, for President R. SARGENT SHRIVER, for Vice President	Democratic	**3** ➔	◯
RICHARD M. NIXON, for President SPIRO T. AGNEW, for Vice President	Republican	**4** ➔	◯
JOHN G. SCHMITZ, for President THOMAS J. ANDERSON, for Vice President	American Independent	**5** ➔	◯

THE NOVEMBER GENERAL ELECTION

The final election for partisan offices and those non-partisan offices in which runoffs are necessary, as well as the vote upon most state and county ballot propositions, is held in every even-numbered year on the first Tuesday after the first Monday in November. All registered voters are eligible to vote, and receive the same ballots regardless of their party affiliation.

Presidential Election Years

The ballot is slightly different in alternating general election years. In every presidential election year no state executive offices are filled, but California's presidential electors are chosen.[11] Each party's list of presidential electors is selected at its state convention in its fall meeting preceding the general election. The names of each party's presidential electors do not appear on the general election ballot, however. The ballot contains only the names of the national party candidates for president and vice-president as shown in the sample above. The votes cast for president and vice-president are officially counted as votes for the bloc of presidential electors of each party. The electors of the party whose candidates receive the highest vote are

---

[11] The number of each state's presidential electors is the same as its total representation in the U.S. Congress (California: forty-three representatives and two senators).

declared elected; and all meet in Sacramento on the first Monday after the second Wednesday in December (as required by act of Congress) to cast California's *entire* electoral vote for their party's two candidates. The California law is explicit in binding the electors to vote for only the official candidates of their party. However, this has never been enforced because a federal law permits an elector to vote for a candidate of any party.

CALIFORNIA'S BALLOT FORM

"Long"

A *long* ballot is one that gives the voter many things to decide. A state like California—in which there are ten state executives to be elected besides the governor, as well as judges and local government officials, and a host of ballot

"Harold's getting in shape to fill out the June primary ballot. . . ."

Graysmith in the San Francisco Chronicle, *April 28, 1974. Reprinted by permission.*

propositions, bond issues, and charter amendments to be approved—may be said to have a very long ballot. A voter in an average precinct who took his suffrage privilege seriously would be obliged to mark a total of about 100 crosses in the primary and general elections! The voters complain of the ballot's length, but appear reluctant to part with their opportunity to choose and approve, as evidenced in their rejection of a 1958 ballot proposition which would have made the position of state superintendent of public instruction appointive.

"Office-Block"

The California ballot is divided by office rather than by political party, as in some states. Under the heading "Governor," for example, are listed all the candidates for that office from all qualified parties. With the office-block, in contrast to the party-column form, there is no time saved by voting a straight party ticket. Advocates of tighter party discipline are dissatisfied with the present California ballot; some, like William Munnell, former Democratic floor leader in the state assembly, have urged the institution of the straight-ticket option in which one cross placed at the head of a party column is counted as a vote for all the candidates of that party.

THE ADMINISTRATION OF ELECTIONS

Election Officials

The chief elections officer of the state is the secretary of state, and copies of nomination and election petitions must be filed with him. He also has the major responsibility for ballot specifications and arrangements, and certifies and publishes the final vote count. However, the actual preparation of election ballots, selection of voting sites, and counting of votes are the responsibility of the county clerk or registrar of voters in each county. And the county board of supervisors appoints the board of election officials who are the precinct election workers seen at polling places on election day. In municipal elections the city council appoints these workers.

The California Voter's Calendar

Dates	Purpose	Frequency
REGISTRATION		
At least 30 days prior to election day	Deadline for new voters or those who must reregister	Before June primaries or November general election
PRIMARIES		
Nominating Candidates		
First Tuesday after first Monday in June	U. S. senators (2) upon expiration of their alternating terms	One every 6 years from 1964 (1970, 1976) and one every 6 years from 1968 (1974, 1980)
	U. S. representatives (43), state senators (half of 40), state assemblymen (80)	Even-numbered years (1972, 1974, 1976)
	State executive officers (10)	Every 4 years (1974, 1978)
Election		
	Party county committeemen	Even-numbered years
	State supt. of public instruction	Every 4 years (1974, 1978)
	Judicial and county officers	Even-numbered years
	Delegates to national party conventions (presidential primary)	Every 4 years (1976, 1980)

Dates	Purpose	Frequency

GENERAL ELECTION

Election

| First Tuesday after first Monday in November | All officers nominated in the June primary All "runoff" contests for minority winners in June elections and primaries for supt. of public instruction, judicial and county officers | In years indicated above |
| | Presidential electors | Every 4 years (1976, 1980) |

Approving or rejecting:

| | State and local ballot propositions (initiative, referendum, amendments) Bond issues (state and local) | Even-numbered years |

MUNICIPAL ELECTIONS
(For all general law cities and most charter cities)

| Second Tuesday in March or second Tuesday in April | City officers: councilmen, mayor, treasurer, clerk, and others | Even-numbered years |

SPECIAL ELECTIONS

| Upon call by governor | For unexpired terms: U. S. representatives, state senators, state assemblymen | When such vacancies occur |
| | For ballot measures | |

General Procedures

Voting precincts of an estimated 200 voters each are established by the county election officials and are consolidated for local elections. Within each precinct a polling place is selected and polling booths erected. The polling place may be in almost any convenient building—a private home, a school, the lobby of an apartment house, or a garage, but not a liquor store or bar (a curious restriction in view of the law that prevents alcoholic beverages from being *sold* on election days). The polls are open from 7 A.M. to 8 P.M. in most counties. As soon as the polls have closed, the precinct boards begin to count the votes (called the first "canvass") in the presence of all bystanders. This is usually done at the polling establishments, but provision may be made by county officials for a central counting. The results are posted at each precinct and released to the press. The second "canvass" takes place when county officials—again in public—add together the returns of the individual precincts. The county sends copies of all returns to the secretary of state, and stores all ballots for six months, after which they are destroyed.

Automatic voting machines, where the voter pulls a lever to indicate his choice, are being used in a few California counties including San Francisco. In some counties, voting is still by the old-style rubber stamp on paper ballots which are counted by hand. But in the majority of counties, including Los Angeles, the voter marks his ballot by some kind of stylus or marking device and the ballots are then counted by electronic machines.

Special Protections

California's election laws have numerous provisions designed to insure fair play and guard against fraud. Each detail, from the opening and inspecting of the empty ballot box on election morning to the defacing and destruction of unused and voided ballots, is carefully outlined in the 11,700 sections of the state Elections Code. All election proceedings, for example, must be conducted in English. No election official while on duty may carry on a conversation in a foreign language. No one may speak to a voter within 100 feet of a polling place about his vote. Employers who include political propaganda in the pay checks of their employees are guilty of a misdemeanor. Voting is secret, behind curtains; but a voter may not remain in a polling booth longer than ten minutes. All business concerns, according to law, must give their employees sufficient time to vote on election day. There are provisions for challenging voters at the polls who are suspected of fraudulent voting and for challenging counts and demanding recounts. Penalties are stiff for voter intimidation or inducements in the form of money, property, or employment.

SELECTED REFERENCES

California, Secretary of State, *Statement of Vote.* Sacramento: State Printing Office. Issued after each general, primary, and special election.

California Voters' Handbook. Pasadena: League of Women Voters of California, 1974.

Elections Code, State of California. San Francisco: Deering, 1973.

The Development of Politics in California

Today's political scene in California presents a curious paradox. It is typical of the politics of the United States as a whole yet at the same time unique. All the characteristic features of American political life appear to be magnified on California's wide technicolor screen—the emphasis on pragmatism over philosophical consistency, side by side with an abundance of utopian cults that have earned for the state the label of "The Land of Loony Schemes and Political Extremes"; the frontier psychology, which admires individualism but is suspicious of excellence, which puts a premium upon material success yet resents the wealthy and worships the glamorous; and the bizarre campaigning, with candidates expected to demonstrate facility in every field of human endeavor, from baby-burping to zoo-tending and Indian smoke-dancing. California has already produced its share of demagogues and statesmen, and indications are that in the future it will continue to make generous contributions in both categories. California is typical; but it is dramatically unique among the other states in being the *most* typical of all!

In the California electorate of the middle 1970's, one can find not only the history of the state, but also a pretty good approximation of the current political sociology of the entire country. To appreciate California's heterogeneity— as well as the headaches it presents to strategists of both major parties—it is helpful to divide the state into four major geopolitical areas:

The San Francisco, Berkeley, Oakland Complex, plus coastal regions up to the Oregon border and down to the Tehachapis (about 25 percent of the state's population): predominantly cosmopolitan, Establishmentarian, intellectual, post-New Deal liberal, internationalist, with a small but visible supply of youth and radical militants.

The Southern California Sunbelt, including Orange, San Diego, and the six other Southern California counties but excluding the city of Los Angeles (about 45 percent of the state's population): mostly middle-class families who originally came from the Middle-American plains states and are now employed by or indirectly dependent upon the research and development and electronics industries of Southern California. This group is made up of a relatively large proportion of engineers, high-paid blue-collar technicians, or construction and service industry people.

The City of Los Angeles, plus Hollywood, Beverly Hills, Culver City, and Venice (about 15 percent of the state's population): a melange of black and Chicano ghettos, blue-collar whites, pensioners, media and academic elites, investment and savings-and-loan executives and their middle-income white-collar entourages. This is a politically volatile area subject to bitter polarization.

The Interior Agricultural Plateau (about 15 percent of the state's population): Dominated by the immense Central Valley, the breadbasket of California is highly dependent upon government-run hydroelectric, irrigation, and agricultural programs; it is also the area that employs the most migrant Mexican farm workers.

The above sketch outlines only the gross topographic features of the California polity today. A more refined picture of its complexities requires a bit of political geology, digging below the contemporary surface to discover the historical strata.

THE PERIOD OF KEARNEYISM

Kearneyism grew out of the overcrowded labor market resulting from the economic depression of the 1870's. The thousands of Chinese laborers laid off by the railroad builders upon the completion of the transcontinental lines made the employment situation especially critical, and gave California's brand of antimonopoly agitation its peculiar racist flavor. Newton Booth won the governorship in 1870 on a platform containing Chinese-exclusion and railroad-regulation planks. But the legislature merely enacted a series of measures that harassed the Chinese and denied them civil rights, without doing anything to keep them from coming, prevent them from staying, or find them work.

When the delayed reaction to the panic of 1873 hit California with full impact, white labor agitation against the "Yellow Peril" and the railroad menace reached the point of hysteria. In 1877, the Workingmen's party under the leadership of Denis Kearney, a young San Francisco drayman, gave organized political expression to the popular anger. In addition to demanding Chinese exclusion acts, the Workingmen's party urged state regulation of the railroads and banks, an equitable system of taxation, an eight-hour day, the abolition of contract labor on public works, compulsory education, and the direct election of U.S. senators. With this program the Kearneyites elected one-third of the delegates to the constitutional convention of 1878–79. Their proposals for regulating big business, Chinese exclusion, and the eight-hour day were enacted, and they succeeded in electing ten senators and sixteen assemblymen to the 1880 legislature. But with a substantial part of their program adopted, and a rapid economic upswing during the next few years, the Workingmen's party became a political nonentity by 1885. Its lasting effect was in firing up resentment against the railroad machine—a popular sentiment the Progressives had no trouble rekindling two decades later.

THE AGE OF THE RAILROAD MAGNATES

In the prosperous eighties, with the demise of the Kearney reformers, the railroad magnates had an open field for molding the state legislature into a responsive political instrument. Economic power—and consequently, political power—became concentrated in the hands of the railroads' "Big Four": Leland Stanford, Collis Huntington, Charles Crocker, and Mark Hopkins. According to California historian John Caughey:

> there was hardly an office, from the seats in the United States Senate down through the governorship and the courts to the most inconsiderable town office, in which the right man could not do the railroad a service.[1]

The domination of California politics by the Southern Pacific Railroad went virtually unchallenged from the decline of Kearneyism to the rise of the Progressive movement. As late as July 4, 1908, the *San Francisco Call* reported that "the railroad company machine" kept an "expert political manager" in every county in California to see that "the right men were chosen as convention delegates, the right kind of candidates . . . elected, and the right things done by the men in office."

THE PROGRESSIVE ERA

Reformist sentiment sweeping the country at the start of the twentieth century, under the leadership of Theodore Roosevelt and Robert M. LaFollette, was organized into a political movement in California by the Lincoln-Roosevelt League. Reacting to the bullying of the 1906 Republican state convention by the Southern Pacific machine and San Francisco's notorious Abe "Boss" Ruef, a group of Republican newspaper editors and publishers began to drum up sentiment against the railroad. In 1907 they called a convention of dissatisfied Republicans and launched the Lincoln-Roosevelt League, pledging the "emancipation" of the California Republican party "from domination by the political bureau of the Southern Pacific . . ."; the enactment of a direct primary to give "the party voter a . . . voice in the selection of party candidates"; the direct election of United States senators; and the "selection of delegates to the next

[1] John W. Caughey, *California*, 2d ed. (Englewood Cliffs, N.J.: Prentice-Hall, 1953), pp. 449–50.

Republican National Convention pledged to the nomination of Theodore Roosevelt for President." [2]

In the election of 1908 the voters approved by an overwhelming majority an amendment to the California constitution instituting the direct primary system. Thus, in the next gubernatorial election the League was given a chance to displace the entrenched Republican leadership. It prevailed upon Hiram W. Johnson—who had just made a name for himself as a prosecuting attorney in the graft trials against Boss Ruef—to be the Lincoln–Roosevelt candidate for governor in 1910. Johnson conducted an aggressive primary election campaign, touring the entire state and promising to "kick the Southern Pacific Railroad out of the Republican Party and out of the state government." [3] He soundly defeated four candidates for the office, including one who was endorsed by the Southern Pacific machine.

Johnson's administration, aided by League majorities in both houses of the legislature, was responsible for a series of far-reaching "Progressive" measures including the establishment of the initiative, referendum, and recall; the cross-filing system; county home rule; the extension of civil service throughout the state government; the revitalization of the State Railroad Commission, extending its power over all public utilities, and giving it the power to fix rates and determine the character of services; the prohibition of child labor; workmen's compensation laws; and the inauguration of many flood control, reclamation, and conservation projects.

The state's first Progressive legislature made such an impact that Theodore Roosevelt called its work "the most comprehensive program of constructive legislation ever passed at a single session of an American Legislature." [4] On the other side of the fence (or should we say the tracks) the conservative *San Francisco Call* branded it the "Legislature of a Thousand Freaks." Similarly, the *San Francisco Chronicle* called the 1913 session "A Legislature of Progressive

[2] George E. Mowry, *The California Progressive* (Berkeley: University of California Press, 1951), p. 70.

[3] Caughey, *California*, p. 463.

[4] Ibid., p. 464.

Cranks," complaining that "the number of tomfool bills is beyond computation."

The national Progressive party rewarded Johnson by making him Theodore Roosevelt's running mate in the 1912 presidential election. (Roosevelt lost to Woodrow Wilson in 1912.) Johnson was reelected governor in 1914. He ran successfully for the U.S. Senate in 1916 and resigned his governorship to go to Washington. The Progressives continued to occupy the gubernatorial mansion at Sacramento as William Stephens, Johnson's handpicked successor, won the election of 1918. By the 1920's, however, Progressivism had spent itself as a potent and dramatic political force. Most of its reforms had become permanent in California, and it was left without a cause to champion.

REPUBLICAN NORMALCY

Postwar prosperity brought popular complacency toward politics and government. A succession of regular Republican governors kept things on an even keel in Sacramento while San Francisco rocked with the jazz age and real estate boomed in Los Angeles. Democrats seemed content to leave mundane official affairs to Republican incumbents. Throughout the 1920's they held no more than 10 percent of the seats in the state assembly, winning only three out of seventy-seven in the 1922 election. The only significant political rivalries of the time were north–south and rural–urban, and these focused on the issue of legislative reapportionment.

While in 1900 Southern California had only 20 percent of the state's population, by 1920 it had nearly 40 percent and was continuing to gain rapidly. This population explosion—especially in Los Angeles—threatened the domination of the legislature by the northern and rural interests. Southern Californians were outraged when the legislature refused to redraw state senate and assembly districts after the 1920 census. Accordingly, a Los Angeles group, the All-Parties Reapportionment Committee, drafted a constitutional amendment making reapportionment mandatory. Northern and rural interests (the Farm Bureau Federation, the State Grange, the Farmers' Union, and the San Francisco Chamber of Commerce) countered with their so-called Federal Plan. The plan also made reapportionment mandatory, but changed the basis of apportioning seats in the upper house: whereas previously senators, like assemblymen, were chosen from districts of approximately equal population, the proposed plan would have them chosen by counties, thus assuring a greater number of northern and rural senators.[5] In the election of 1926 both measures came up for a vote. Only the voters of Los Angeles County favored their own plan, however, while the Federal Plan carried the state.

DEPRESSION POLITICS

The effects of the Great Depression of the 1930's were especially severe in California since many of the state's major industries—motion pictures, tourist attractions, and olive, date, fig, and citrus production—were nonessentials. Despite the lack of jobs, thousands of persons from other hardhit areas flocked to the "Promised Land."

> "Oh, but she's worth it," said Wilson [in John Steinbeck's *The Grapes of Wrath*]. "Why, I seen han' bills how they need folks to pick fruit, an' good wages. . . . An' with them good wages, maybe a fella can get hisself a little piece of land an' work out for extra cash. Why, hell, in a couple years I bet a fella could have a place of his own."

The ranks of the unemployed were swelled dangerously. The resulting wage cutting and scramble for jobs intensified labor bitterness and encouraged rivalry between organized and unorganized workers. Severe strikes, especially in the agricultural and shipping industries, were frequent. The stage was set for reformers, demagogues, and cure-all plans. Visionary groups such as the Technocrats and the Utopian Society brought new illusions to the disillusioned, while religious cults of the Aimee Semple McPherson variety made heaven not much different from Hollywood. However, the period did produce movements with a definite political impact: Upton Sinclair revived dor-

[5] See pp. 139–40 for the effects of this system upon representation in recent years.

mant Progressivism and brought it into the Democratic party in socialist dress. California's aged were organized into a powerful lobby that is a weighty political factor today. And the state got its first Democratic governor in forty years.

The Epic Crusade

Upton Sinclair, famous novelist and former Socialist gubernatorial candidate, captured the Democratic nomination for governor in 1934. He built his campaign around the EPIC (End Poverty in California) plan, calling for: state-owned-and-operated farms and factories to provide jobs for the unemployed, state distribution of the products of these farms and factories, and the printing of a special state currency to finance the new state projects; replacing the sales tax by a steeply graduated income tax to fall most on large corporations and wealthy individuals, tax exemption for small property owners, a modified form of the Henry George single tax; and a pension of $50 a month to those who were needy because of old age, widowhood, or physical incapacity.

Sinclair was a popular candidate, but his extreme program stimulated a highly organized counterattack by more conservative Republicans and Democrats alike. Even Socialist Norman Thomas said that Sinclair had "promised the impossible," and that his election would be "a tragedy to himself and the cause of radicalism." [6] In the November election he was defeated by the lackluster Republican Frank Merriam, receiving 879,557 votes to Merriam's 1,138,620. However, two candidates supported by EPIC were successful. Culbert Olson was elected to the state senate (he became governor in 1938) and Sheridan Downey was elected U.S. senator in 1938. Sinclair went into retirement and continued to write novels.

The Pension Fever

During Sinclair's election campaign the competing plan to cure the Depression was advanced by a retired physician of Long Beach, Dr. Francis Townsend. Every

[6] Robert G. Cleland, *California in Our Time, 1900–1940* (New York: Alfred A. Knopf, 1947), p. 226.

person over sixty would receive $200 a month with the requirement that each installment be spent within three months. The plan was to be implemented nationwide, financed by a 2 percent federal tax on all commercial transactions. Sinclair denounced the Townsend Plan. But Merriam, conscious of the enthusiasm with which California's great number of senior citizens greeted the scheme, endorsed it a few weeks before election. (As governor, Merriam could conveniently brush off the Townsendites since their program called for national implementation.)

The Townsend movement generated a pension fever, however, which soon reached epidemic proportions. In advance of the next gubernatorial election a new wave of it broke out, with the "Thirty-Dollars-Every Thursday" (alias "Ham and Eggs") scheme the most prominent. Sponsored by a group of professional promoters, it appeared on the 1938 ballot as a constitutional amendment providing that every Thursday all unemployed persons over fifty would receive "state warrants" worth $30 and redeemable after one year. The program was to be financed by a stamp tax and by bonds sold to the California public. The Democratic candidates for governor and U.S. senator both went on record as favoring the amendment. Both Democrats won by narrow margins, and although "Ham and Eggs" lost, it was considered to have helped the Democratic cause.

The Democratic Interlude

In 1936, two years prior to Culbert Olson's election as governor, the California Democratic party was swept along in the New Deal landslide, winning fifteen of California's twenty congressional seats and forty-five of the eighty state assembly seats—the best year for California Democrats until their 1958 sweep. When Olson won the governorship and Sheridan Downey the senatorship in 1938, the tide had already turned away from the Democrats. The Democratic delegation to Congress was reduced to twelve and Democratic assembly seats to forty-two. And despite Olson's victory the Republicans retained the offices of attorney general, secretary of state, controller, and treasurer.

Culbert Olson, a reformer at heart, had the misfortune of becoming governor during the later stages of the Depression. Not only did his party have a diminished majority in the assembly, but an "economy bloc" of Democrats in the legislature cooperated with Republicans to frustrate him. He was able to accomplish some reforms, however, in the state's penal system and in the areas of youth corrections and mental hygiene.

During Olson's administration the "Yellow Peril" was rediscovered—this time in different garb. After Pearl Harbor the California Joint Immigration Committee (sponsored by the State Grange, the State Federation of Labor, the American Legion, and the Native Sons and Daughters of the Golden West) agitated for evacuation of the Japanese from the state. Olson disliked the idea at first but eventually cooperated with federal authorities in evacuating the 94,-000 Japanese living in California to special security camps. Critics suspected that the federal order reflected more than "security" considerations since it ordered the evacuation of *all* Japanese, but only those German and Italian aliens suspected of espionage and sabotage were evacuated. The judgments by American historians of this episode in the California story are understandably harsh. The following comment is typical:

> In retrospect the evacuation of the Japanese appears both cruel and unnecessary. . . . That Olson took no stronger line [opposing it] than he did is clear evidence that even a man of liberal instincts and genuine humanitarianism could be bewildered by the forces set in motion by the waving of "California's Bloody Shirt." [7]

THE WARREN ERA

Earl Warren always considered himself a Hiram Johnson Progressive. Entering public service in 1919, he rapidly rose to the position of district attorney of Alameda County. In 1936, still only forty-five years old, Warren became chairman of the Republican State Central Committee and led California's delegation to the Republican National Convention. In 1938, he won the nomination of the Republican, Democratic, and Progressive parties in the primaries for the

[7] Robert E. Burke, *Olson's New Deal for California* (Berkeley: University of California Press, 1953), p. 206.

position of attorney general under Democrat Culbert Olson. So began his successful nonpartisan career.

Warren tried for both the Democratic and Republican gubernatorial nomination in 1942, but Olson led in the Democratic primary. In the general election campaign Warren continued to style himself a nonpartisan. Olson was disturbed by the lack of a well-defined target and called Warren a "puppet pretender." On election eve the Democratic incumbent charged:

> Anyone who is so cowardly as to put on the cloak of non-partisanship in an election like this, either acknowledges that he is a political eunuch and does not know what it is all about, or that he is a political hypocrite. This non-partisan, non-political propaganda is a piece of colossal deceit. It is essentially a lie.[8]

The following day Warren handily defeated Olson at the polls, receiving 57 percent of the vote to Olson's 42 percent. If it is a misfortune that "only men of very loose political affiliations, like Warren, can be elected," commented one analyst, "the blame must be attributed to the [Hiram] Johnson crusade which pounded the ruling party into so many fragments that no one has ever put it together again." [9]

Warren's nonpartisanship paid off spectacularly in 1946 when he won the nomination for governor in both the Republican and Democratic primaries. In 1950 James Roosevelt was able to capture the Democratic nomination, but Warren beat him by more than a million votes in the November general election. The Warren formula for success has been aptly summed up by political scientist Joseph P. Harris.[10] Warren had a keen awareness of the controlling features of California politics: the large proportion of independent voters, and the necessity for a candidate for governor to appeal to the liberal urban vote as well as the conservative elements in the state. He followed essentially a middle-of-the-road course which was displeasing to both the

[8] Ibid., p. 216.

[9] Raymond Moley, in *The Politics of California: A Book of Readings*, eds. David Farrelly and Ivan Hinderaker (New York: Ronald, 1951), p. 220.

[10] Joseph P. Harris, *California Politics*, rev. ed. (Stanford: Stanford University Press, 1961), p. 8.

extreme right and the extreme left but was agreeable to the large body of voters in between. He was able to retain the support of both organized labor and the business community.

Warren's ten-year governorship—the longest in California's history—was highlighted by a greatly expanded state welfare program, including old age pensions, workmen's compensation, mental hospital and prison reforms. His political popularity allowed him to press through the legislature almost anything he requested. The outstanding exception was his compulsory health insurance plan, which, after determined opposition by the powerful California Medical Association lobby, was defeated in the legislature.

The popular California governor received the Republican vice-presidential nomination in 1948, becoming the running mate of Thomas E. Dewey. He was considered a leading contender for the Republican nomination for president in 1952 until the Eisenhower candidacy was announced. In 1953, Eisenhower appointed him chief justice of the United States Supreme Court. With Warren no longer active in California politics, leadership of the state Republican forces was divided among three men: the new governor, Goodwin J. Knight (Warren's lieutenant governor); U.S. Senator William F. Knowland; and Vice-President Richard M. Nixon.

THE DEMOCRATIC RENAISSANCE: 1958–1964

From 1934 to 1956, more than two decades, California was a political enigma: the majority of its voters were registered Democrats and the majority of its elected officeholders were Republican. This disproportion between party registration and election results emerged at every biennial statewide election until 1958. Finally, in 1958, Californians voted in more partisan fashion. Democrats, led by gubernatorial candidate Pat Brown, won 62 percent of the contested offices. Suddenly, they found themselves in control of both the executive and the legislature.[11]

[11] The year 1958 was the first since 1888 in which the Democrats won control of the legislature; and their popular vote margin was the largest won by either party since 1883.

However, when the absentee ballots gave California to presidential candidate Nixon in 1960 by 35,623 votes, many Democrats were abruptly returned to reality for the first time since election eve two years previously. Although the Democrats retained their sixteen to fourteen hold on California's congressional delegation, kept their forty-seven to thirty-three majority in the state assembly, and even gained three seats in the state senate, they were once again unable to translate their huge registration majority into a voting majority.

Election postmortems fixed on the following factors: organized Democrats were divided, while the Republican organization—with Knowland and Knight out of the klieg lights—was united behind the Nixon wing of the party. Moreover, Republican financial sources, which seemingly evaporated in 1958, had again begun to flow—particularly as the sharp drop in Pat Brown's prestige following the Chessman case (see pp. 196–97) gave them hope of regaining the governorship in 1962. And Nixon's home-town-boy-makes-good campaign had been effective.

Nixon's Bid for the Governorship in 1962

In 1962 California's "nonpartisan" tradition was underlined once again by the electorate's ambivalence in reelecting a Democratic governor (by a margin of about 300,000) and a Republican U.S. senator (by a margin of over 700,000).

Nixon was faced with a painful dilemma: *either* effect Republican party unity by taking a swing to the "right," *or* continue to run down the center at the risk of losing the considerable financial and organizational, as well as enthusiastic, "grassroots" backing that conservatives could throw his way. Nixon attempted to avoid this dilemma by simultaneously taking *both* prongs of the fork in the road. To maintain the image of moderation he continued to repudiate the ultraright John Birch Society and those congressional candidates running under its banner, and he refused to join in the right wing chorus of condemnation of Chief Justice Earl Warren.

As a balance to the "liberal" image, Nixon gave increasingly more attention to the domestic communism issue as the campaign progressed, attempting to suggest that somehow the incumbent state administration was responsible for the problem in California. The result was a fragmented image, and the Democrats were handed the easy-to-exploit "same old Nixon" issue.

Governor Brown was more successful in maintaining the image of nonpartisanship. He stressed those issues with a minimum of ideological content such as the state water plan and school construction.

The hard factors of party organization and finance also played a considerable role. The Democrats ran a coordinated, efficient, and unusually well-financed operation —this time it was Republican unity that fell off the wall.

The 1964 Election

In 1964, California once again showed itself to be a "split ticket" state. President Johnson won the state's forty electoral votes from Barry Goldwater by a huge margin of 1.3 million, while the Democratic nominee for the U.S. Senate, Pierre Salinger, was losing to Republican George Murphy by 200,000. The Democrats secured a twenty-three to fifteen seat hold in the California delegation to the U.S. House of Representatives and retained twenty-seven out of the forty seats in the state senate. But the GOP picked up four seats in the state assembly, making the line-up in that body: Democrats forty-eight, Republicans thirty-two.

The major choice facing George Murphy was whether or not he should ride the coattails of the Republican presidential nominee. If Murphy were to present himself as a Goldwater Republican, and still hope to *win*, not only would he be bucking the thrust of recent California political history and all the latest public opinion polls, but he would also be giving up any chance of playing the role of happy conciliator between the "right" and "moderate" wings of California Republicanism after the election. Accordingly, in the words of the *Los Angeles Times*, "he danced in the middle of the stage . . . in the matter of Senator Goldwater," [12] as he also did on the controversial ballot measure Proposition 14, the state constitutional amendment to re-

[12] *Los Angeles Times*, November 8, 1964, Part II, p. 4.

peal California legislation outlawing racial discrimination in real estate transactions.

In some postmortems on Pierre Salinger's defeat by Murphy, Proposition 14 figured prominently. Salinger supported the "no" side; this increased his appeal among ethnic-minority communities and was important in regaining support from liberal volunteer Democrats of the California Democratic Council (CDC). Salinger's stand on Proposition 14 probably did him more harm than good among the non-committed, "nonpartisan" elements of the electorate and the nominal Democrats, many of whom are recent migrants from the South. The "carpetbagger" charge also hurt Salinger, as opponents played up his last-minute flight to California to beat the primary election filing deadline and his failure to meet the legal residence requirements.

REPUBLICAN 1966: TREND OR ANOMALY?

After the Goldwater Republicans took control of the Republican party in 1964 and lost the state badly to Johnson that fall, it was widely assumed that the California voting majority was now more than ever urban Democratic. The Brown organization was anxious for Ronald Reagan (who in recent years had shared the marquee with Barry Goldwater) to defeat San Francisco's former mayor, George Christopher, for the Republican nomination. The center of the road would again be for the Democrats. The Republicans would be off on the slippery right shoulder.

However, Reagan was cast in the nonpartisan mold for the general election. He played the part well and with dash. Moreover, it was a fresh Reagan. Brown was an old pro at the role of Mr. Everyman; but for him it was a rerun.

The returns tell the story: Reagan got 59 percent of the 6,370,000 votes cast. There were only 3,350,000 Republicans registered, as opposed to 4,720,000 Democrats. This means that *at least* 316,000 registered Democrats crossed party lines and voted for Reagan. The successful gubernatorial candidate brought into office with him the entire slate of Republican candidates for the other state executive offices—except attorney general, which was won by incumbent Thomas Lynch. The Republicans also severely cut into the Democratic control of the legislature, leaving only a four-member Democratic majority in the eighty-seat assembly, and a two-member Democratic majority in the newly apportioned senate. Similarly, the existing Democratic majority of eight in California's congressional delegation was halved to four.

This was the first statewide election since the rioting of blacks in Watts (see pp. 238–39) and since student demonstrations at Berkeley had caused the near paralysis of the University of California. In addition, 1966 was the first statewide election since the state supreme court had overruled the electorate's 1964 vote on Proposition 14 to repeal the Rumford open-occupancy legislation. Governor Brown seems to have been associated in the minds of some voters with the Watts riots and Berkeley disorders; and the Reagan campaign drummed it in by calling explicitly for a legislative repeal of the Rumford Act, calling for a more efficient system of law enforcement, and promising an investigation of the University of California—the implication being that the Brown administration was overzealous in sponsoring civil rights legislation and overpermissive on matters of law and order.

Partly to blame for Brown's poor showing in some traditionally liberal election districts was his failure sufficiently to inspire the more radical grassroots elements in his own party, and to galvanize the CDC and the professionals into coordinated precinct work. If he was unable to keep the "swing" vote because of Reagan's success in painting himself as a moderate, his take-it-easy approach on matters dear to the Democratic left prevented him from gaining overwhelming support among the liberals and ethnic voting blocs to counter his other losses.

The Republicans displayed a remarkable degree of unity, which was helped in part by the intervention of former President Eisenhower. Even during the primary election the bitter split that had developed between Goldwater Republicans and Kuchel Republicans was subdued under the authority of state chairman Gaylord Parkinson's eleventh commandment: "Thou shalt not speak ill of any other Republican."

Reagan was helped by the deft campaign management

of Spencer-Roberts and Associates [13] to purge his rhetoric of the more abrasive Goldwaterisms he had thrown around in 1964 and to stick to the standard Republican complaints against excessive government spending and against centralization of control in Washington and Sacramento at the expense of private initiative.

Reagan's only concessions to the more fundamentalist type of Goldwater conservatism were his endorsement of the CLEAN (antiobscenity) ballot proposition and his refusal to disavow the Birch society.

1968: THE POLITICS OF TRAUMA

The effects in California of the traumatic events experienced by the nation during 1967 and 1968—ghetto burnings, the assassinations of Martin Luther King, Jr., and Robert Kennedy, the withdrawal of Lyndon Johnson from the presidential contest, the increasing resort to tactics of violent confrontation on the campuses—seemed by the summer of 1968 to be leading to a left–right polarization. Whereas previously the broad "middle-of-the-road" was clearly the preferred position for the politician or party hoping to command the support of a statewide majority, extremist positions now appeared to have the greatest political magnetism.

The primary election contests in the spring of 1968 reflected and reinforced this apparent polarization. The Republican voters denied renomination to the politically moderate Senator Thomas Kuchel, selecting instead Max Rafferty, the superpatriotic superintendent of public instruction. Meanwhile California's Democrats overwhelmingly repudiated the Johnson-Humphrey administration. The administration-backed slate of convention delegates, headed by state Attorney General Thomas Lynch, received less than 12 percent of the vote. The differences between Senator Robert Kennedy (who won the presidential primary with 46.3 percent of the vote) and Senator Eugene McCarthy (who obtained 41.8 percent) were less significant

[13] See pp. 99–101 for further details on the activities of public relations firms.

than the fact that they both were strong antiadministration "doves" on Vietnam and also vitriolic critics of administration responses to the urban crisis in this country.

The murder of Senator Kennedy in Los Angeles during his California victory celebration on election night had the immediate effect of intensifying the left–right polarization. Kennedy and McCarthy supporters saw Kennedy's violent death in the context of the meanness, distrust, and violence associated with the Vietnam war. The Rafferty and Reagan camps attributed the rising tide of violence to the disrespect for authority, law, and order spread by the New Left and the black militants.

One of the few remaining links with the more solid tradition of California politics was assembly speaker Unruh, widely expected to seek the Democratic gubernatorial nomination in 1970. Dropping his sideburns a few inches and dropping the "e" from his first name, "Jess" Unruh stepped swiftly onto center stage to claim the starring role in the drama of the New Politics. Unruh was now in a position to make the McCarthy-supporting CDC come to him. Old pro Unruh turned out to be surprisingly convincing in his new role as leader of the dissident Democrats. He exploited the fact that he had early been a vocal opponent of the Johnson administration's handling of the war in Vietnam; and now, when it might have been tempting for a politician with gubernatorial ambitions to join the Humphrey forces in advance of the Chicago convention, he risked being passed over in 1970 rather than compromise his outspoken anti-administration views.

The national spotlight was on Unruh throughout the Democratic convention in Chicago. As leader of the huge 172-member California delegation previously committed to Robert Kennedy, Unruh was in the enviable position of being able to clinch a dramatic unity movement for Humphrey at any time. But his holdout to the last, and his tactical leadership among the shifting Kennedy-McGovern-McCarthy elements of the dissidents, gained him the admiration of the same people who used to regard Unruh as a symbol of machine politics. Upon his return to California he was affectionately adopted by the CDC as their new hero.

Humphrey's loss to Nixon of California's forty electoral

votes cannot be attributed mainly to the left–right polarization that seemed to characterize the period of the primaries. Nixon did get a 164,000-vote margin in Orange County and a 92,000 margin in San Diego County, but this expected showing in Southern California conservative country would have been insufficient to overcome Humphrey's strong pull in San Francisco, Alameda, San Mateo, and Sacramento. Nixon also needed his 39,000 margin in Los Angeles County and victories in San Bernardino, Ventura, and Santa Barbara counties to push him over the top with 48 percent of the popular vote as opposed to 45 percent for Humphrey and 7 percent for George Wallace.[14]

Humphrey was seriously handicapped by his inability to balance Nixon's suburban pluralities with a heavy turnout in black and Mexican-American precincts. To the extent that they voted, these groups went overwhelmingly for Humphrey, but the Humphrey organization did a poor job in its registration and get-out-the-vote drives in the ghetto areas. It was the Kennedy organization that had pull among the poor and the ethnic minorities, but the young activists who could have sparked saturation drives in the slums were numbed by the tragedy of June 5. On top of this, the Chicago convention did nothing to inspire them to work for Humphrey.

Even though California elected Alan Cranston, a Democratic senator, the pivotal figure in shaping the opposition to Reagan's administration over the next two years would be—more than ever—Jess Unruh. However, Unruh would have to work from a reduced power base. The November election changed the lineup in the state assembly from forty-two Democrats and thirty-eight Republicans to forty-one Republicans and thirty-one Democrats, thus depriving the Democratic party of the powerful position of speaker of the assembly, a post Unruh had occupied for ten years. But this was not an unmixed blessing for the Reagan administration. With Republicans in control of the assembly

[14] Wallace's 7 percent in California contrasted with his 14 percent of the national popular vote—another indication that polarization in California did not proceed as far as it had seemed to in the early summer of 1968.

and tied for control of the senate, Governor Reagan would have to bear a greater share of the responsibility and blame for the actions and inaction of the state government.

1970: CONTEST FOR THE MIDDLE MAJORITY

In 1970, state politics were more affected than in most nonpresidential elections by the national contest between the Democratic and Republican parties. That year, deliberately and openly, the contest was for the vast middle of the electorate, the 60 percent or so of the voters who are middle class in socioeconomic status and usually oriented toward stability and security in their political preferences.

The Republican party, still in the minority both nationally and in California in terms of registration, was attempting to draw a large chunk of the middle class (many in blue-collar occupations) from its traditional attachment to Democratic candidates. The key voters were thought to be those most upset by the increase in crime, the radicalization of racial minorities, the militancy and disrespect for authority of affluent youth and young faculty in the high schools and colleges, and the breakdown of traditional moral standards. Middle America, in the eyes of Republican strategists, was disillusioned with the traditional Establishment types in government, academia, the media, and industry for allowing such a disintegration of social order to take place. And because the Establishment has been identified in the popular mind, ever since the New Deal, with the northeastern Democratic party and its local satraps throughout the country, the GOP now had an opportunity to recapture the progressive-populist segments of America that used to vote Republican in the days of Teddy Roosevelt and Hiram Johnson.[15]

The interpretation of the Democratic party strategists was similar, but they were not about to allow the Republicans to exploit Middle America's growing fears and con-

---

[15] This view of Republican opportunities in the 1970's, misnamed "the Southern Strategy" by journalists, was set forth in an influential book by Kevin Phillips (an aide to Attorney General John Mitchell), *The Emerging Republican Majority* (Garden City, N.Y.: Doubleday, 1969).

fusion. Their main campaign objectives were to neutralize life-style and law-and-order as partisan issues and to get the voters to focus on economic issues, such as the recession and growing unemployment. Public opinion surveys showed that most of the electorate still believed the Democrats were better at handling these economic problems. Candidates across the nation were counseled to talk up the pocketbook and to be wary of Republican efforts to identify Democrats with pot, pornography, and permissiveness.[16]

The election results showed that although the mood of the electorate was basically conservative and concerned about the breakdown of social order, in areas of growing unemployment the traditional attachment of vulnerable elements of the population to the Democrats held quite firmly. All in all, aside from a few peculiar local races, the Democrats' strategy worked and the Republicans' failed in both California and the nation.

Nothing else could account for (1) Governor Ronald Reagan's victory over Jess Unruh by a margin of half a million votes *less* than he had had over Pat Brown four years before; (2) Democratic challenger John Tunney's 597,000-vote margin over Republican incumbent Senator George Murphy; (3) the Democrats' success in wresting control of the state legislature from the Republicans, and their ability to hang on to a majority in the congressional delegation; and (4) the dramatic upset victory by Wilson Riles over the incumbent superintendent of public instruction, Max Rafferty.

Postelection surveys of middle-income precincts around the state showed Reagan getting from 45 to 55 percent of the vote against Unruh, where he had won 60 to 70 percent against Pat Brown. In precincts of high unemployment, often containing a high percentage of blacks and Mexican-Americans, Unruh almost invariably came out on top, frequently with as much as 80 percent of the vote. Even in Orange County, the heart of California conservatism, Unruh cut Reagan's total to 67 percent (in comparison with the 71 percent he piled up against Brown four years earlier).

---

[16] The Democratic bible for the 1970 campaign was the popular book by Richard Scammon and Ben Wattenberg, *The Real Majority* (New York: Coward-McCann, 1970).

In the northern coastal counties Unruh averaged a 4 percent lead over Reagan, but this was not nearly enough to compensate for the governor's margins in Southern California.

Statewide, Reagan gained 53 percent of the vote, Unruh 45 percent, with the remaining 2 percent split evenly between the American Independent and the Peace and Freedom candidates. Surprisingly, in view of Reagan's presumed charisma, three of his running mates for state executive office did better than he. Ed Reinecke won the lieutenant governorship with 55 percent, Houston Flournoy the controller's office with 60 percent, and Ivy Baker Priest the treasurer's office with 58 percent, causing wags to quip that she swept Reagan in on her skirt-tails. Nor did the Republicans make an easy sweep of all state executive posts. Evelle Younger just barely edged out his Democratic challenger, Charles O'Brien, in the attorney general's race —and probably would not have won if the Peace and Freedom candidate had not siphoned off 3 percent of the vote. And reversing the usual pattern, a Democrat, Edmund G. Brown, Jr. (the son of the former governor), won the office of secretary of state that has been held for the last fifty years by a Republican. Contrary to all expectations, it was decidedly not Reagan's year.

To the California Republican party the most embarrassing part of the election results was seeing the Democrats gain control of both houses of the state legislature just one year after the Republicans had won control in special off-year elections. It was a hard blow to Governor Reagan, who had campaigned across the state for Republican candidates, concentrating in particular on defeating five of the "dirty dozen" (some Democratic senators he wanted to purge for defeating his tax reform legislation). All of those men were reelected.

The numerical lineup in the legislature—forty-three Democrats and thirty-seven Republicans in the assembly; twenty-one Democrats and nineteen Republicans in the senate—only told part of the story. A close look at individual races showed that in almost every case where Democratic incumbents ran, they won by bigger percentages than in 1968; but where Republican incumbents ran, they either won by smaller margins than the previous time or were, in some cases, defeated.

1972: THE AFFAIR WITH MCGOVERN

A plurality of California Democrats responded to temptation in the spring and summer of 1972 by saying yes to a more ideological exemplar of liberalism than usually wins California statewide elections. The affair with George McGovern ended in the fall as many of the conventional, mainline Democrats had warned, with an embarrassing national repudiation of the party's dramatic move to the left—the counterpart of the 1964 electoral repudiation of the Republicans move to the right with Goldwater. Somewhat surprisingly, however, the decisive national and statewide defeat of the top of the Democratic ticket in 1972 (nationally, Nixon 61 percent, McGovern 38 percent; in California, Nixon 55 percent, McGovern 41.5 percent) could not be translated into a Republican victory in the contests for congressional and state legislative seats. Once again, California showed itself to be a rather accurate political barometer of the nation.

Humphrey vs. McGovern

The fact that the winner of the Democratic primary would grab all of California's 271 votes in the party's national convention—one-sixth of the total needed for nomination—made California the final "make-or-break" preconvention arena for all candidates who survived the contests in other states. Early in the year, moderate Edmund Muskie of Maine led the pack, boosted by the endorsement of Senator John Tunney, and the speaker of the California assembly Bob Moretti. But the deflation of the Muskie balloon in a series of disappointing primaries (New Hampshire, Florida, Wisconsin, Massachusetts, Pennsylvania), and the refusal of Edward Kennedy to run, left the California field to George McGovern and the party's former standard-bearer, Hubert Humphrey. McGovern's meteoric rise in California paralleled his national ascendence. Whereas opinion samples in February 1972 showed the South Dakotan to be favored by only 7 percent of California's Democrats, by the end of May he was the front-runner.

Senator McGovern's June 6 primary election victory

virtually assured his nomination the following month at the national convention.[17] But Humphrey's tough campaign in California exposed overstatements and vulnerabilities in the McGovern program that were to contribute significantly to the latter's national undoing in November.

On every issue, from the conditions of United States' withdrawal from Vietnam to the role of bussing to achieve racial balance in the schools, Humphrey maneuvered to the more conservative, seemingly more prudent position, and from this stance vigorously attacked McGovern's less cautiously formulated proposals. In the closing stretch of the California primary campaign, in three nationally televised debates, the Minnesota senator pushed McGovern to explain how his plans for cutting military expenditures would be consistent with maintaining full employment in a state so heavily dependent upon defense contracts. With an eye to California's Jewish voters, Humphrey also attempted to establish a connection between McGovern's leaner defense posture and his somewhat equivocal support for Israel's stands in the Middle Eastern conflict (during the campaign McGovern moved toward a pro-Israeli position almost identical to Humphrey's; but his juxtaposition of the military-budget and Middle East issues put McGovern on the defensive). On the issues of welfare reform and taxes—fields in which Humphrey's credibility was well established, especially with organized labor—McGovern's more extreme positions, while integrating him somewhat with blacks and various poor peoples' lobbies, apparently were looked upon rather suspiciously by the broad middle classes. Nor was McGovern's appeal to blue-collar workers helped by his associations with various upper-middle-class liberal positions on amnesty, abortion, and marijuana.

Although McGovern carried fifty counties and Humphrey only eight, the McGovern victory in popular votes was

[17] However, McGovern's claim to all 271 of California's votes became a major issue at the convention. Humphrey and Muskie forces got the Democratic credentials committee to overturn California's winner-take-all outcome, awarding the votes instead by percentage: McGovern now had only 120, losing 151. After two weeks of wrangling, including litigation in the courts, the convention took up the question; and by a solid margin the McGovern forces won back the 151 delegates stripped from them earlier.

only by 45 percent to 40 percent—reflecting Humphrey's solid majorities in Los Angeles and Orange counties. Portending trouble for McGovern in November, blue-collar precincts gave Humphrey an average margin of 50 percent to 30 percent. Among blacks the two candidates ran neck and neck. About 60 percent of the Jewish vote went to Humphrey, while McGovern had a solid edge among college youth. In Los Angeles County Mexican-American precincts, Humphrey did slightly better than McGovern, but statewide, and especially in the farming areas, the South Dakotan came out ahead. Looking toward the national election, the most worrisome feature of the California primary election returns for the McGovern forces was their discovery that much of the Humphrey vote was less a solid pro-Humphrey expression than an expression of dislike for McGovern's presumed "radicalism." It was evidently a weakly committed Democratic vote that could switch to Nixon in the two-party contest.

The Nixon Triumph

Nixon's California victory was probably one of the most satisfying of all state wins, occurring several years after his humiliating loss in the race for the California governorship. For the McGovernites, the inability of their hero to woo California successfully was, next to losing nationally, probably the worst disappointment of the campaign. At least if they had won California, the McGovernites could claim that theirs was the progressive wave of the future, and they could keep control of the national party for a grand comeback in 1976, and certainly in the meantime retain control of the state party. As it turned out, McGovern's California loss would be used by the more conservative elements of the Democratic party as final proof of their thesis that the surest way to guarantee the election of Republicans was for the Democrats to follow the liberal *avant-garde*.

The slippage of McGovern support in traditionally Democratic socioeconomic groups would give state strategists much to ponder as they approached the critical 1974 election, with two big plums dangling—governor and U.S. senator. In 1968 Nixon had been able to win only a third of the state's blue-collar vote; in 1972 he received nearly half. McGovern was the easy favorite of those earning under $7000 a year, but the president increased his showing among this group by about 5 percent over 1968. The South Dakota senator got nearly 95 percent of the state's black vote, and almost three-quarters of the Spanish-speaking vote; but among these groups, too, the president registered net gains. Though over two-thirds of Democrats supported McGovern, Mr. Nixon improved his 1968 showing by about 15 percent. It clearly was insufficient for McGovern to explain his California loss simply by the fact that most of the votes Governor George Wallace of Alabama got in California in 1968 went to Nixon in 1972.

1974: RUNNING AGAINST WATERGATE

Once again California's 1974 elections mirrored the mood of the nation. Generally Democrats benefited locally from the nationwide discontent with Richard Nixon's misuse of presidential power. In California they won five out of the six statewide offices elected on a partisan basis—a reversal of the 1966 and 1970 results—and expanded their majorities in the legislature (55 Democrats to 25 Republicans in the assembly; 25 to 14, with one vacancy, in the senate). The Democrats also gained four seats in the California congressional delegation, giving them 28 out of 43; and Alan Cranston was reelected U.S. senator by a margin of 1.4 million votes. But large numbers of Californians apparently doubted the effectiveness of the ballot as a means of turning the country around from political and economic mismanagement. Many voters stayed at home; the turnout was the state's lowest percentage of registered voters in more than thirty years.

No single factor can adequately explain the complexities of a California statewide election. Yet the aura of Watergate—political dirty tricks, bought candidates, policy-level payola, the confusion of personal success with the public interest—seemed to be all-pervasive. President Nixon's humiliating resignation and return home to California in August thickened the oppressive presence of the national scandal between the primaries and the general election. Even more than the increasing stagflation (prices higher than ever; unemployment in the state reaching 8 percent in the fall), the pall of Watergate became necessary for each candidate to run against—or away from. Expectations by some Democrats that Watergate would be a drag only on Republicans proved too simple, as candidates from both parties maneuvered somehow to associate their opponents with the practices it symbolized and to give themselves the appearance of incorruptible, independent-minded reformers.

The Race for the Statehouse

The Watergate factor weighed heavily in the selection of the gubernatorial candidates of both parties and had some paradoxical impacts on the general election campaign.

Early in the jockeying for the Republican nomination, Robert Finch, probably the most formidable candidate, removed himself from consideration, apparently deterred by the developing scandal in the national administration with which he had been closely associated. Two other Californians of national prominence, Caspar Weinberger and David Packard, also withdrew from the race. A fourth popular prospect, state attorney general Evelle Younger, decided that running for reelection was safer than trying for the governorship in 1974. These withdrawals seemed to leave the field to Governor Reagan's heir-apparent, Lieutenant Governor Edward Reinecke. A Goldwater-Reagan conservative, Reinecke had been appointed to fill the unexpired term of Robert Finch, who had resigned his state post in 1969 to join the Nixon administration.

The only hope of the progressive Republicans—and it was a long shot—was the state controller, Houston Flournoy. Flournoy had been elected to the assembly while still in his early thirties after a brief career as a political science professor. He established himself as a moderate Republican on state issues, and supported Rockefeller against Goldwater in the 1964 primaries. In 1966, Flournoy defeated the incumbent controller, Alan Cranston, in the Republican sweep of statewide offices. Then in 1970 he established himself as a leading vote getter in his own right, winning reelection by a comfortable margin of 1.3 million votes, and receiving more total votes than any Republican in the country in that nonpresidential year. Clearly his own man now, and a favorite of the voters, Flournoy felt free to differ with Reagan on important policy issues such as oil drilling and taxes.

As 1974 began most bets were on Reinecke. But it was soon revealed that he was being investigated by the federal government's special prosecutor for possible perjury before the Senate committee looking into the role of ITT in connection with efforts to bring the 1972 Republican convention to San Diego. By the time Reinecke was indicted for perjury by the Watergate grand jury in April, most Reagan financial "fat cats" had already dropped him in favor of the likely primary winner, Flournoy. Meanwhile, Flournoy had been assuming a more conservative stance to appeal to the party's rank and file. Flournoy beat Reinecke handily in the primary (63 percent to 30 percent, with minor candidates splitting the rest) and did well with conservative as well as progressive Republicans.

Jerry Brown's success in garnering the Democratic nomination was also due in no small measure to his ability to translate voter disillusionment with "politics as usual" into personal support. Elected secretary of state in 1970 at age thirty-two, mainly on the strentgh of voter recognition that he was the son of former Governor Pat Brown, he aggressively converted the traditionally mundane responsibilities of his office for elections administration into a base for prosecuting violators of the laws on campaign expenditures. In suing three oil companies for illegal campaign contributions, the young secretary of state not only recalled the heroic legacy of California progressivism but also established himself early as a fighter against the sins of political corruption symbolized by Watergate.

The secretary of state and his small but energetic staff also played a central role in formulating the most controversial legislative initiative measure for the 1974 June elections: Proposition 9, on the reform of campaign spending and related practices (for details on Proposition 9, see pp. 104–5). Opposed by organized labor and by some of his opponents for the gubernatorial nomination, the campaign reform initiative solidly demonstrated Brown's instinct for anticipating the central issues of the day.

By the start of 1974 Jerry Brown already had taken the lead in the race for the nomination. The only two candidates thought capable of overtaking him were Robert Moretti, speaker of the assembly, and Joseph Alioto, the mayor of San Francisco. Moretti underestimated the political reform issue, waffling on Proposition 9, and hitched his effort to the standard Democratic vote gainers, tax reform and mismanagement of the economy, while trying to denigrate Brown's youth, inexperience, and personal ambition. Alioto appealed to the New Deal, Fair Deal, Hubert Humphrey establishment within the Democratic party, and to its base among organized labor and voters of Italian and East European ancestry. But some old journalistic allegations that he had connections with the criminal underworld and had engaged in illegal attorney fee-splitting lingered to tarnish his image. Moreover, he was hurt in mid-campaign by a public altercation with his wife on nationwide television and some bumbling on law-and-order crackdowns in the San Francisco black community. His campaign organization was never able to put the pieces back together.

In the June primary Brown drew 38 percent of the vote, Alioto 19, Moretti 17, and William Roth (a patrician Rockefeller-type, favored by various intellectually oriented groups) 10. Brown performed well across the socioeconomic strata. The association with father Pat helped him in the ethnic and blue-collar districts; and he ran very strongly in black, Chicano, and Jewish precincts. He led the pack in all areas of the state except San Francisco.

Everything seemed to be going Jerry Brown's way at the start of the general election campaign. The campaign reform initiative, passed overwhelmingly by the voters in June, was identified with him. His willingness to take on the "big boys" gave him a David versus Goliath charisma. The Field poll showed him a good 14 percentage points ahead of Flournoy in early August. Other Democratic candidates were anxious to ride Brown's coattails. Yet on November 5, he was able to obtain only 198,691 more votes than Flournoy (out of a total of 6 million) for 50.2 percent of the total vote. Members of both camps were agreed that if election day had been one week later, Flournoy might well have beaten Brown. What happened between June and November?

Houston Flournoy (left) and Edmund G. Brown, Jr. (right), engage in debate during their campaigns for governor. *Jack Miller photo for* Santa Ana Register.

Their series of TV debates and their respective media campaigns showed the positions of the two candidates on substantive issues to be remarkably close, while giving their very different personalities greater exposure. This apparently benefited Flournoy and hurt Brown.

Brown's previous rather abstract image of the former Jesuit seminarian—intellectually honest, morally committed—appears under sustained TV coverage to have come across to many voters as cold, humorless, overly aggressive, power hungry—paradoxically, some of the very traits that characterized the Nixon White House "Mafia." By contrast, Flournoy's less sharply defined image and lack of flair came across as moderation and unpretentiousness. Any attempt by Brown to resort to guilt-by-association tactics in trying to saddle Flournoy with the burden of Watergate would have been futile at best and at worst would have backfired, especially with California voters who remembered such tactics as Nixon's stock in trade. Other contrasts between the two men may also have helped Flournoy as the campaign programmed: Flournoy as the stable family man as opposed to Brown the bachelor; fourteen years as an elected official for Flournoy against only four years for Brown.

Jerry Brown would take up his duties as governor in January 1975 without a mandate for a new set of programs or the impressive personal victory that would have given him leverage over legislature and party. Nor was it the kind of victory that would make him an automatic favorite for a place on the national ticket in 1976.

Other Highlights

Mervyn Dymally won the lieutenant governorship without much support from the regular Democratic organization and joined the roster of black politicians able to appeal to the broad California electorate (others being Mayor Bradley of Los Angeles and state superintendent of public instruction Wilson Riles, who was reelected to this nonpartisan office in the primary).

The most impressive plurality for state executive office was obtained by a woman of Oriental ancestry, March Fong, in the contest for secretary of state.

Ken Cory was elected controller in a close race with fellow assemblyman William Bagley. He campaigned on the statement, "Cory—the man the oil industry fears most!"

Jess Unruh, in being elected treasurer, won statewide office for the first time in his colorful career as a California politician.

Evelle Younger, a moderate, was the only Republican to hold onto statewide office. His victory, along with Flournoy's impressive showing, would allow the moderates to attempt to reassert control over the California Republican party for the first time since Reagan's 1966 sweep.

Implications

All in all, this was a highly idiosyncratic election. Without providing a mandate *for* anyone or anything, the voters returned a Democrat to the statehouse for the first time in eight years and elected heavily lopsided Democratic majorities in both houses of the legislature. Given party discipline, the new governor would have an opportunity rarely available to the state's chief executive to develop and implement public policy. But as will be shown in the following chapter, such party discipline would be out of character with the usual workings of the political process in California.

SELECTED REFERENCES

ANDERSON, TOTTEN J., "Bibliography on California Politics," in *Bibliography on Western Politics*, ed. Frank H. Jones, a supplement to *Western Political Quarterly* 11 (December 1958): 23–51.

————, and EUGENE C. LEE, "The 1966 Election in California," *Western Political Quarterly* 20 (June 1967): 535–54.

BROWN, SEYOM, "Fun Can Be Politics," *The Reporter* 21 (November 12, 1959): 27–28.

California, Assembly Committee on Legislative Representation, *List of Legislative Advocates and Organizations*. Sacramento: State Printing Office. Issued periodically.

California, Secretary of State, *Statement of Vote*. Sacramento: ƴ State Printing Office. Issued after each general, primary, and special election.

Constitution and By-Laws of the California Democratic Council. Obtainable from California Democratic Council headquarters in San Francisco and Los Angeles.

HARRIS, JOSEPH P., *California Politics*, rev. ed. Stanford: Stanford University Press, 1961.

LEARY, MARY ELLEN, "California: A Report," *Atlantic* (February 1968), pp. 224 ff.

MOWRY, GEORGE E., *The California Progressives*. Berkeley: University of California Press, 1951.

OWENS, JOHN R., EDMUND CONSTANTINE, and LOUIS F. WECHSLER, *California Politics and Parties*. Toronto: Macmillan, 1970.

WILSON, JAMES Q., "A Guide to Reagan Country," *Commentary* (May 1967), pp. 34–45.

5

The Political Process
in California

In a state as large as California it is virtually impossible
for anyone to influence public policy unless he works
through an organization composed of like-minded members. He may become active in a political party or a party-
oriented organization, or he may work through a pressure
group purporting to represent his interests. These organized
groups employ various methods in their attempts to affect
policy: direct support for candidates for public office, publicity campaigns, and lobbying in Sacramento. Together
these functions make up the political process, which will be
elaborated below under four headings: political parties,
campaigns, interest groups, and lobbying.

POLITICAL PARTIES

Currently, four organizations have legal status as
political parties in California: the Democratic party, the
Republican party, the American Independent party, and
the Peace and Freedom party. Legal status as a political
party gives an organization the right to have the names of   91

its candidates for public office printed on the official election ballot. Legal status also obligates a political organization to keep its structure and procedures in conformity with explicit provisions in the Elections Code. Without legal recognition a political organization may still run candidates for office, but their names must be handwritten on the ballot by their supporters on election day.

Requirements for Legal Status

Legal recognition as a political party in California is conferred upon an organization that obtains *either* a registration of at least 1 percent of the total number of registered voters, or files a petition signed by a number of voters equal to 10 percent of the vote cast for governor in the preceding election. Once recognized, a party continues to appear on the ballot as long as it passes *both* of the following tests: in any gubernatorial election, one of its candidates for statewide office must receive at least 2 percent of the vote cast, and it must maintain at least one-fifteenth of 1 percent of the total registration. (The Prohibition party and the Communist party are among those organizations once on the official ballot but now disqualified for failing to meet the state requirement.)

Formal Structure and Functions

To say that California law is explicit concerning the structure and basic functions of political parties is an understatement. The Election Code goes into such detail that it seems as if about the only thing left to the discretion of party leaders themselves is the preparation of a menu to be served convention delegates.[1]

THE STATE CONVENTION   State law provides that every recognized political party must hold its state convention at

[1] For example: "The convention shall be called to order at 10 o'clock . . . by the retiring chairman of the state central committee. It shall at once proceed to the election of a temporary chairman by a roll call read from an alphabetical roll . . ." (Section 2807). "The convention shall . . . adopt a State platform for its party which shall be made public not later than 6 o'clock in the afternoon of the following day" (Section 2809).

CALIFORNIA'S FORMAL PARTY ORGANIZATION
(as prescribed by state law)*

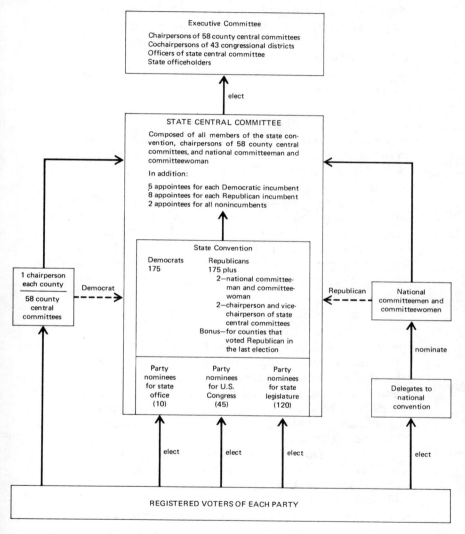

Executive Committee

Chairpersons of 58 county central committees
Cochairpersons of 43 congressional districts
Officers of state central committee
State officeholders

elect

STATE CENTRAL COMMITTEE

Composed of all members of the state convention, chairpersons of 58 county central committees, and national committeeman and committeewoman

In addition:

5 appointees for each Democratic incumbent
8 appointees for each Republican incumbent
2 appointees for all nonincumbents

State Convention

| Democrats 175 | Republicans 175 plus 2—national committeeman and committeewoman 2—chairperson and vicechairperson of state central committees Bonus—for counties that voted Republican in the last election |

1 chairperson each county

58 county central committees

Democrat

Republican

National committeemen and committeewomen

| Party nominees for state office (10) | Party nominees for U.S. Congress (45) | Party nominees for state legislature (120) |

nominate

Delegates to national convention

elect   *elect*   *elect*   *elect*

REGISTERED VOTERS OF EACH PARTY

*For details see Elections Code, Secs. 8401–6.

Sacramento every year, and in election years between the primary and the general election. The convention usually lasts for one day only. Its principal functions are to draft the state platform and to select presidential elector candidates. The members of the convention consist of all party nominees and holdovers for statewide and congressional offices,[2] and the Republicans have recently added certain party officials to this number (refer to the chart on political party organization).

THE STATE CENTRAL COMMITTEE   The day after the state convention has finished its deliberations, the central committee meets, also at Sacramento, to elect the officers of the party's executive committee and to propose certain legislation.

The state central committee is a large body of party leaders composed of all members of the state convention and a number of their appointees. In addition, the chairpersons of all county central committees and the national committeeman and committeewoman serve as members of the state central committee (refer to organization chart).

THE EXECUTIVE COMMITTEE   The executive committee of each party has the *formal* responsibility to oversee party affairs and campaigns. Occasionally the committee appoints district campaign committees to assist congressional and state legislative candidates. The day-to-day management of the affairs of the formal party organization is carried on by the chairperson and vice-chairperson. These top offices provide no monetary compensation and have little formal power.

Membership of the executive committee consists of the chairpersons of the 58 county central committees, the cochairpersons of the 43 congressional districts, the state officeholders, and the elected officers of the state central committee—a group of about 160 persons.

---

[2] If the party has no holdover incumbents or nominees for a given office, an "appointive delegate" is named by the party committee in the district concerned.

COUNTY CENTRAL COMMITTEES   The members of the county central committees of the party are chosen by the voters in each county. County committees are elected in the *biennial* partisan primaries for terms of two years. In larger counties they are elected by assembly districts, in smaller counties by supervisorial districts. In addition to the elected members, party nominees for state offices and incumbents living in the county are ex officio members of the committee. County committees vary in size, but none may have fewer than twenty-one elected members. Los Angeles is an anomaly with about 250—57 elected from each of its assembly districts, plus the nominee for each assembly and senate district in the county.

LIAISON WITH THE NATIONAL PARTY ORGANIZATION There is very little formal connection between the official state parties and national organizations. The main links are provided by national committeemen and women who serve on the national committee. The national committees' operations are largely devoted to presidential election activities. Because of the manner of selection of national committeemen their ties to their official party organization in California may be quite tenuous.

The Democratic National Committee revised its rules of representation in the early 1970's to better reflect the country's population. California, by the new formula, is allotted ten places, five for committeewomen and five for committeemen. The Republican National Committee allots two places to each state, and also allows the state chairman of a state that voted Republican in the previous presidential election to be a member of the national committee —giving California three members as of 1974.

Factional Organizations within the Parties

Partly because of the amorphous and inchoate nature of California's major statewide political parties, and partly because of the encumbrances of the Elections Code, unofficial factional organizations have played a large role in the state's political process. These groups usually consist of people with similar political viewpoints who get together to make sure that their kind of Republicans or Democrats get nominated by the party and elected to office.

THE CALIFORNIA REPUBLICAN ASSEMBLY (CRA)   Following the defeat of the Republican presidential candidate, Herbert Hoover, in 1932—a year that also saw the California congressional delegation controlled by Democrats for the first time in a century—a group of young Republicans dissatisfied with official party conservatism formed a committee to reassert "progressive" Republicanism. Among the founding members was Earl Warren, then district attorney of Alameda County. Today the CRA plays a far different role within the state Republican party. During the last decade the CRA membership took a decidedly rightward swing, so that the organization is now regarded as one of the party's more conservative voices.

The stated purposes of the CRA include the development of a statewide aggressive Republican organization, the provisions of political programs for the betterment of California, and the improvement of the party's public relations. The CRA endorses and provides financial and other campaign support to candidates, particularly in the primary elections, that it feels best represent the standards of true Republicanism.

In its early years, nearly all the candidates endorsed by the CRA won the Republican primary. The organization was instrumental in making Earl Warren, Goodwin Knight, and Richard Nixon major political figures. CRA endorsement is no longer a free ticket to victory in the primaries, however, as other organizations within the party have emerged to siphon off some of its clout. (Thus the CRA-endorsed candidate for governor, Ed Reinecke, lost the 1974 primary race to Houston Flournoy.)

The annual convention of the CRA, held regularly since 1934, carries on many activities of the type one can find at a national party convention. Party notables speak, policy resolutions are adopted, and, during election years, candidates are endorsed. The convention is composed of delegates elected from local and county Republican assemblies. Any fifteen or more registered Republicans may form a local assembly unit and apply for a charter from the state organization. The local units in turn support the state organization through fees assessed on the basi of membership. Republican assemblies are active in all of the state's fifty-eight counties and most major cities, with a total membership of approximately 9500.

THE UNITED REPUBLICANS OF CALIFORNIA (UROC) Chartered in 1963 by a group of Goldwater Republicans who felt the CRA was too liberal, the UROC piled up an impressive record in its early years. It endorsed Ronald Reagan for governor in 1966, and supported Max Rafferty in his primary election upset of incumbent U.S. Senator Thomas Kuchel in 1968. In recent years UROC candidates have continued to do well in primary elections, but have not fared so well in the November elections.

The UROC, like the Republican Assembly, operates through local clubs and a statewide convention; but unlike the CRA, all UROC members may vote in the convention.

THE CALIFORNIA REPUBLICAN LEAGUE (CRL) The CRL is the most prominent moderate Republican group within the party, and also the most recently formed. Organized in 1964 as a haven for the more liberal Republicans who had found themselves outnumbered in the CRA, the CRL has had difficulty in getting its endorsees nominated in the primary election. But 1974 may have marked a turning point for the moderate faction, as the Republican voters selected a more liberal slate than they had for a decade.

THE CALIFORNIA DEMOCRATIC COUNCIL (CDC) The CDC is the statewide organization of the once-powerful liberal Democratic club movement. The statewide organization was born in 1953 through the federation of already existing local grass-roots clubs. Alan Cranston, now California's senior senator, was elected the first CDC chairman. Its rise to influence in California politics was stunning. In 1954 and 1958 every statewide candidate endorsed by the CDC won in the Democratic primary. During its high success period more than 400 local clubs were affiliated with the CDC, and its paid-up membership reached 70,000.

But, paradoxically, the CDC may have succeeded too well. By helping to make possible the Democratic landslide of 1958, it put into office a large number of professional

Democratic politicians who no longer felt dependent upon the CDC and who were critical of the "amateurish" tactics of the volunteer organization. Democratic party regulars cooperated with their Republican counterparts in passing a 1963 law prohibiting unofficial organizations like the CDC from publicizing candidates they favor in upcoming primaries as "officially endorsed."

The CDC's outspoken stance against the Vietnam war during the Johnson administration also contributed to the backlash against the organization from party loyalists. In the mid-1960's many members dropped out of the organization, and its rolls dipped to 10,000 in 1967.[3]

In recent years the CDC has enjoyed a rejuvenation of sorts. It made peace with long-time foe Jesse Unruh during the National Democratic Convention of 1968, and the 1972 Democratic party platform reflected CDC positions. CDC members point with pride to the fact that their membership has returned to 150 affiliated clubs with 20,000 members. But it appears doubtful that the CDC will ever return to the dominant position it once held within the Democratic party in the late 1950's and early sixties.

The statewide Democratic Council is composed of delegates from local clubs, apportioned on the basis of paid-up membership, as well as representatives from assembly, county, and congressional district councils. The official Democratic organization is supposed to be represented on the CDC by the officers of the state central committee, delegates from county central committees, and Democratic officeholders and nominees. CDC's current activities, in addition to preprimary endorsements, are recommending action on important issues in state and national politics and providing California Democrats with the type of enthusiasm and volunteer legwork which is often lacking in the official party.

CAMPAIGNS

The process of running for office is long and arduous. Statewide candidates must lay the foundations for a race years in advance. Each candidate must examine the issues

[3] Interview with Toni Kimmel (former CDC Southern California vice-president), July 10, 1974.

and analyze the needs of the constituency he hopes to represent. A successful campaign needs to be well scheduled and financially managed, and to project its message and candidate to the state's 10 million-plus registered voters.

Campaign Management

Candidates in California are relying increasingly on public relations firms for the management of their campaigns. Firms that arrange for and direct advertising on a year-round basis for commercial clients are often better able to provide advantageous advice and connections than are temporary publicity committees organized around individual candidates in election years.

MAJOR FIRMS [4] Whitaker and Baxter is the oldest campaign management firm in the country. Originally started in 1933 to oppose a ballot initiative, Whitaker and Baxter today rarely handles candidates but concentrates on ballot propositions. The firm managed the campaign against the coastline initiative (Proposition 20) in 1972, and received criticism for its method of sloganeering. Prominent Whitaker and Baxter clients have included Earl Warren, Pacific Gas and Electric Co., and the California Teachers Association.

Another old Republican-oriented management firm is the Baus and Ross Company, established in 1948. Baus and Ross probably has the best record of any firm, having won a high percentage of its campaigns, and is also known for its high fees (ranging from $20,000 to $100,000 per campaign). It has had a few tough losses, among them Pat Brown's 1966 unsuccessful try for a third term as governor. Baus and Ross, unlike some other firms, usually limits itself to a small load. Attorney General Evelle Younger was one of its clients in the 1974 elections.

Spencer-Roberts specializes in total management of campaigns, from research (extensive polling) to ads. Since 1966, when it managed Ronald Reagan's election as governor, Spencer-Roberts and Associates has hit a losing

---

[4] For a recent description of major campaign management firms see Nancy Boyarsky, "The Image Makers," *California Journal* 5, no. 5 (May 1974): 149–55.

streak. They had planned to sit out the 1974 campaign, but in March of that year signed on with Houston Flournoy's gubernatorial campaign.

The best-known Democratic firm is Cerrell and Associates, headed by Joe Cerrell. Cerrell began by working on the campaigns of former Governor Edmund G. Brown in 1958 and 1962, and with John F. Kennedy in 1960. Cerrell's firm operated on a very large scale in the 1974 elections; but only one of its statewide candidates (Merv Dymally, the lieutenant governor) made it past the primary and general elections. Cerrell's forte is the use of free media, making sure his candidates get stories in the papers and evening TV news.

Other firms that usually have Democrats as clients also have thrived recently, partly as a result of the Republicans' entanglement with Watergate in 1973 and 1974. Notable are Weiner and Company (who managed liberal Republican Norton Simon's unsuccessful, but surprisingly strong, showing in the 1970 senatorial primary against George Murphy) and the newly formed C. and L. Winner Associates (who helped out in the Morretti and Brown campaigns for governor in 1974).

THE FIRM AT WORK Campaign management is a business with ups and downs. Most firms sustain themselves in the off season with commercial clients, but reduced income often forces them to lose valuable workers, many of whom never return once they leave.

Firms establish their reputations over the years. Some have been more successful over the long run; others, while less successful, have established good rapport with officeholders who continue to use them. Usually a candidate comes to a firm and asks for help, although on occasion firms have pursued candidates who look like sure winners.

Campaign management firms can perform a variety of services. Depending on the candidate, a firm may be involved only in a consulting role, or it may direct all aspects of the campaign—from the use of media and scheduling public appearances to polling the voters on the issues of the day. Their operations have been changing in recent years. Costs have spiraled, average constituency size has grown, and computers are now commonly used.

The public relations firm goes into a campaign to win, and attempts to use the strengths of a candidate to his best advantage. A firm hired by a physically attractive candidate might emphasize television commercials, while another, in the service of a candidate with a good voice, will likely emphasize radio. One common technique is to identify a candidate with one popular issue. Often a catchy slogan will do the trick; partly because of this, campaign management firms have come under attack for steering campaigns away from the deeper issues and toward superficial slogans.

In the sixties it seemed that any candidate who hired a firm to help his campaign automatically increased his chances of being elected. The aura of firms has dimmed somewhat in recent years, but they have established a reputation as important parts of the electoral process.[5]

The Media

With the rapid growth of population making it impossible for candidates to have personal contact with all of California's voters, an office seeker must rely on other means, especially the newspapers, radio, and television.

THE PRESS Newspaper coverage is important to all candidates, but especially to the lesser known. In recent years, investigative reporting has hurt the chances of some well-known political figures, as detailed day-to-day exposés eroded their support. A notable example was the 1970 coverage of Senator George Murphy's contract with Technicolor Inc., which was a significant factor in Murphy's loss to Democrat John Tunney.

Editorials are another aspect of press power. Republican candidates get this coveted support more often, though in recent years the Democrats have been gaining endorsements. (Editorial support can also be reflected in the amount of daily news space allotted.) The *San Francisco Chronicle, Oakland Tribune,* and Copley Hearst chain are rather consistently Republican. The McClatchy papers—the *Modesto Bee, Fresno Bee,* and the *Sacramento Bee*—are

[5] The discussion of campaign firms at work relies in part upon insights gained from an interview with Joe Cerrell of Cerrell and Associates, July 9, 1974.

prominent Democratic papers in the state. California's best-known (and nationally respected) paper is the *Los Angeles Times*. The *Times* tends to favor the Republican party, but has moved toward the liberal wing in recent elections. A *Times* endorsement can have major impact, especially in nonpartisan races or ballot propositions, as in its support of Wilson Riles over Max Rafferty in the 1970 superintendent of public instruction race and in its staunch editorial defense of Proposition 9 in 1974.

TV AND RADIO   Ever since the Kennedy–Nixon debates of 1960, television has become a major part of campaigns for public office. (Today candidates may well overemphasize the importance of television.) In California, as in other states, voters are subjected to a last-minute TV "blitz" before elections, as each candidate attempts to portray himself as the most honest, hardworking, intelligent, and best-qualified person on the ballot. Consequently, handsome and trustworthy faces have become increasingly valuable political assets.

Expenses for radio and TV advertising often account for as much as 50 percent of a statewide candidate's expenditure. There are indications that candidates, the public, and media executives themselves may be beginning to reevaluate the heavy use of media. And there is agitation for stations to donate free time for debates and speeches in the public interest.

The Money Game

Prior to the 1974 regulations on campaign financing, it took about $3 million to wage an effective campaign for governor. In the 1972 primaries candidates for the legislature spent on the average about $65,000, with some in divided races costing as much as $100,000. But with the passage of Proposition 9, future candidates for governor and other offices will be limited to less than half those amounts, and will have to prove that they have not exceeded it.

CAMPAIGN FINANCING   The biggest contributors to California campaigns are corporations, labor unions, and special interest groups. Such donations are obtained by

Democrats no less than Republicans. Several "fat cat" individual donors also donate large amounts of money.

Some individuals or interests, particularly those who make frequent demands on officeholders, contribute to more than one candidate's campaign for the same office, in order to cover all bases. Often a well-to-do candidate has contributed hundreds of thousands of dollars to his own campaign

"O, deliver me from this sinful corruption. But not just yet."

Engelhardt in the Sacramento Bee, *August 31, 1974. Reprinted by permission.*

(such as Norton Simon, Republican candidate for senator in the 1974 primary, and William Matson Roth, candidate for the 1974 Democratic gubernatorial nomination. Both lost, but surprised pundits by their surprisingly strong showings).

With the Waxman-Dymally disclosure bill going into effect in January 1974, that year's primary featured the first detailed look at the sources of election money. The most financially powerful groups in the 1974 election, with war chests of over $300,000, were the California Teachers Association, the California State Employees Association, and California doctors and dentists. In addition, during the primary, four Southern California donors contributed a total of almost $1 million.[6]

CAMPAIGN SPENDING Once money is raised (and sometimes even before it is) the candidate and his supporting organization spend it in the way they feel is most conducive to his campaign. An analysis of both the 1966 and 1970 campaign expenditures for governor by both parties indicates that about 45 percent was spent for radio and television, 20 percent for campaign personnel, 15 percent for travel expenses, 10 percent for billboards and posters, 5 percent for public opinion polling, and another 5 percent for office supplies, telephone bills, and store-front rentals. The estimated figures for the 1974 campaigns generally follow this same line.

The total campaign costs for California state and congressional elections in 1970 totaled more than $26 million. This was the highest in the state's history—but may well have been topped in 1974.

IMPACT OF PROPOSITION 9 Until 1974, regulations concerning campaign contributions and expenditures were pretty loose. Reports were sometimes filed, but their accuracy was questionable. Undoubtedly, the Watergate affair accelerated attempts to clean up the use of money in politics. And as a result of Proposition 9, candidates running for office must now follow a new, stiffer set of rules.

[6] William Endicott, "Big Donors Emerge in Campaign Fund Reports," *Los Angeles Times,* July 25, 1974.

Any candidate for elective office in California (congressional elections are under federal guidelines) who spends over $200 in an election is subject to the new laws, as are all committees acting on his behalf. All contributions of $50 or more must be reported (along with the name, address, and occupation of the contributor) to the secretary of state. The total sum of contributions under $50 must also be reported. Candidates must file reports forty and twelve days before, and sixty-five days after the election. Anonymous and cash contributions over $50 are prohibited. Proponents and opponents of ballot measures are covered under similar provisions.

In addition to reporting the source of contributions, the same procedure must be followed for filing expenditure reports (reporting dates, cash limits, etc.). Total expenditures are also limited. Gubernatorial candidates may spend up to 7 cents per voting-age citizen in the primary, 9 cents in the fall election. All other statewide candidates, excepting congressmen and senators, are limited to 3 cents per voting-age citizen in the primary and general elections. Total expenditures for or against an initiative may not exceed the lower of the following: 8 cents times the voting-age population or $500,000 more than the amount those on the opposite side of the measure report they intend to spend.

In 1974, the disclosure laws were in effect but spending limits were not. The candidates, as usual, spent a lot, although an effort of sorts was made by Brown and Flournoy to limit themselves to $1.3 million apiece in the fall campaign.

INTEREST GROUPS

The political parties, and even intraparty factions, tend to be broad coalitions of interests and ideologies, as a result of their need to appeal to broad constituencies at the polls. Consistent and persistent advocacy and support of more specific public policy proposals and legislation, therefore, is left to organizations that are primarily concerned with policy outcomes and only secondarily concerned with the success of particular candidates or political parties.

Special Interests

Groups representing certain occupations or segments of the economy set up associations specifically designed to exert pressure on the state administrative agencies, the legislature, and the political parties to assure that their demands are given attention. Some of the more prominent special interest groups are briefly described below.

The California Chamber of Commerce represents an alliance of business and agricultural interests. The Chamber is a nonprofit association of 4000 firms plus trade association members. It often speaks for, but lacks authority over, 378 local chambers of commerce.

The California Chamber's main goal is to promote a favorable business climate in the state of California. In the Chamber's Sacramento headquarters all legislation is monitored and analyzed in terms of its possible impact on business. The Chamber endorses no political candidates, but does take stands on propositions—recent examples being its support of Proposition 22 in 1972, which would have limited the effectiveness of the farm workers' union, and opposition to the coastline initiative (Proposition 20, fall 1972) and Proposition 9 on the June 1974 ballot.[7]

The political arm of the AFL-CIO is the Committee on Political Education (COPE). More than most special interest groups, COPE acts openly and directly to influence elections: registering voters, getting out the vote on election day, and endorsing candidates for office. COPE flexes its muscles with officeholders in two major ways. One is with its great wealth of voting power. The other is by backing up its endorsements with large campaign contributions. As a result, many officeholders, when elected, are "in debt" to labor, and are heavily pressured to vote the union line. Election years feature politicians, usually Democrats, engaged in elaborate courtships of labor. In recent years the AFL-CIO has increasingly sided with agribusiness interests, reflecting a nationwide trend. The most recent example is their opposition to Proposition 9 in June 1974.[8]

---

[7] Interview with George Sawyer (general manager of programs, California Chamber of Commerce), July 17, 1974.

[8] Interviews with Bill Schward and Jim Wood of AFL-CIO (COPE), July 8, 1974.

Typical of more specialized interests are the oil companies, who characteristically employ their vast monetary resources in pushing for or opposing legislation affecting their interests, and the California Medical Association, which has been lavish in its spending on political candidates and is very active in Sacramento.

As the new campaign disclosure laws and spending limits go into effect, along with tougher provisions as to the use of money by lobbyists, special interest groups could lose some of their power. (See discussion of Proposition 9, above, p. 104, and below, pp 110–12.)

Citizen Groups

Organizations of citizens with similar views on a range of public policy issues such as political reforms and improving the environment are also active in the state's political process. In contrast to the special interest groups, citizens' groups are often broadly based, with members of various occupations and classes. Over the past few years citizens' groups have been increasing their membership and carrying more weight with the voters.

Perhaps the best-known citizen group is the League of Women Voters. Born out of the suffragette movement, the League now operates on local, county, state, and national levels. The California League has 15,000 members, most of them white housewives over thirty (perhaps in deference to "men's lib" the League has now opened its membership to males!). Each member pays $15 annual dues, and this money is divided among each of the four operative levels (national, state, county, and local). The League's main activities include voter services, study programs, and endorsements of legislation (action). Long known for its thorough and unbiased research of issues, the League is widely respected by voters and lawmakers alike. In recent years the League of Women Voters has supported the coastline initiative (Proposition 20, November 1972) and June 1974's Proposition 9. The League was also at the forefront of the opposition to Governor Reagan's ill-fated tax initiative in 1973.[9]

[9] Interview with Yvonne Gottlieb (president, Los Angeles County League of Women Voters), July 11, 1974.

Nineteen seventy-four was a banner year for a new nonpartisan citizens' group, Common Cause. Conceived in Washington, D.C., in 1969, Common Cause established its California branch in 1972, with Ken Smith as director. Members pay $15 annual dues, which go to the national headquarters. Contributions beyond the regular dues support the state office. Common Cause's program calls for open legislative meetings, lobbying disclosure, conflict-of-interest laws, and public campaign financing. Its preferred means of change being via the legislature, Common Cause lobbies in Sacramento, using letters of support from its 60,000 plus members as leverage. In 1973, realizing that the legislature was not going to move on reforms, Common Cause went the initiative route, joining the People's Lobby as sponsors of Proposition 9. Common Cause also successfully backed Proposition 6 on the June 1974 ballot, which made legislative committee meetings open to the public. Although elated with the passage of Proposition 9, Common Cause feels the state's campaign legislation still is not adequate. Its next push is to be for public financing of elections.[10]

More radical than Common Cause and smaller, the People's Lobby started in 1969 under the leadership of Joyce and Ed Koupal. The People's Lobby aims to improve government by subjecting more decisions to direct voter approval. Like the early California progressives, the People's Lobby believes that the initiative process is the only effective way to force substantial changes in the state. It has become expert in signature drives for initiatives, playing a major role in sponsoring the unsuccessful clean environment initiative in June 1972, and the successful coastline initiative of 1972, plus Proposition 9 in 1974. Other People's Lobby goals include the closing of tax loopholes and restriction of oil companies. The organization is self-sufficient, sustained by annual dues of $10 per member, most of whom are young people.[11]

Environmentalists have formed some of the most powerful of citizen's groups. The Sierra Club is the most prom-

[10] Interviews with Lee Sanders and Ken Smith of Common Cause, July 16, 1974.
[11] Interview with Joyce and Ed Koupal of the People's Lobby, July 2, 1974.

inent, combining thorough research with an effective lobbying team in Sacramento. Other well-known environmental groups include the California Coastal Alliance, Friends of the Earth, and Environmental Protection Center.

LOBBYING

Special interest and citizen groups of the kind discussed above attempt to shape government programs by directly influencing the legislature in Sacramento. Over 600 organizations, covering the gamut from the Farm Bureau Federation to the National Hot Rod Association, employ individuals who are formally registered as "legislative advocates." The most important function of these legislative advocates—or lobbyists, as they are commonly called—is to make sure that the legislation passed in the state capital is in the best interests of their organizations. Many interests believe that because of the volume of bills in Sacramento, and the number of groups competing for attention, something more than moral persuasion is required to get their "foot in the door." This is a special concern of lobbyists representing special interest groups and private associations lacking a broad constituent base that would enable them to win statewide elections.

Lobbyists employ various methods. They provide bill-drafting services and counseling on issues. Every group comes to Sacramento with facts and figures to back up its program, but advice given from a "friend" often has more of an impact. Fraternization of lobbyists with legislators can take many different forms, ranging from picking up the tab for lunch, to yacht cruises complete with dinner, drink, and pretty young women. Other favorites which sometimes serve to remind the legislator of the interests of his friends are bottles of wine, desk calendars, or other assorted gifts for the office, and, probably most important, *campaign contributions*.

Regulation of Lobbying

EARLY REFORM   A series of magazine articles published by *Colliers* in 1949 gave California lawmakers a slap on their wrists. The embarrassing articles exposed the activities of the notorious Arthur H. Samish, lobbyist for the beer industry. Samish, who reportedly said he could tell "if a man wanted a baked potato, a girl, or money," was supposed to have raised $1 million over a six-year span from a nickel-a-barrel levy on beer. His lieutenants monitored all meetings dealing with liquor, horse racing, and other gambling activities, and he held virtual control over the Public Morals Committee. (Repeatedly the target—and survivor —of investigations, he was finally jailed for sixteen months beginning in 1953 as a result of income tax evasion. He never returned to lobbying, and died in February 1974.)

The Samish revelations helped bring about the passage of the Collier Act (in 1949) which, subsequently amended, required all lobbyists to register and to file monthly statements with the legislature, and for legislators to report any employment they accepted as advocates for special interest groups. Violations were punishable by fines up to $5000 and /or twelve months in jail. But no one was ever convicted under the Collier Act, and some observers claimed that little, if any, improvement was made after its passage. It was, they said, business as usual.

LOBBYING AND PROPOSITION 9   Further lobbying reform was advocated by the late Earl Warren, while he was governor, but little attention was paid to reform until the early seventies. In 1973 a package of reform bills was introduced in the legislature. Some of the bills, given last-minute attention by worried lawmakers, were passed, but no action was taken on those related to lobbying. Lobbying disclosure and regulation had been prime aims of both Common Cause and the People's Lobby since their beginnings several years earlier. At the same time, then Secretary of State Jerry Brown and his staff were also looking for stricter controls on lobbying. It was apparent to all three groups that the legislators were not anxious to pass laws that would in effect restrict their own activity (just as they had been reluctant to enforce the provisions of the Collier Act), and so in 1973 the three reformist groups joined forces and, after much heated discussion and argumentation, agreed on the political reform initiative of 1974, which appeared as Proposition 9 on the June primary ballot. The proposition had a wide scope, including campaign financing, financial disclosure by public officials, and, of course, lobbying.

Approved by the voters, and effective as of January 7, 1975, Proposition 9 clearly defines a lobbyist as any person who receives compensation for the purpose of influencing legislative or administrative actions as a regular part of his/ her employment. The major lobbying provisions are as follows: (1) all lobbyists must register with the secretary of state, and regularly file detailed reports describing all financial activity (including to whom gifts were made, for what reason, and how much); (2) employers of lobbyists must make periodic reports; (3) lobbyists' expenditures are limited to $10 per month per legislator (enough for two hamburgers and a Coke, in the words of Proposition 9 backers); and (4) lobbyists are prohibited from making campaign contributions. All lobbyists' reports are to be made available to the general public and all lobbyist activities and complaints about them will be monitored by the Fair Political Practices Commission. This commission is responsible for overseeing all of Proposition 9's regulations and will, in the words of People's Lobby director Ed Koupal, act as a "political police force." It is composed of five members, with no more than three members from one party. The governor appoints two members, and the attorney general, secretary of state, and controller appoint one each. The commission proposal came under heavy attack during the June 1974 campaign, opponents charging that the commission would be too powerful and that appointments would be politically motivated. Supporters of the commission responded that a powerful enforcing body was needed, that the 3–2 party split and overlapping terms were as nonpolitical as any commission could be, and that proceedings would be public.

EFFECTS OF THE NEW REGULATIONS   As 1975 began there appeared to be no clear consensus as to what impact the new laws would have. Opponents of the new provisions complain (a) that they are too confusing and will create havoc; (b) that the regulations invite violation by their ambiguity and that these new violations will doubtlessly be more intricate and discreet than those in the past; (c) that groups will be deterred from constructive lobbying by all the paperwork; and (d) that lobbyists will be restricted to talking to administrative assistants rather than legislators. Those who supported the restrictions foresee a democratizing effect—with citizens' groups and other nonprofit organizations being given a fair chance to air their views, regardless of their lack of funds. Supporters also see the public as being better informed of the activities of their legislators. Not only will full disclosure insure fairness, they say, but also the press will be better able to expose illegitimate activity.

SELECTED REFERENCES

BAER, MARKELL C., *Story of the California Republican Assembly*. Obtainable from the Republican Assembly of Los Angeles County.

BOYARSKY, NANCY, "The Image Makers," *California Journal* V, 5 (May 1974): 149–55.

California, Assembly Committee on Legislative Representation, *List of Legislative Advocates and Organizations*. Sacramento: State Printing Office. Issued periodically.

Constitution and By-Laws of the California Democratic Council. Obtainable from California Democratic Council headquarters in San Francisco and Los Angeles.

People's Lobby, *Proposition Nine: A Fact for California, A Proposal for America*, 1974. Obtainable from People's Lobby headquarters in Los Angeles.

SAMISH, ARTHUR H. and BOB THOMAS, *The Secret Boss of California*. New York: Crown Publishers, 1971.

VELIE, LESTER, "The Secret Boss of California," *Colliers* 124 (August 13, 1949): 11–13, 71–73; (August 20, 1949): 12–13, 60, 62–63.

Referendum, Initiative, Recall: Democracy through Petition

Popular petition for legislation and the recall of elected officials, along with the direct primary and cross-filing, were part of the reform program sponsored by the Progressives to rid the state of control by political bosses and the railroad machine. Direct democracy can be traced back to the New England "town meetings," or even back to ancient Greece. The Progressive reformers, however, were primarily inspired by the successful operation of the initiative and referendum in Switzerland in the late nineteenth century. J. W. Sullivan, "the father of the modern initiative and referendum in the United States," [1] carried his campaign to California at the turn of the century. In California the movement was championed by the Direct Legislation League, headed by the prominent Los Angeles physician John Randolph Haynes. At the instigation of Haynes and his associates, petition devices were adopted in several cities, including Los Angeles and San Francisco, from 1902 to 1910. The election campaign of the Progressives in 1910

---

[1] Dewey Anderson, *California State Government* (Stanford: Stanford University Press, 1942), p. 191.

113

contained the promise to institute a statewide initiative and referendum system. And upon election Governor Hiram Johnson sponsored a series of constitutional amendments which, when approved by the voters in 1911, extended the initative, referendum, and recall to the state and to local governments that had not yet adopted the system. California is now one among twenty-eight states where initiative and referendum devices and recall are employed. There are only twelve states that permit amendment of the constitution by initiative.

REFERENDUM BY PETITION

Referendum by petition is used to prevent laws already passed by the legislature and signed by the governor (or passed over his veto) from going into effect. This should not be confused with the so-called "compulsory referendum," whereby constitutional amendments and bond issues passed by the legislature must always be approved by the people in order to become law. Referendum by petition is a popular device for *interrupting* the normal legislative process. Any law passed by the legislature may be held up on referendum, "except acts calling special elections, acts providing for tax levies or appropriations for the usual current expenses of the State, and urgency measures necessary for the immediate preservation of the public peace, health or safety. . . ." [2] To qualify for an "urgency" label a bill must be passed by two-thirds of the membership in each house. [3]

Signatures Required

The referendum petition must be signed by registered voters amounting to at least 5 percent of the vote cast for governor in the last election in order to place the measure on the ballot.

[2] Constitution of the State of California, Art. IV, sec. 8d.
[3] During the economic depression of the 1930's as many as 11 to 14 percent of the laws passed as "exempt" or "urgent." Winston W. Crouch, *The Initiative and Referendum in California* (Los Angeles: Haynes Foundation, 1950), p. 26.

Procedure

To prevent a statute from taking effect, a petition bearing the requisite number of signatures must be filed with the secretary of state within ninety days after the enactment of the bill. This period must elapse anyway before legislation, with the exception of emergency measures, takes effect in California. If the petition qualifies, the act to which it refers is not enforced until the next election when the people have a chance to accept or reject it.

Before each election the voter receives in the mail, along with his sample ballot, a booklet containing all of the ballot propositions with arguments pro and con. These arguments are written by legislators or citizens whom the presiding officer of the senate or assembly has designated as legitimate spokesmen for each side. At the polls, a majority of "yes" votes allows the measure to become law. A "no" majority defeats the measure.

Extent Used

During the first thirty years of its use in California, the popular referendum was applied to thirty-four legislative acts. Twenty-one of these were voted down by the people. Since 1942, only one referendum proposition has appeared on the ballot: a legislative act that exempted nonprofit private and religious schools from the property tax was held up by a referendum petition, only to be approved by the voters at the 1952 election.

The referendum subjects that in the past have aroused much public attention include granting courts the power to close "red-light" districts by injunction (upheld), levying a special tax upon chain stores (defeated), and creating a State Oil Conservation Commission (defeated).

DIRECT INITIATIVE

Through the direct initiative method the people themselves originate and pass laws and constitutional amendments without recourse to the legislature. No subjects are exempted from the direct initiative. The only constitutional restriction is that a given initiative proposal must deal with only one main subject. The governor may not veto an initiative measure.

Signatures Required

Under the 1966 revision of the state constitution, the direct initiative *statute* petitions must be signed by a number of registered voters amounting to at least 5 percent of the vote cast for governor in the last election in order to place the measure on the ballot. If the direct initiative is proposing an amendment to the constitution, the petition must carry signatures amounting to at least 8 percent of the previous gubernatorial vote.

Procedure

The attorney general must approve the official title and summary of the initiative proposal that appears on the petition to be circulated. From the date of this approval, a maximum of 90 days is allowed for sponsors to secure the required number of signatures. The petition is transmitted to the secretary of state for final verification of signatures and placement on the ballot. (If the secretary of state does not receive the petition at least 130 days prior to the state election, it is held over until the following election.)

The title of the initiative measure, its summary prepared by the legislative analyst, its complete text, and arguments pro and con appear in the ballot booklet sent to all registered voters in advance of the election. If the measure receives a majority affirmative vote it becomes law. A law thus passed may not be amended or repealed by the legislature (unless so provided in the measure) without approval by the voters. In the event that conflicting initiative measures appear on the same ballot and are passed, the one receiving the highest vote becomes law.

Extent Used

The direct initiative accounts for the great majority of petition measures submitted to the voters of the state. Up to the present time, approximately 165 direct initiatives have been presented to the California voters. In 1914, a record seventeen initiative measures were on the ballot, though on the average only about four or five qualify and in some elections there are none. However, in 1972 there were nine initiative measures on some very controversial issues such as coastal zone protection, penalties for the use and possession of marijuana, and the death penalty. In the past years there has been a wide range of subjects covered by initiatives, including the use of the Bible in public schools, prohibition on the sale of intoxicating beverages, the single tax, old-age pensions, regulation of oil monopolies, "right to work" legislation, and racial and religious discrimination in housing. More direct initiatives have been constitutional amendments rather than statutes. This is due to the fact that constitutional amendments may be changed only by a two-thirds vote of the legislature and approval by the electorate whereas statutes can be revised by a simple majority vote of the legislature. Further, initiative statutes are subject to judicial review and may be declared unconstitutional by the courts.

THE REAGAN TAX INITIATIVE

For the first time in the state's history, a governor called a special election on an initiative sponsored by himself. Following rejection of this measure by the legislature, Governor Reagan campaigned for a new constitutional amendment initiative and personally solicited signatures for the petition. The necessary 520,000 signatures were secured and Proposition 1 was presented as the only issue on the ballot in November 1973.

The prime purposes of this initiative were to limit and reduce taxes, provide for refunds to taxpayers of surplus state revenues, and to require voter approval of taxes that exceeded limits set forth in the amendment. Expenditures for 1974–75 from state tax revenues were to be limited to their current percentage of state income for 1973–74, which was estimated at 8.3 percent. The allowable ratio between expenditures and income was to be decreased by one-tenth of 1 percent a year until 1989–90, when it would reach the limit of 7 percent. Thereafter, the state would have to operate under that fixed ceiling for the future unless the voters chose to alter or abandon it. If state revenues for any fiscal year exceeded the state tax limit, the excess (no more than two-tenths of 1 percent of that year's state income) would be transferred to a tax surplus fund to be used for economic emergencies created by natural disasters,

Governor Reagan collects a signature for a petition to qualify Proposition 1 in the November 1973 special election. Los Angeles Times *photo.*

inflation, and other similar causes. All surplus tax revenues above those so allocated were to be disposed by the legislature as refunds or future tax reductions.

Other provisions of the measure included: a plan to require a two-thirds vote of the legislature for the institution of a new tax or a change in any current levy; tax rate limits for cities, counties, and special districts; and a proposal for a one-time credit of 20 percent on personal income taxes for 1973 out of the state's surplus of that year.

Governor Reagan, supported by groups including the California Taxpayers Association, the California Real Estate Association, and the California Chamber of Commerce, contended that constantly increasing taxes have created big government and a bureaucracy that is a burden upon the people. It was also argued that government tends to perpetuate itself and that the bureaucracy has become the most powerful lobby in Sacramento, seeking more government spending to serve its own purposes.

A. Alan Post, state legislative analyst, and Robert Moretti, speaker of the assembly, became the principal spokesmen opposing the governor. They argued that government spending is not increasing at the rate claimed and that which is spent is in response to the public need. Also, as all appropriations are subject to approval of the legislature and the governor, the initiative was viewed as an attack against representative government. The limitation on state expenditures would "hamstring" both the legislature and the governor. It was also claimed that certain loopholes in the initiative would allow the state to reduce allocations to local governments, schools, and the courts. Thus, these needs would have to be financed by increased local property taxes, retail sales taxes, or higher taxes on private businesses.

Among the state organizations opposing the Reagan tax initiative were the League of Women Voters, the League of California Cities, the California Supervisors Association, and the California Teachers Association.

It is estimated that the Reagan forces spent about 2 million dollars on a statewide campaign, spending some $390,000 just for securing sufficient signatures for qualifying the petition. The campaign included tape recorded "personal" messages from the governor sent by telephone to thousands of voters in the state. Expenditures for those groups opposing Proposition 1 totaled about $375,000.[4] In addition, the cost of administering the special election was approximately $19 million.

The voters rejected the Reagan tax initiative by a 54 percent to 46 percent margin. This was the first defeat for

[4] Bruce Keppel, "An Offer Californians Did Refuse," *California Journal* 4, no. 12 (December 1973), p. 402.

the governor at the polls and was viewed by his opponents as a possible factor in case Reagan became a candidate for president. Most observers believed that the defeat of the proposition was due to the complexity of the measure and the fear that it would be detrimental to schools and local governments.

INDIRECT INITIATIVE

Prior to 1966, the state constitution contained a provision for an indirect initiative. Like the direct initiative statute, it began with a petition to enact or change a statute. The petition required a number of signatures equal to 5 percent of the votes cast at the last election for governor. The indirect initiative was directed to the legislature rather than to the people for a vote. If the legislature approved the proposed statute, it became law; if the legislature did not approve the proposed statute, it was submitted to the people for their approval or rejection.

Extent Used

The indirect initiative was one of the least used of the petition devices, and though the indirect initiative was authorized in 1911, it was not used until 1937. It has been used only four times since then and only once has this type of proposition ever been approved by the voters. This infrequent use, plus the fact that under constitutional revision in 1966 the percentage of signatures for statutory direct initiatives was reduced, led the Constitutional Commission and the legislature to abandon the indirect initiative as a device for direct legislation.

RECALL

By means of the recall, voters in California may remove from office any *elected* state official before the expiration of his term. A proposition approved by the voters in 1974 provided that all elected state and local officials are subject to recall at any time after their election. In contrast with one who has been impeached (where a misdemeanor is the required indictment for removal), the recalled official need not have violated any law.

Signatures Required

To recall an officer elected by the entire state, the petition must be signed by registered voters amounting to at least 12 percent of the total vote cast for the involved office in the last election. The petition must also contain signatures of voters in at least five counties equal to not less than 1 percent of the vote cast for the office in each of these counties.

If the recall involves state officers elected by districts (members of the legislature, district courts of appeal judges, and members of the Board of Equalization), the petition must contain signatures of voters in the district equal to at least 20 percent of the vote cast for the office in the last election. This relatively large percentage coupled with a lack of public interest in these offices has resulted in virtually no recall of state officers elected by districts.

Procedure

The procedure for circulating the recall petition and the verification of signatures is the same as for referendum and initiative petitions, except that there are *no time requirements for circulation or filing*. The recall petition must contain a statement of grounds for removal; but as there is no requirement for specific charges, the petition may in fact say no more than "we don't like the way he's doing his job." Upon certification of the petition by the secretary of state, the governor is required to call an election to take place between sixty and eighty days from the date of qualification.

Candidates wishing to replace the officer to be recalled are required to file a petition twenty-five days before the election, signed by at least 1 percent of the vote cast for that office at the last election.

A recall election ballot contains the question: "Shall (incumbent) be recalled from the office of ———?" If the voter indicates a "yes" vote, he may then choose from among the other contestants for the office whose names are listed on the ballot. Also included on the ballot are the charges against the officer and his own statements in self-defense.

If the recall fails, the state reimburses the incumbent for his election expenses.

Extent Used

The recall has seldom been used against state officers. In three recall elections involving state senators, held shortly after the institution of the recall in California, two senators lost their offices. A petition was circulated to recall Governor Culbert Olson in 1940, and in 1960, after the reprieve of Caryl Chessman, an attempt was made to recall Governor Edmund Brown. Both efforts were unsuccessful. More recently, in 1968, a petition to recall Governor Ronald Reagan fell some 300,000 signatures short of the 780,414 needed to place the measure on the November ballot.

DEMOCRACY THROUGH PETITION IN COUNTIES AND CITIES

Referendum, initiative, and recall originated in California on the local level at the turn of the century. When the state adopted these devices, provisions regarding their local use were included in the constitution.

Local Referendum and Initiative

SPECIAL REQUIREMENTS   Local governments organized under charter may set their own special requirements for legislative petitions. Other counties and cities are prevented by state law from requiring more than 10 percent of their electors to qualify a referendum, and 15 percent to qualify an initiative. The usual practice is for local governments to require signatures amounting to 5 percent of the vote in the last general election for referendum petitions and 10 percent for initiative. In most jurisdictions financial matters and public works are not subject to popular petition.

EXTENT USED   The referendum and initiative have been more frequently used on a statewide basis than locally. And on the local level they have been used more often in the more populous cities and counties. The rule at work seems to be that there is less need for direct legislation when government is close to the people.

Subjects put before local voters by petitioners have included policemen's and firemen's salaries and pensions, garbage and refuse collections, and regulation of liquor establishments and dance halls. A local referendum that received nationwide attention, and on which much money and wrath were spent, concerned a contract between the Los Angeles (formerly Brooklyn) Dodgers and the city of Los Angeles to sell public land to the baseball club for the construction of a stadium. Backers of the referendum charged that the city council had no right to grant land that was planned for a public park and public housing to a private corporation. Opponents of the referendum claimed that a vote against the contract was a vote against the Dodgers and against major league baseball in Los Angeles. The Dodger fans thought they had won when the contract was approved by the voters in June 1958, but a superior court judge ruled that the contract violated the city charter. Outraged Dodger fans appealed his decision to the state supreme court. Finally, in January 1959, the supreme court in a unanimous decision upheld the original contract with the Dodgers as approved by the voters.

Recall of Local Officers

SPECIAL REQUIREMENTS As with direct legislation, local governments may set their own recall procedures in their charters; however, California's constitution prohibits local governments from requiring petition signatures amounting to more than 25 percent of the vote cast in the previous election for the office involved. Recall procedures must also conform to state law in the following respects: County recall petitions must be signed by at least 20 percent of the vote cast at the last election for the office involved. And recall petitions in general law cities need a minimum of 12 percent of the total number of registered voters. Notice of intention to file a petition and reasons for the recall must be published, and the officer must be given two weeks to publish his reply followed by a three-week waiting period *before the petition can be circulated.* The five-week interim between first notice and petition circulation is required to give the voters a chance to become acquainted with the evidence before signing. Otherwise, the petition procedure is the same as it is for the recall of state officers.

The local recall ballot differs somewhat from the state ballot. Instead of including the names of candidates attempting to succeed the incumbent, the voters are asked to decide whether the local legislative body should fill the vacancy or call a special election.

EXTENT USED   The local recall has practically never been used except in cities. Mayor Frank Shaw of Los Angeles was recalled in 1938 on charges of corruption in office, and was succeeded by Fletcher Bowron. In 1946 an attempt was made to recall Mayor Roger Lapham of San Francisco on the grounds that he had raised municipal railway fares and that, being a businessman, he was unfit for public office. Lapham squashed the attempt by offering to sign the petition himself—a dramatic gesture to demonstrate his desire to fight the issue in the open. Arthur Snyder, a Los Angeles city councilman, was subjected to a well-publicized but unsuccessful recall election in 1974. An outspoken and controversial veteran of six years on the council, he was charged with criminal fraud, and it was contended that he did not truly represent the newly reapportioned 14th councilmanic district, which was over 70 percent Mexican-American in population. All five challenger candidates were Mexican-Americans. There have been literally hundreds of recalls initiated against local elected officials including city councilmen, mayors, and others. Various charges of bribery, graft, and corruption have been used, and in one instance, a Duarte councilwoman was recalled after she was convicted of shoplifting in a local supermarket.

EVALUATIONS OF REFERENDUM, INITIATIVE, AND RECALL

California's experience with the petition devices, especially in recent years, has highlighted many features of direct democracy unforeseen by the Progressives who championed the 1911 constitutional amendments. Much could not be foreseen, as the "great game of politics" has been transformed dramatically since the days of Hiram Johnson and the Lincoln-Roosevelt League. Thus some of the criticisms against referendum, initiative, and recall are new, and cannot be dismissed by reference to the standard theories of democratic government and popular sovereignty. Other criticisms, however, are perennial, recurring each time the matter comes up for discussion. Yet a balanced evaluation must grant the possibility that even the old criticisms may assume a new validity with changing conditions.

The various criticisms leveled against the petition devices fall into five groups.

A Cluttered Constitution

It is often alleged that our bulky and unwieldy constitution has resulted from the many amendments initiated by the voters. However, the record shows the great majority of constitutional amendments to have originated in the state legislature. For example, in the 1972 election, of the fifteen proposed constitutional amendments only four were placed on the ballot by popular petition, and only one of these initiatives was approved by the voters. The lengthiness of the California constitution is more correctly attributed to its detailed nature as drafted in 1879. Unlike the U.S. Constitution, which contains broad and general provisions allowing for statutes to meet changing conditions, California's basic document itself has to be altered to provide for nearly every change in statutory law. The cluttered state constitution is less a *result* of constitutional initiatives than a *cause* of them.

"Crackpot" Legislation

Critics charge that the initiative device opens up the floodgates to a deluge of radical and unworkable cure-all legislation. The frequent appearance on the ballot of such proposals as the single tax, "Thirty Dollars Every Thursday," and other magnanimous pension plans is cited as evidence. But it should be noted that from among all these so-called "loony schemes" only the 1948 McLain initiative was approved by the voters. This measure provided for immediate large increases in pension payments and instituted sweeping changes in the state's social welfare administrative setup, making the director of social welfare an elected official and installing a McLain coworker as director until the following election. However, the electorate salvaged its reputation for intelligent judgment by enacting a 1949 initiative that threw out the whole plan.

Voter Confusion

A long list of complicated fiscal, administrative, and technical matters frequently confronts the voter as ballot propositions. It is contended that he does not have the time or the training to cast an informed vote on laws relating to land titles, mortgage foreclosures, highway construction and administration, and judicial procedure—all of which have appeared on the California ballot. To add to the confusion, contradictory measures appear on the same ballot. As recently as 1964, Propositions 13 and 16 relating to a state lottery were in direct opposition to each other. The

"The woods are full of 'em."

Bastian in the San Francisco Chronicle, *1960.*

booklet the voter receives in the mail prior to each election does little to help him. It is lengthy (often containing as many as fifty pages in fine print), legalistically worded, and complicated in its meaning and language.[5] Note, for example, some typical passages from the text of the 1972 initiative proposition (#14) on taxation:

> Sec. 2 From and after the effective date of this article the State shall not levy an ad valorem tax for any tax whatsoever: provided, however, that in each year that the State Controller certifies that no other source of funds or method of taxation is available, the State may levy a statewide ad valorem property tax sufficient to service and retire debts or liabilities of the State authorized or outstanding on the effective date of this Article; and provided further no subordinate taxing agency shall levy an ad valorem property tax for the purpose of paying the costs of social welfare services.

> Sec. 5 From and after the effective date of this section, subordinate taxing agencies may levy ad valorem property taxes for the debts or liabilities provided the proposition for incurring each debt or liability of each subordinate taxing agency shall have been approved by a two-thirds majority of the votes cast on such a proposition within the subordinate taxing agency at a statewide primary or general election or if the subordinate taxing agency is uninhabited, by a petition approved by a two-thirds majority of property owners within such agency. . . .

The initiative measures are often presented in an incomprehensible legal jargon and the voter is hit with a barrage of propaganda and pros and cons in argument which is not necessarily designed to stimulate considered judgments. Proponents and opponents of the same measure often use the same pitch on billboards and spot announcements. The flagrant case in 1972 involved Proposition 20 (Coastal

---

[5] As a result of legislative action, a revised form of the voter's pamphlet was issued in 1974. Printed in larger type and using a new format, the various propositions with analyses and arguments pro and con were presented in more readable form. The new law was sponsored by the office of the secretary of state and supported by the League of Women Voters.

Zone Conservation), with both sides advertising "save our Coast." A billboard announcing "Don't lock up our Coast" advocated a "no" vote, whereas the proposition itself would allow more people greater access to the coastline and would prevent private ownership of the beaches.

Mervin Field, director of the California Poll, who has followed the progress of initiative proposals says, "Voters seldom have clearly defined opinions about most measures even on the eve of voting. Many have a limited and even erroneous understanding of the issues. Opinions of this type are often subject to quick change under the pressure of massive propaganda and emotional appeals." [6] Members of the legislature displayed doubts as to the electorate's ability to judge ballot propositions on their merits in a 1957 amendment to the Elections Code. Whereas previously the secretary of state decided which number to assign a proposition on the ballot, the Code amendment prescribes a specific formula for the order in which measures must appear.[7] The discretion was taken away from the secretary of state because of the belief that voters tend to approve measures appearing at the top of the ballot and to reject those near the bottom of the ballot, especially when the list is long. If the secretary of state could juggle the order of propositions, he could influence the outcome of the vote—or at least so ran the argument.

In rebuttal to the argument that the citizen is asked to vote on measures that are too complicated for him to evaluate wisely, it is contended that the experience is good for him: it contributes to his civic education. And in answer to the charge that in initiative and referendum campaigns the voter is made a captive of the public relations consultants hired by pressure groups, it can be observed that misleading advertising is not a problem exclusive to the area of direct legislation. Although in recent years the "PR" boys are frequently found in the coaching box during political

---

[6] "Initiative Makes a Big Comeback as Groups Seek to Bypass the Legislature," *California Journal* 2, no. 7 (August 1972): 229.

[7] The secretary of state still determines the order of legislative proposals, then come initiative measures in the order in which they qualify, and finally referendum measures, also in the order in which they qualify. Elections Code, Section 3812.

campaigns, the basic question is really how to secure an enlightened public opinion in this age of mass communications.

Use by Pressure Groups

The most severe criticism is that the expense of petition circulation and ballot proposition campaigns discourages all except highly organized interest groups from using

Proposition 22, which dealt with agricultural labor relations, attempted to create a labor relations board that would have restricted agricultural labor union activities. In an amazing 58–42 percent victory, Cesar Chavez's group defeated the supporters of the proposition, and in so doing spent only one-third the amount spent by their opponents. *Conrad in the* Los Angeles Times, *1972.*

the direct legislation approach. In 1974 it took 325,504 signatures to qualify a direct initiative petition and a referendum, and 520,806 to qualify an initiative constitutional amendment. With the growth in population, the requirements will continue to increase. Notable among the firms who will circulate petitions for a fee are those of Joseph Robinson in San Francisco and Morgan Keaton (California Initiative and Referendum Bureau, Inc.) in Los Angeles. At going rates—35 to 50 cents per signature—it cost at least $100,000 to place an initiative measure on the ballot in 1974. After qualification, an effective campaign on a controversial measure—requiring billboards up and down the state's multitudinous highways, television and radio time, newspaper advertising, and direct mail circulars— often takes, these days, about a million dollars. Reported figures (somewhat less than actual expenditures) are filed after every campaign by the proponents and opponents of the various propositions.

State records for 1972 showed that the California Employees Association spent $1.8 million for its salary initiative (Proposition 15), with more than $250,000 of this amount expended just for securing the necessary signatures to qualify the petition. Opponents of this proposition under the banner of "The Committee to Stop the Blank Check" spent about $30,000. The measure was defeated. Supporters of Proposition 14, the Watson property tax initiative, spent $1.3 million in their unsuccessful campaign while opponents calling themselves "Citizens against Higher Taxes" reported spending $794,575. One of the most interesting contests in 1972 involved Proposition 18, which proposed the enactment of strict new controls to crack down on what supporters said was an avalanche of obscenity in California. Citizens against the measure, bankrolled by movie theaters, film makers, and publishers, reported spending $746,852 on the campaign. *Playboy Magazine,* the trailblazer of the nude centerfold, contributed $125,000 of this amount. The unsuccessful proponents consisting of many small contributors reported spending $162,000, with the biggest single contribution coming from P. J. Frawley, the Los Angeles razor mogul. The final reports show that the opponents of Proposition 20 (Coastal Zone Conservation), which included the California Real Estate Association, Building and Construction Trades Council of California, Allied Workers

Union, Council of Carpenters, California Manufacturers' Association, California Chamber of Commerce, and the Teamsters' Union spent about $2 million in their unsuccessful efforts to defeat this proposition.

In total, almost $11 million was spent on the twenty-two propositions in 1972. It is not surprising, therefore, that the most active organizations sponsoring or opposing ballot propositions in recent years have been well-financed pressure groups representing oil producers, the trucking industry, liquor interests, real estate associations, the medical profession, manufacturers' associations, and labor unions. It would appear that the original purpose of direct democracy, namely, to eliminate the control of government by powerful economic interests, has been frustrated. How mercenary the process may be is indicated by the fact that the firm that circulated the petitions for the successful McLain pension initiative in 1948 also gathered the signatures for its repeal one year later!

This condition led Governor Brown, in his 1965 message to the legislature, to comment as follows:

> In recent years, it [initiative] has often been used to turn the ballot into a field for jousting among public relations men wearing the colors of special interests. . . . I believe legislation is needed to prevent special interests from turning the initiative to private gain through the use of professional petition circulators and large sums of money. If such a law can be written, I will support it. At the same time, I will not support any bill that would restrict the value of the initiative.

Yet it seems that at times the general citizenry has produced needed government reforms through popular petition. Noteworthy examples are the merit system for government employees, a centralized executive budget, coastline conservation, and permanent voter registration. Were it left to the legislature, these reforms might never have come about.

Intimidation through Recall

The threat of removal at any time may make elected public officers reluctant to alienate political factions or organized interests. Though difficult to prove, should this threat prevent an official—a judge especially—from making unpopular decisions, a sacrifice of the public interest might well be the result. The *accepted* use of the recall, however, is to give the voters a chance to remove from office officials who have demonstrated incompetence and corruption, but who are not necessarily guilty of criminal action.

SELECTED REFERENCES

Ballot Measure Reports. Los Angeles: Town Hall, 1974.

"Ballot Propositions, 1972 General Election," *California Journal* V, 5 (May 1974): 160.

CROUCH, WINSTON W., *The Initiative and Referendum in California.* Los Angeles: Haynes Foundation, 1950.

"Initiative Makes a Big Comeback as Groups Seek to Bypass the Legislature," *California Journal* II, 7 (August 1972): 229.

Pros and Cons of State Ballot Measures (pamphlet). San Francisco: League of Women Voters of California, October 1974.

7
The Legislature

COMPOSITION AND STRUCTURE

S imilar to the Congress of the United States and to the
legislatures of all states in the Union but one, California has a bicameral (two-house) legislature. At the
1849 convention the proposal for a two-house legislature
was passed unanimously and without debate. The more
numerous house was named the *assembly,* the less numerous the *senate.* Since 1849, however, California politicians
have rarely been unanimous on anything. Not only the
number of the legislative houses, their size, and the basis
of their representation have been heatedly debated, but also
the name of the most numerous house—"assembly" being
considered less dignified than "house of representatives" or
even "legislative assembly."

Representation

Prior to 1926, representation in both houses was based
on population. In that year a constitutional amendment
instituting the "federal plan" was approved by the voters.   133

This plan retained population as the basis of representation in the assembly and provided for geographical-area representation in the senate. However, the "federal plan" was replaced in 1966 under the Reapportionment Act of 1965, which returns to population as the basis for representation in both houses.

APPORTIONMENT OF ASSEMBLY SEATS   The assembly has eighty members, somewhat fewer than most state legislatures. According to the California constitution, assemblymen are to be elected from districts "as nearly equal in population as may be." To paraphrase the old saw, all assembly districts are created equal but some are more equal than others. Although each district is supposed to contain one-eightieth of the state's population, some districts have contained as much as 50 percent more people than others. Unequal districts came about naturally through population growth and shifts between the reapportionment the legislature made after each ten-year census. However, they also occurred because of the provisions in the apportionment law; assembly districts must contain complete counties, or be contained entirely within a county, in which case they may not cross congressional district lines.

APPORTIONMENT OF SENATE SEATS   California's second constitution (1879) set the number of state senate seats at forty, and the size has not been changed since. The difficulty under the "federal plan" was how to divide forty senators equally among the state's fifty-eight counties. It was decided that county lines should be the basis of division and that no county could have more than one senatorial district; however, it was further provided that a senatorial district could cover as many as three sparsely populated counties. As a result of apportionment by the legislature in accord with this formula, the majority of counties had one senator each representing them in Sacramento, but some counties were represented by only one-third of a senator. California's "federal" arrangement was thus markedly different from strict federalism (such as exists in the United States Senate), where each geographical unit has equal voting strength in the upper house. Under the state's 1961 Reapportionment Act, five senatorial districts contained three counties each, eight districts each had two, and the remaining twenty-seven consisted of one county each. Measured against the geographical-equality principle of federalism, some of the rural counties like Modoc, Mono, and Mariposa were sold short.

However, if another yardstick was applied—that of "equal population, equal representation"—the tight shoe was on the city dweller's foot. Approximately 60 percent of the state's population (concentrated in San Francisco, Alameda, Los Angeles, and San Diego counties) voted to fill only one-tenth of the state senate seats, while the remaining 40 percent of the population had control over nine-tenths of the seats. The senator from Los Angeles County, for example, represented over 6.5 million constituents; but the senator from District 28 (Alpine, Mono, and Inyo counties) represented fewer than 15,000—a ratio of about 440 to one! This particular imbalance had the dubious honor of being more severe than in any other upper house in the United States.

OPPOSITION TO SENATE APPORTIONMENT   From time to time there has been organized opposition to the so-called "federal plan" as a formula for the apportionment of state senate seats. The original measure instituted by an initiative in 1926 was sent to the legislature in order that senatorial districts be constituted. In 1927 opponents of the plan drafted by the legislature invoked the referendum to prevent the legislation from going into effect. However, in 1928 the voters sustained the action of the legislature by a vote of 692,000 to 570,000. Then after the 1931 reapportionment under the new law, a petition was circulated to protest the allocation of senate seats, but this failed to get sufficient signatures to qualify for the ballot.

In 1948 a constitutional amendment was proposed by an initiative that would have moved in the direction of restoring apportionment of the senate on the basis of population. Counties and groups of counties were to make up the senatorial district, but the more populous counties would be given more than one seat. For instance, Los Angeles County would be assigned ten senators, San Francisco would be allocated five, and two would go to Alameda

County and perhaps to Contra Costa County. However, the voters rejected this proposal by a vote of 2,251,000 to 1,070,000.

BONELLI PLANS   The issue of senate apportionment was again brought to the fore by Proposition 15 on the 1960 ballot. This initiative measure became known as the "Bonelli Plan," since it was sponsored by Southern California interests led by Frank G. Bonelli, chairman of the Board of Supervisors for Los Angeles County. It would have kept the number of senators at forty, but would have redrawn the districts in such a way that twenty senate seats would be allocated to thirteen southern counties and twenty seats would be shared by the remaining forty-five northern counties. This first Bonelli Plan was denounced in Northern California as a power grab by Los Angeles, even though the northern counties with only 40 percent of the state's population would still have one-half of the senators. Proposition 15 was defeated by a vote of two to one, Los Angeles being the only county to give it a majority.

Mr. Bonelli and his associates placed another constitutional amendment on the November 1962 ballot as Proposition 23. It would have increased the senate to fifty members and would have assigned five of the ten additional seats to Los Angeles County and one each to San Francisco, Alameda, Santa Clara, Orange, and San Diego counties. The same charges of a power grab were hurled against the second Bonelli Plan. The proponents of reapportionment polled a much larger vote than in 1960, carrying populous Orange and Los Angeles counties, but they still fell short of a majority by about 300,000 votes out of a total of more than 4 million cast.

THE U.S. SUPREME COURT AND REAPPORTIONMENT The move for California senate reapportionment was given tremendous impetus by the U.S. Supreme Court in the decision of Baker *v.* Carr (1962), in which the Court declared that state legislative reapportionment was within the purview of the federal courts.

On June 15, 1964, the U.S. Supreme Court, in a historic decision involving six different suits in six different states, held that the districts in *both* houses of state legisla-

STATE SENATE DISTRICTS BY COUNTIES

(Reapportionment by state supreme court effective 1974. Each senate district had an approximate population of 499,332.)

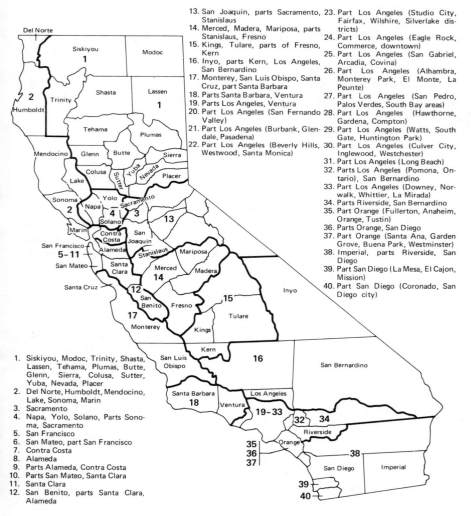

13. San Joaquin, parts Sacramento, Stanislaus
14. Merced, Madera, Mariposa, parts Stanislaus, Fresno
15. Kings, Tulare, parts of Fresno, Kern
16. Inyo, parts Kern, Los Angeles, San Bernardino
17. Monterey, San Luis Obispo, Santa Cruz, part Santa Barbara
18. Parts Santa Barbara, Ventura
19. Parts Los Angeles, Ventura
20. Part Los Angeles (San Fernando Valley)
21. Part Los Angeles (Burbank, Glendale, Pasadena)
22. Part Los Angeles (Beverly Hills, Westwood, Santa Monica)

23. Part Los Angeles (Studio City, Fairfax, Wilshire, Silverlake districts)
24. Part Los Angeles (Eagle Rock, Commerce, downtown)
25. Part Los Angeles (San Gabriel, Arcadia, Covina)
26. Part Los Angeles (Alhambra, Monterey Park, El Monte, La Peunte)
27. Part Los Angeles (San Pedro, Palos Verdes, South Bay areas)
28. Part Los Angeles (Hawthorne, Gardena, Compton)
29. Part Los Angeles (Watts, South Gate, Huntington Park)
30. Part Los Angeles (Culver City, Inglewood, Westchester)
31. Part Los Angeles (Long Beach)
32. Parts Los Angeles (Pomona, Ontario), San Bernardino
33. Part Los Angeles (Downey, Norwalk, Whittier, La Mirada)
34. Parts Riverside, San Bernardino
35. Part Orange (Fullerton, Anaheim, Orange, Tustin)
36. Parts Orange, San Diego
37. Part Orange (Santa Ana, Garden Grove, Buena Park, Westminster)
38. Imperial, parts Riverside, San Diego
39. Part San Diego (La Mesa, El Cajon, Mission)
40. Part San Diego (Coronado, San Diego city)

1. Siskiyou, Modoc, Trinity, Shasta, Lassen, Tehama, Plumas, Butte, Glenn, Sierra, Colusa, Sutter, Yuba, Nevada, Placer
2. Del Norte, Humboldt, Mendocino, Lake, Sonoma, Marin
3. Sacramento
4. Napa, Yolo, Solano, Parts Sonoma, Sacramento
5. San Francisco
6. San Mateo, part San Francisco
7. Contra Costa
8. Alameda
9. Parts Alameda, Contra Costa
10. Parts San Mateo, Santa Clara
11. Santa Clara
12. San Benito, parts Santa Clara, Alameda

tures must be "substantially equal" in population. The Court said there was no valid analogy between state legislatures and the federal Congress in which the Senate is based not on population but on two members for each state. The specific provision in the Constitution for the Senate, the

Court said, resulted from a compromise among the sovereign states that formed the Union. But counties and other subdivisions of states have never been sovereign, and states are subject to the Constitution's overriding requirement of equality.

The decision cited the Fourteenth Amendment of the Constitution providing that "no state shall . . . deny to any person within its jurisdiction the equal protection of the laws." Chief Justice Earl Warren, a former governor of California, said, "Legislators represent people, not trees or acres. Legislators are elected by voters, not farms or cities or economic interests." [1] The chief justice specifically said that both houses of a bicameral legislature must be based on population. To apply the rule to only one house, he said, would permit a minority veto in the other and thus stalemate or frustrate the will of the majority.

The Supreme Court decision held that the federal district courts would implement the redistricting of state legislatures based upon population. And although only six states were involved in the first series of cases, nine more were included a week later and cases were pending in forty states, including California. A special panel of three federal judges in California issued an order in December 1964 that the California senate must achieve reapportionment not later than July 1, 1965. This ruling was then modified by the California state supreme court, which ordered legislative reapportionment by December 9, 1965. The state court further proposed that districts should not vary in population more than 15 percent from the norm (median-size population), nor should a majority of the senators be elected by fewer than 48 percent of the electorate.

REAPPORTIONMENT ACT OF 1965   Though there was considerable discussion of reapportionment during the 1965 general session of the legislature, no agreement was reached on any of the proposed plans. Thus, to forestall threatened court redistricting, Governor Brown called a special session to produce a new legislative reapportionment. Finally, in October, the two houses passed a measure that drew new senate districts on a population basis and realigned the

[1] *New York Times*, June 16, 1964, p. 28.

STATE ASSEMBLY DISTRICTS BY COUNTIES
(Reapportioned by state supreme court effective 1974. Each assembly district had an approximate population of 249,661.)

1. Siskiyou, Modoc, Trinity, Shasta, Lassen, Tehama, Plumas, Glenn, part Butte
2. Del Norte, Humboldt, Mendocino, Lake, part Sonoma
3. Colusa, Sutter, Yuba, Sierra, Nevada, Placer, part Butte
4. Yolo, Solano
5,6. Sacramento
7. El Dorado, Amador, Alpine, Calavaras, Tuolumne, Mono, parts Sacramento, San Joaquin
8. Napa, part Sonoma
9. Marin, part Sonoma
10,11. Contra Costa
12,13,14,15. Alameda
16,17. San Francisco
18. Parts San Francisco, San Mateo
19,20. San Mateo
21,22,23. Santa Clara
24. San Benito, part Santa Clara
25. Santa Clara
26. Parts San Joaquin, Stanislaus
27. Merced, part Stanislaus
28. Santa Cruz, part Monterey
29. San Luis Obispo, part Monterey
30. Mariposa, Merced, Madera, part Fresno
31. Parts Fresno, Tulare
32. Kings, parts Tulare, Kern
33. Kern
34. Inyo, parts Kern, San Bernardino, Los Angeles
35. Santa Barbara
36. Ventura
37,38. Parts Ventura, Los Angeles
39-65 (inclusive). Los Angeles
66,67. San Bernardino
68. Riverside
69,70,71,72,73. Orange
74. Parts Orange, San Diego
75. Imperial, parts Riverside, San Diego
76,77,78,79,80. San Diego

eighty assembly districts. In the redistricting, the legislature was forced to disregard state constitutional provisions concerning county lines and the number of counties to be contained in districts.

This new reapportionment act brought about far-reaching changes, with twenty-three senate districts in

Northern California combined into eight. Los Angeles
County jumped from one senate district to 14⅓ seats. Under the 1965 reapportionment, eight Southern California
counties had twenty-two of the forty senate seats and forty-
six seats of the eighty-member assembly.

THE 1970–72 REAPPORTIONMENT CONTROVERSY Un-
der the California constitution the legislature must reappor-
tion itself during the regular session following the decennial
federal census. A legislative reapportionment plan was
passed by the assembly and senate at its 1971 First Extraordinary session but was vetoed by the governor. The Democrats had won control of both houses in 1970 and the reelected Republican, Governor Reagan, felt the legislature
had been gerrymandered in favor of Democrats so he vetoed
the measure.

A constitutional amendment in 1926 had provided for
a reapportionment commission headed by the lieutenant
governor to carry out legislative reapportionment in case the
legislature failed to do so after a decennial census. However,
this amendment had been passed when the senate districts
were based on a geographical basis and prior to the U.S.
Supreme Court decision that the provisions of the California
constitution had violated the one man, one vote principle.

All of this resulted in a controversy over the question of
who constitutionally could make the reapportionment decision in California.

In January 1972, the state supreme court handed down
a ruling consolidating its decisions on three separate cases
involving reapportionment. Its decision upheld the governor's power to veto any bill, including reapportionment bills,
and also recognized that the reapportionment commission
was unconstitutional under the circumstances as cited
above.

At the same time, the court realized that there was not
enough time to develop a new plan that would meet the approval of both the legislature and the governor before the
1972 elections. Therefore, it was ordered that the existing
districts be used in the primary and general elections of
1972. In the case of congressional districts, however, the
addition of five new seats in California led the court to approve the forty-three-seat plan of 1971 (an addition of five

new U.S. representatives in Congress due to growth in California from 1960 to 1970).

REAPPORTIONMENT FOR 1974   Due to the inability of the legislature and the governor to approve a new reapportionment, the California supreme court appointed three retired judges as special masters to prepare new reapportionment plans. Ending the tradition of drawing districts that guaranteed the election of incumbents, the panel made an attempt to eliminate the crazy quilt boundaries of previous legislative and congressional district maps. The masters panel used a computer instead of friendship, sentiment, and politics in drawing new district lines. Their redistricting was based upon the criteria of population equality, contiguous and compact districts, keeping counties and cities intact if possible, preserving the integrity of basic geographic regions, consideration of "community of interest," forming state senatorial districts by combining two adjacent assembly districts wherever possible, and following assembly district lines to form congressional districts.

The Supreme Court approved the Masters Plan in December 1973 and ordered the first court reapportionment in California history to be implemented in the 1974 elections. It was recognized that the staggered system of electing half the senate members every two years for four-year terms must be preserved under the state constitution. Therefore, the court ordered elections in 1974 in the even-numbered senate districts and voting in 1976 in those with odd numbers rather than in all 40 new districts in 1974.

Because of population changes since the reapportionment of 1965, one state senate district and two assembly districts were shifted from the north to the south. Thus, the eight Southern California counties now have twenty-three of the senate seats and forty-eight of the eighty-member assembly. Assembly districts vary no more than 1.94 percent from the ideal one-person, one-vote population of 249,661, based on the 1970 census figures. Senate districts vary no more than 1.92 percent from a population of 499,322 and congressional districts no more than 0.24 percent from 464,486. Dozens of legislators faced loss of their prize districts; with the new boundaries, many now found themselves living in the same district as another incumbent. The redistricting also increased the chances for additional blacks and Mexican-Americans to be elected to the state legislature and the Congress.

Terms of Office, Compensation, Qualifications

State senators serve terms of four years, with half the membership elected every two years. There is no restriction on the number of terms an individual legislator may serve. When a vacancy occurs before a term has expired, the governor is required to call a special election.[2]

Prior to the constitutional revision of 1966, legislative compensation was set at $6000 per year. The new provision allows the legislature to set its own compensation by statute, though any salary adjustment may not take effect until after the next general election. In addition, such an action takes a two-thirds vote of each house and is subject to the governor's veto. Individual increases may not exceed 5 percent per year. A 1966 statute effective upon passage of Proposition 1A set legislator's salaries at $16,000 per annum, and, in 1970, they were increased to $19,200. An additional raise in pay to $23,332 became effective in 1976.

In addition to their salaries, California lawmakers are paid $30 a day for living expenses while the legislature is in session, which is most of the time. They also receive these per diem expenses when serving on interim committee assignments. Each enjoys a state-leased car and unlimited charges on an oil company credit card for official business. Each assemblyman and senator has a private office and some have office suites and adjoining rooms. All have paid personal aides and secretaries who work in Sacramento and in the legislator's home district.

Legislators have also voted themselves generous retirement plans. In 1971 a bill was passed that allowed a legislator elected before 1974 who had served a minimum of two terms to receive benefits immediately and before he reached retirement age. Thus a defeated incumbent could be paid "retirement" benefits at the age of thirty or forty and receive this for the rest of his life. This was the subject of such

---

[2] In case of wartime disaster, creating vacancies of one-fifth or more of the members of the legislature, the legislature itself may provide for the filling of the vacancies.

severe criticism that a special session called late in 1974 repealed this action.

An individual is eligible for election to either house of the legislature if he (or she) is twenty-one years old, a U.S. citizen and resident of the state for three years, and a resident in his district for one year previous to election.

Legislative Officers

IN THE SENATE   The lieutenant governor of the state is the president of the senate. He presides over senate sessions but may not introduce a bill or vote upon a measure except in the case of a tie vote. The senators elect a president pro tempore from their membership to preside over the senate when the lieutenant governor is absent. The president pro tem is regarded as the most important officer of the senate, serving as chairman of the powerful rules committee and as majority floor leader. Under the constitution he becomes the acting governor when both the governor and lieutenant governor are out of the state. In 1968 when both Governor Reagan and Lieutenant Governor Finch were in Florida attending the Republican convention, Senator Hugh Burns, president pro tem, successfully invoked this power and adjourned the legislature despite the opposition of Assembly Speaker Jess Unruh. Nonmembers are elected by the senate to serve as secretary, sergeant-at-arms, chief clerk, and chaplain.

IN THE ASSEMBLY   The speaker of the assembly is the presiding officer. An assemblyman himself, he is elected to the speakership by the members of the house, and retains all his voting and debating rights. He selects a majority floor leader to serve as his personal representative on the floor during proceedings. (The minority floor leader is selected by the minority party.) The speaker is the most powerful officer in the assembly, indeed, in the entire legislature. He makes all appointments to committees except the rules committee,[3] appoints all committee chairmen, and refers all bills

[3] The speaker's power was diminished in 1951. Previously he had the power to appoint the rules committee. Now this committee is elected by the members of the assembly.

to committee. A speaker pro tempore, also elected from the assembly, presides in the absence of the speaker. Nonmember officers include the chief clerk, the sergeant-at-arms, the minutes clerk, and the chaplain.

SERVING BOTH HOUSES   The post of auditor general was created in 1955 to keep close scrutiny over the financial management of the executive branch and to make annual reports to the legislature. The auditor general, an experienced certified public accountant, is appointed by the Joint Legislative Audit Committee and serves at the pleasure of the committee.

The legislative analyst (formerly called the legislative auditor) is mainly concerned with fiscal matters but should not be confused with the auditor general. The analyst's most important job is to review and analyze the governor's annual budget proposals. The legislative analyst has the additional duty of maintaining a registry of legislative advocates (lobbyists) and keeping files on their activities. He is appointed by the Joint Legislative Budget Committee and is directly responsible to this body.

The legislative counsel is the legislature's legal specialist and bill-drafting expert. He is selected by concurrent resolution of both houses. He maintains a permanent office and staff in the state capitol within easy access of the legislative chambers, and prepares or assists in preparing any measure when requested by a legislator. He also writes digests of bills for use by the legislators.

Party Organization in the Legislature

California's atmosphere of nonpartisanship (or *bipartisanship,* as state legislators prefer to call it) used to prevail at the state capitol. "The words 'Democrat' and 'Republican' are not often heard on the floor of the houses," reported the secretary of the senate in 1957, "and when they are heard it is frequently in some friendly or humorous connection." [4] When the Democrats assumed control of the administration and the legislature in 1959, and since that time, party alignments have become more marked.

Yet, in contrast with the U.S. Congress, where the com-

---

[4] Joseph A. Beek, *The California Legislature* (Sacramento: State Printing Office, 1957), p. 152.

mittees and their chairmen are selected on a partisan basis, there is no such formula for committee assignments in the California legislature. A bitter partisan fight over the budget in 1963 resulted in an assembly rule providing that all committee chairmen must be members of the majority party. However, this rule was rescinded in 1964. At the same time, it is still true that in both houses the majority party retains the chairmanships and majorities on the important committees, including finance and rules.

In the assembly each party maintains a caucus and "whips," but the Democratic organization is more formal than the Republican. Members of each party meet weekly to decide which of the bills to be considered by the legislature should become matters of party policy. But there is no means of disciplining dissident members, and assemblymen are free to vote independently on the floor or in committees. The tone of the Democratic caucus deliberations is set by a steering committee consisting of the Democratic floor leader and his three assistants. The Republican caucus elects a chairman but does not have a steering committee.

Prior to 1959 there were no caucuses in the senate. Shortly after the 1959 session convened, however, the Republicans summoned a caucus to chart legislative strategy; the Democrats have since organized in a similar manner. The legislative sessions beginning in 1961 have been marked by an increase in political partisanship in both the assembly and the senate.

SESSIONS

Most state legislatures are in session for only short periods during the year, and generally the length of the session is limited by law. More than half the states convene only once every two years for legislative sessions (California had this arrangement from 1862 to 1946). These practices are quite in contrast with the U.S. Congress, which convenes in early January and usually does not adjourn until late in the summer or early in the fall when it deems it has finished its annual business. Until California changed its plan for legislative sessions with constitutional revision in 1966, New York was the only state having annual year-long legislative sessions.

The General Session and the Budget Session

From 1946 until 1967 the California legislature met in general session in every *odd*-numbered year and met in a budget session in every *even*-numbered year. As the titles indicate, bills dealing with all types of legislation (including the budget) were handled in the general session whereas the budget session was limited to the consideration of the budget bill.

The general session convened on the first Monday after New Year's Day and continued in session for 120 calendar days excluding Saturdays and Sundays. A "split" session instituted by the Progressives in 1911 provided for a compulsory thirty-day recess after the first thirty days of the session. The purpose of this "split" or "bifurcated" session was to allow ample time for the public to examine and express its opinion on pending legislation. However, a constitutional amendment was voted in 1958 which set no time limit upon the introduction of bills and also eliminated the *compulsory* thirty-day recess. It further provided for a thirty-day waiting period after introduction before any bill, except the budget bill, could be heard by a committee or acted upon by either house. (In effect, this meant that most bills had to be introduced within the first ninety days of the 120-day session.) However, the thirty-day waiting period could be dispensed with for emergency legislation and by the consent of three-fourths of the members of the house. This device could also be used for emergency legislation.

The budget session commenced on the first Monday in February and could last no more than thirty calendar days. However, after the submission of the budget bill by the governor, a recess of both houses was generally taken, but it could not exceed thirty days. In recent years, the legislature had been unable to agree upon a budget within the thirty-day period, thus making it necessary for the governor to call the legislature into a special or extraordinary session so that a budget could be passed to make funds available for the various state agencies.

Extraordinary (Special) Sessions

The legislature could be called into extraordinary session by the governor at *any* time—between regular sessions or even concurrently with regular sessions. To call an extraordinary session the governor issued a proclamation stating the purposes for which he was convening it and listing the subjects he wished to be considered. On such occasions the legislature had "power to legislate only on subjects specified in the proclamation. . . ."[5] The governor thus had tighter control over legislation in extraordinary sessions than in regular sessions.

The legislature was called into extraordinary session on fifty-three different occasions from its first session in 1849 through 1970, thirty-five since 1940. The record was set in 1940, when Governor Olson called five extraordinary sessions, some running concurrently. The chief clerk of the assembly, Arthur Ohnimus, describes what happened:

> During this period, at the time appointed, each of the sessions was called to order, the roll was called, the prayer was offered by the Chaplain, and all organizational matters were performed. After proceeding with the "Order of Business," the daily session was adjourned, and the next extraordinary session was immediately called to order. This procedure . . . [required] five separate publications of the Journal, History, and File (which, in order to properly identify the sessions, were printed in different colors of ink for each session: black, brown, blue, green, and purple . . .).

Not to be outdone, the 1960 senate, when it was called into extraordinary sessions, also made use of different colored flags on the presiding officer's desk so that the legislators would know which session was in progress! Extraordinary sessions have lasted from one day in length to 312 calendar days.

Legislative Reorganization

The revision of / California's constitution approved in 1966 provided for annual sessions of the legislature beginning on the Monday after January 1. There was to be no limit on the length of the annual session: if the legislature had finished its business it would adjourn; if it had not, it would continue in session uninhibited by an arbitrary termination.

---

[5] Constitution of the State of California, Art. IV, sec. 3b.

"I'll have this thing working in a minute . . . ."

Renault in the Sacramento Bee, *August 27, 1974.*
Reprinted by permission.

Under the approved Proposition 4 in 1972, the legislative calendar has been changed from one-year to two-year sessions. Under the terms of the measure, the legislature convenes in even-numbered years on the first Monday of December and remains in session until November 30 of the following even-numbered year, with the provision that either or both houses can go into recess. The governor may call extraordinary sessions of the legislature to deal with specified matters, but such sessions would appear to be likely only in the event that both houses had agreed to recess for an extended period before the final adjournment.

Bills may be introduced in either the first or second year and bills introduced in the first year are automatically carried over to the second, except in the case of bills that have not been passed by their house of origin by January 30 of the second year. No bill may be passed by either house on or after September 1 of the even-numbered year except statutes calling elections, providing tax levies, or appropriations; "urgency measures"; and bills passed over the governor's veto. The legislature may not present any bill to the governor after November 15 of the second year. Most newly enacted statutes go into effect after January 1 but only after ninety days have passed since enactment; otherwise they do not go into effect, in the absence of an urgency clause, until the next January 1.

This new plan should cut down on waste of time and expense in the reorganization of the legislature each year. In many respects, it resembles the system now used in the United States Congress.

LEGISLATIVE ACTION

The legislature may take action in any of three basic ways: it may express an opinion; it may pass a law; or it may refer a measure to the voters for approval, which is required with bond issues and constitutional amendments.

Resolutions are used for expressions of opinion by one or both houses of the legislature. *House* resolutions are made by one house only and may pertain to any matter. *Joint* resolutions are expressions by both houses relating only to national government matters. These are usually expressions of approval or disapproval by the California legislature of legislation pending in Congress. *Concurrent* resolutions are used for all other matters on which both houses wish to express an opinion or must act jointly, as for adjournment or recess or to commend individuals for public service and for approval of amendments to city and county charters.

Constitutional amendments and bond issues (see

Chapter Six) are treated as regular bills but are submitted to the voters for final adoption or rejection at the following general election instead of being sent to the governor for his signature. Constitutional amendments require a two-thirds vote of both houses.

How a Bill Becomes a Law

1. Introduction The act of introducing a bill consists of a legislator submitting a signed copy to the clerk of the house to which he belongs. Though all bills must be formally introduced by members of the legislature, most of them originate in government agencies, the office of the governor, or with pressure groups. In fact, more often than not the legislator acts merely as an intermediary for other interested parties. After submission of the signed copy, the bill is numbered, given its "first reading," and assigned to

The California assembly in session. *Wide World Photos.*

an appropriate committee. (Committee assignment is the responsibility of the speaker in the assembly and the committee on rules in the senate.)

2. Consideration by Committee   The fate of most bills is determined by the committee to which they are assigned. Public hearings are scheduled for important legislation, and anyone wishing to testify is usually given an opportunity to appear. Committees have the authority to subpoena witnesses and documentary evidence related to their investigations (failure to honor a subpoena is grounds for legal prosecution). A committee may dispose of a bill in any of the following ways: (*a*) table it—that is, postpone action indefinitely; (*b*) report it out (back to the whole house) without recommendation; (*c*) report it out with the recommendation "do pass," either in its original form or as amended by the committee. Many bills (more than half in the assembly) are never reported out of committee—are "pigeonholed," to use the legislative vernacular. However, a bill can be forced out of committee by a majority vote of all members in the house concerned; but this process is rarely used. Usually the house follows the committee's recommendations.

3. Consideration on the Floor   After the bill has been reported from committee it is given a "second reading," at which time committee amendments and amendments from the floor are adopted. It is then reprinted with the amendments for the "third reading," which opens floor debate. Debate may be closed and the question brought to a vote in each house by a majority vote, so there can be no minority "filibusters" in the California legislature. A bill may be passed with or without amendments, referred back to committee, or rejected. The final vote on passage of a bill is by roll call—the vote of each member placed in the record—in each house. The senate retains the traditional oral roll call, the clerk droning out the name of every member. The assembly uses an instantaneous electric recording device which simultaneously flashes all votes on a scoreboard in view of everyone as members press the "yes" or "no" buttons at their desks. It takes forty-one votes in the assembly to pass an ordinary bill and twenty-one in the senate (a majority of the total membership of each house). To pass a constitutional amendment, an urgency measure, a budget bill, or to override a governor's veto, fifty-four assembly votes and twenty-seven senate votes (a two-thirds majority of each house) are required. Once a bill is passed by either house, it is signed by the presiding officer and sent to the other house for consideration. Final passage by the legislature requires approval by both houses.

4. Referral Conference Committee If the second house to consider a bill passes it with amendments and the originating house refuses to concur in these amendments, a conference among selected members of both houses is called to iron out the differences. The conference committee is composed of three assemblymen appointed by the speaker and three senators appointed by the committee on rules. Two of the members from each house must be from the majority which voted to pass the bill and one from the minority. If the report of the conference committee is not accepted by both houses, another conference committee is convened; but there can be no more than three such committees for one bill. If the two houses still fail to agree the bill is dead.

5. To the Governor for Approval After an agreed-upon version of a bill has been passed by both houses it is technically referred to as a legislative act. If signed by the governor, most bills go into effect the following January 1, providing ninety days have passed since signing. If the governor fails to sign the bill within twelve days after receiving it and the legislature is still in session, the bill becomes a law without his signature. A bill passed within the last twelve days of a general session will become law unless the governor vetoes it within thirty days after the end of the session.

6. Overriding the Governor's Veto A bill returned to the legislature by the governor with his objections can be passed and become law over these objections only by a vote of two-thirds of the elected members of each house. If the legislature is unable to obtain such a vote against the governor's action, the bill fails to become a law. A special five-day veto session of the legislature, called for the purpose of considering and possibly overriding the governor's vetoes as established by the 1966 constitutional revision, was eliminated by Proposition 4 in 1972. No governor's veto was overridden by the legislature from 1946 until 1974, when a Reagan veto was overruled. (For a full discussion of the veto power, refer to Chapter Eight.)

Amount of Legislation

Approximately 4500 different bills are now being introduced at each session of the legislature. About one-third of these are almost immediately abandoned and never receive serious consideration by the committees or on the floor of the legislature. Most of these have been introduced by legislators to satisfy their constituents and the authors themselves have little enthusiasm or hope for passage. Another third of the measures introduced are killed either by the committee, on the floor of the assembly or the senate, or are vetoed by the governor. Thus, in recent years, about 1300 to 1500 bills have finally become law during each legislative session.

PROPOSALS FOR IMPROVING THE LEGISLATURE

There has never been a final answer to the question of what is the primary function of an elected legislator. Should he cast his votes on the basis of the wishes of his constituents? or of the interests of the state? or of what is "right" or "just"? Similarly, there is no unanimity on the question of whether the legislature should be an agency for registering the majority will, or for reconciling and compromising the conflicting demands of interest groups. The citizen, the politician, the interest group, and the political scientist are likely to take sides on proposals for *procedural* and *structural* changes according to their answers to the problem of the *role* of the legislator and the legislature. Thus, what appears an improvement to one often seems an impairment to another. Three of the most prominent proposals that have been advanced in recent years as "improvements" upon the present system are discussed in the following pages.

Establishing a Unicameral Legislature

There has been renewed interest in the establishment of a one-house (unicameral) legislature since 1964 when the U.S. Supreme Court handed down its so-called one-man, one-vote doctrine. Now that both the state assembly and the senate represent population, it is argued that there is no logic in retaining two houses, as they basically represent the same constituencies.

It is contended that a unicameral legislature would be more economical as it most likely would have a smaller number of members with a proportionate reduction in staff. Supporters also point out that two houses create duplication of effort and unnecessary delay in passing bills and this costs money and time.

Proponents believe that the centralization of legislative and political responsibility in one house would prevent the practice of "passing the buck" between the two houses or between political parties when each house is controlled by a different party. Lawmaking and lawmakers would be more "visible," thus decreasing the influence of lobbyists and special interests. The unusual power now held by the conference committee (up until recently meeting behind closed doors) would be eliminated and transferred to the whole membership representing statewide constituencies.

Many proposals for a one-house legislature in California have been made in past years. Prominent political leaders including former Governor "Pat" Brown, his son "Jerry" Brown, and Jess Unruh have urged this as a legislative reform. A plan promoted by Judge Lewis Sherman, a former state senator, was presented in a bill to the 1974 legislature. This proposal would have established one house of 99 senators serving staggered four-year terms. Jess Unruh, arguing unsuccessfully for the bill, said, "If we need a two-house legislature, why not have two city councils or two boards of supervisors?" After its defeat in the legislature, the proponents conducted a vigorous, but unsuccessful, campaign to secure sufficient signatures to qualify an initiative for the November election.

Unicameralism has made little headway in the United States, with Nebraska in 1937 being the only state to adopt and implement the system. The tradition of the two-house system set by the U.S. Constitution is deeply ingrained and there is strong resistance to any change on the part of politicians and active legislators. Pressure groups and special interests find bicameralism congenial as it allows more time and points of contact for their lobbying activities. Two houses do afford more time for consideration of legislation, resulting in more deliberate action on important matters. A differential in terms of office between the members of each house could provide some added degree of perspective in the consideration of legislation.

So far, it appears difficult to arouse sufficient enthusiasm to establish a unicameral legislature in California.

Increasing Legislative Efficiency

Many legislators and political scientists are concerned with the duplication and wasted effort cited by proponents of unicameralism, but claim that much of this could be lessened even *within* the bicameral system. More joint committees could be established to avoid duplicate hearings and unnecessary differences in the treatment by both houses of the same pieces of legislation. A permanent secretariat, or headquarters with a staff of paid specialists, has been suggested to facilitate committee work and recordkeeping. A less drastic proposal would be merely to expand the services of the legislative analyst, making specialized information more accessible to committees.

A majority of states have established a council of legislators to serve as a master interim committee. The council prepares and recommends a legislative program in advance of each session so that haphazard calendars and duplicate bills are avoided. Some legislators object to such a council, however, feeling that it unduly concentrates legislative power in the hands of a few.

Increasing the Terms of Assemblymen

Periodically, the proposal to increase the terms of assembly members from two to four years is brought forward.[6] It is contended that a two-year term barely allows the new member to become familiar with the technicalities of legislative procedure before he has to run for reelection. Staggered four-year terms, with half the membership elected at each biennial election, would guarantee continuity of membership as it exists in the senate. And the expense of an

---

[6] Proposition 2 to increase the terms of assemblymen to four years was defeated in the 1960 election.

election campaign every two years would be eliminated. Those who resist such a change maintain that standing for election every two years forces the assemblyman to keep his "ear close to the ground," to be responsive to shifts in public opinion, and that this is all to the good of democracy.

CALIFORNIA LEGISLATURE RANKED BEST IN NATION

The California legislature was ranked first among the legislatures of the states in an evaluation made public in 1971. The study was conducted by the Citizens Conference on State Legislatures, a respected national association dealing with state government.

Overall comparative rankings were based on evaluations in five criteria of functionality, accountability, information handling capacity, independence, and representativeness. The California legislature secured the highest combined ranking in all categories of all states. New York and Illinois secured the second and third places in the study.

Certain improvements for the California legislature were recommended in the study. It was pointed out that the legislature has too many committees and legislators have too many committee assignments. There is also need for better minority member representation on committees. In addition, published rules of committee procedure are needed, as well as public access to committee reports and roll calls showing how each member voted. It was also recommended that better preparation of bill summaries was desirable.

SELECTED REFERENCES

BAKER, GORDON E., *The Reapportionment Revolution: Representation, Political Power, and the Supreme Court.* New York: Random House, 1966.

"Ballot Propositions 1972 General Elections," *California Journal* III, 8 (September 1972): 263.

BELL, CHARLES, JOEL FISHER, and CHARLES PRICE, *The Legislative Process in California,* Washington, D.C., American Political Science Association, 1973.

BLAIR, GEORGE S., and HOUSTON I. FLOURNOY, *Legislative Bodies in California.* Belmont, Calif.: Dickenson, 1967.

BUCHANAN, WILLIAM, *Legislative Partisanship: The Deviant Case of California.* Berkeley: University of California Press, 1963.

California, Assembly Interim Committee on Elections and Reapportionment, *Reports.* Sacramento: State Printing Office, 1957, 1961, 1965.

California, Legislature, *Final Calendar of Legislative Business.* Sacramento: State Printing Office. Issued annually.

Los Angeles Times. For daily coverage of the legislature.

Sacramento Bee. For daily coverage of the legislature.

"The Two-Year Session: Success or Failure?" *Cailfornia Journal* V, 1 (January 1974): 11, 12.

U.S. Bureau of the Census, *Congressional District Data Book.* Washington, D.C.: Government Printing Office, 1971.

The Executive and the Administration

Unlike the federal government but like most state governments, the California government has several elected executive officers. In addition to the governor, there are ten state executives—lieutenant governor, attorney general, secretary of state, controller, treasurer, superintendent of public instruction, and four members of the Board of Equalization—all elected directly by the people. Originated to prevent excessive concentration of power in the hands of

THE PLURAL EXECUTIVE

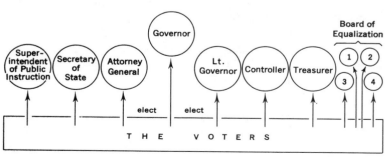

one person, this arrangement has contributed to a divided administrative structure. Though the state constitution vests the governor with "supreme executive power," the other executive officers have independent constitutional status and are responsible only to the electorate. On two occasions California voters have elected a Democratic governor and at the same time chosen a lieutenant governor who was a Republican. And in most elections, at least one of the other executive officers is a member of the opposite party from the governor. As can be noted in the chart on page 162, Edmund Brown, a Democrat, served as attorney general in the Republican administration from 1951–1959. And Frank Jordan, Republican, was elected secretary of state when Brown became governor. Thomas Lynch, attorney general, and Edmund Brown, Jr., secretary of state, both Democrats, were executive officials serving while Republican Ronald Reagan was governor. Attorney General Evelle Younger, a Republican, is now serving with a Democrat as governor. This "plural executive" system contrasts with the national government in which the president and vice-president are always of the same party and the president has the power to appoint and remove the major executive officers. Though the power of the governor has been augmented by the establishment of the executive budget and the item veto (see below), the dominant fact is that the ten executive officers mentioned are not dependent upon him for their jobs.

THE GOVERNOR

As the state's chief executive, the governor has the responsibility of carrying out the laws enacted by the legislature and those initiated by the people. This broad executive power plus the governor's other constitutionally delegated powers makes him the most important public official in the state.

Major Powers

A governor's ability to *direct* public policy depends upon his use of the constants and variables attached to California governorship. The constants are the constitutional powers inherent in his position. The variables are his administrative and political leadership in exercising these powers. These constant and variable powers, when used strategically or aggressively, can have a significant impact on public policy.

THE EXECUTIVE BUDGET   Probably the most important grant of authority to the governor was in the constitutional amendment of 1922, which placed the duty of originating the annual state budget in the governor's office. Where formerly each department and agency submitted its own request for funds to the legislature, under the present system all requests for appropriations must be channeled through the governor. The aim was to eliminate piecemeal and happenstance financial legislation and to diminish the interplay of politics between the legislature, individual departments, and pressure groups.

The governor has the final responsibility for preparing and submitting to the legislature an annual budget containing the bulk of anticipated state income and expenditures. The technical and detailed work of reviewing and making budget estimates for the various departments, holding hearings, and composing the budget documents is the task of the Department of Finance, which is directly responsible to the governor. After the governor has approved the budget document, he submits it to the legislature with his message outlining and defending the year's financial program. Until the budget has been passed, the legislature may not take up any other appropriation measures except those for operational expenses of the legislature itself, unless the governor specially requests an emergency bill.

The executive budget places the governor in the driver's seat of the state's financial program, though the legislature still retains the power to regulate the "fuel supply."

THE VETO   The governor can also influence legislation through the exercise of, or the threat to use, his veto power. He has two classes of veto—the general veto for rejecting an entire bill, and the item veto for rejecting only portions of bills.

1. The General Veto   The governor may disapprove a bill within twelve days after its passage by sending it back to the legislature. The vetoed bill is usually accompanied by

ELECTED STATE OFFICERS, 1951–1979

Term of office	Governor	Lt. Governor	Attorney General	Secretary of State	Controller	Treasurer
1951–55	Earl Warren (Goodwin J. Knight, 1953–55)*	Goodwin J. Knight (Harold J. Powers, 1953–55)*	Edmund G. Brown	Frank M. Jordan	Thos. H. Kuchel (Robt. C. Kirkwood, 1953–55)*	Chas. G. Johnson
1955–59	Goodwin J. Knight	Harold J. Powers	Edmund G. Brown	Frank M. Jordan	Robert C. Kirkwood	Chas. G. Johnson (A. Ronald Button, 1956–59)*
1959–67	Edmund G. Brown	Glenn M. Anderson	Stanley Mosk (Thomas Lynch, 1964)*	Frank M. Jordan	Alan Cranston	Bert A. Betts
1967–71	Ronald Reagan	Robert Finch (Ed Reinecke, 1969–)*	Thomas Lynch	Frank M. Jordan	Houston Flournoy	Ivy Baker Priest
1971–75	Ronald Reagan	Ed Reinecke	Evelle Younger	Edmund G. Brown, Jr.	Houston Flournoy	Ivy Baker Priest
1975–79	Edmund G. Brown, Jr.	Mervyn Dymally	Evelle Younger	March Fong	Kenneth Cory	Jess Unruh

*Served out the unexpired term of the elected officer

☐ Republican   ▨ Democratic

162

a written statement from the governor indicating his objections. A vetoed bill can be passed over the governor's objections only by a two-thirds vote of the elected members of both houses.[1] If the governor neither signs nor formally rejects a bill within twelve days of receiving it, as long as the legislature has not yet adjourned, the bill becomes law without his signature. Until Proposition 6 was passed in 1966, if the legislature adjourned before the ten-day period had expired, the governor was allowed thirty days after adjournment in which to sign the bill. And if after the thirty-day period the bill remained unsigned, it was considered "pocket vetoed" and there was no possibility for the legislature to override the veto.

Prior to the constitutional revision in 1966 more than 80 percent of all vetoes had been of the "pocket variety." The high percentage resulted from the frequent pile-up on the governor's desk of bills that had been passed in the final rush of the legislative calendar due to limited time for sessions.

As noted in Chapter Seven, Proposition 4 providing for legislative reorganization was passed by the voters in 1972. Under its provisions, the legislature is in a continuous two-year session, other than when it declares a recess. Hence, pocket vetoes were effectively eliminated as the legislature can consider all vetoes while in session.

A survey of the 1958–74 period shows that Governors Knight, Brown, and Reagan refused to approve about 6 percent of all the bills passed by the legislature. A frequent use of the gubernatorial veto is evident in other large states, such as New York and Pennsylvania. These veto rates are substantially higher than the incidence of presidential vetoes, which for recent national administrations totaled approximately 2 percent of all bills passed.

2. The Item Veto California's governor, like the chief executives of four-fifths of the states, but unlike the president, may reject individual items in any appropriation bill.[2] He may either *strike out* an item completely or *reduce* it;

[1] The California legislature has rarely been successful in overriding a governor's veto. For the first time since 1946, both houses in 1974 secured the necessary two-thirds vote to override Governor Reagan's veto of a bill relating to closure of state hospitals.

[2] A few states go even further and allow their governors to apply the item veto to all legislation.

but he may make *no increases* in expenditures. The legislature has the same power to override an item veto as it does for the general veto. However, it rarely uses this device, almost always allowing a bill that has received an item veto to take effect.

The purpose of the item veto, instituted along with the executive budget in 1922, was to strengthen the governor's hand in the formulation of the state's fiscal program. Whereas previously the governor had either to accept a bill or to reject it *in toto*—thus encouraging legislators to add unrelated "riders" to the budget bill or other vital legislation —the governor may now reject only those provisions he finds objectionable, while retaining the basic measure.

The item veto is not used often by California governors. However, its infrequent use is no measure of its effectiveness. As a gubernatorial weapon it serves as a threat, like the gun in the holster of a California sheriff. As such it is a major source of the governor's "legislative" power, helping him to compel the legislature to consider only those matters he deems important.

CALLING SPECIAL SESSIONS The state constitution provides that "on extraordinary occasions the governor by proclamation may convene the legislature in special session. When so convened it has power to legislate only on subjects specified in the proclamation but may provide for expenses and other matters incidental to the session" (Article IV, section 3b). Governors have used this device frequently. They may, and often do, call these extraordinary sessions to meet at the same time the legislature is sitting in regular session, and on these occasions the results are sometimes truly extraordinary.[3] The effect of the governor's power to call sessions and specify their business is readily seen: senate and assembly leaders know they cannot ignore a governor's legislative program.

The governor has no corresponding power over adjournment, however. He may adjourn the legislature only when both houses fail to agree upon a date.

APPOINTING STATE OFFICERS Though the governor's power of appointment is limited by the plural executive sys-

[3] See discussion of *extraordinary sessions* in the chapter on the legislature, pp. 146–47.

tem providing for direct election of many important officers, and by the large state civil service program, it is nonetheless a substantial power. He appoints all *department* heads, with the exception of two, both elected officials: the attorney general, who directs the Department of Justice, and the superintendent of public instruction, who heads the Department of Education.[4]

There are twenty-five to thirty top state administrative positions that the governor fills by appointment, including the directors of finance, public works, corrections, agriculture, social welfare, employment, motor vehicles, industrial relations, and alcoholic beverages control. He also names the members of several important boards and commissions —the Public Utilities Commission, state Personnel Board, state Board of Education, Board of Health, Trustees of the State Universities and Colleges, and the Regents of the University of California—many of whom have terms overlapping the governor's four-year term; thus any one governor may not have the opportunity of making all board and commission appointments.

In addition, the governor is given the privilege of naming the members of some of the advisory and administrative boards created by the legislature as needs arise. The Water Rights Board, Veterans Board, Building Standards Commission, Colorado River Boundary Commission, and Advisory Board on Furniture and Bedding (which regulates product standards) are examples.

The governor's appointment power is somewhat limited, however, by the necessity for senate approval of the appointment and removal of many important state officials. The governor has full appointment and removal power over most department heads. But among those subject to senate concurrence are members of the Personnel Board, fish and game commissioners, the director of corrections, and wardens of the state prisons. When the legislature creates new agencies in the executive branch of government it likes to keep some voice in their staffing. But too much legislative

[4] A constitutional amendment to have the superintendent appointed by the state Board of Education (rather than elected) failed to pass in the November 1958 election. And an attempt to change the method of selection, allowing the legislature to determine how the superintendent of public instruction should be chosen, was defeated in the 1968 attempt to revise Article IX of the constitution.

intervention tends to obliterate whatever separation of powers still exists between the branches.

Another facet of the governor's appointment power is his responsibility for filling the unexpired terms (because of resignation, disability, death, or conviction of crime) of certain elected officers; U.S. senators, state executive officers, and judges of the supreme, district, superior, and municipal courts.[5] Filling vacancies on the court bench has become a frequently exercised and important duty.

POWER AS POLITICAL LEADER   Occupancy of the office itself brings to the governor, whether he be a strong or a weak leader, a position of political prominence second to none in the state. He is looked upon as the titular leader of his party, often becoming its "favorite son" at the presidential nominating convention; and with the increased electoral weight of California, the governor is automatically regarded as a presidential possibility. The position's prestige, and its resultant influence over public opinion, may be used—if a governor is so inclined—as a whip to corral would-be mavericks in his party or in the state government. Such influence can be exerted through informal conferences, breakfasts, press conferences, and "phone calls from the governor's office."

Other Powers

The governorship carries with it many other responsibilities in addition to the major powers already discussed. Many of these are the traditional duties of any governmental chief executive in the United States, whether president, governor, or mayor.

COMMANDER IN CHIEF OF THE STATE MILITIA   Whenever police officers of the state, counties, or cities are unable to handle emergency situations such as fires, earthquakes, or floods, or to quell such civil disturbances as riots, insurrections, or strikes, the governor may call out the state militia. The militia—now integrated with California's National

---

[5] When vacancies occur in many other elective offices, as in the state senate and assembly, the governor issues writs for special elections. In any office in which there is no provision for filling a vacancy, the governor has general constitutional authority to make an appointment.

Guard units—is a stand-by military reserve composed primarily of men who have served in the nation's military forces. Though the governor may order the militia about at his own discretion, he rarely ever calls upon it except upon request from a local law enforcement official.[6] The actual administration of the militia is delegated to the adjutant general of the California National Guard, an appointee of the governor subject to presidential approval.

CIVIL DEFENSE RESPONSIBILITIES Related to his emergency powers is the governor's position as head of the state's civil defense program. In accord with the Civil Defense Act of 1950, as amplified by the 1956 extraordinary session of the legislature, the California Disaster Office and the Disaster Council were established to assist the governor in mitigating the effects of enemy attack or sabotage. It is the governor's duty to insure the coordination of local and state plans with those of the national government.

EXECUTIVE CLEMENCY Except in the case of impeachment, the governor has power to grant pardons, reprieves, and commutations of sentence to individuals convicted of any felony. The governor may not grant a pardon or commutation to a person twice convicted of a felony except on the recommendation of the supreme court. The difficult nature of such decisions, and the large number of requests, place a heavy strain upon the chief executive. "I'd bleed from every pore each time I went over a case," recalls Goodwin Knight. "You realize that all you have to do is scratch your name on a piece of paper—you do it as governor about twenty times a day anyhow—and a man can live. A flick of the wrist and I can let him breathe, I'd tell myself. And if you did not many people would know. . . . Executive clemency appeals are strenuous and the toughest thing a governor has to face. The evening before the day of execution isn't pleasant." [7] The burden is eased somewhat

[6] Occasionally the guard may be called into national action; for example, in 1950 California's 40th Division was sent to Korea. The National Guard was also called to quell the Watts riot in the Los Angeles area, August 1965.

[7] *Sacramento Bee,* June 11, 1959, Sec. A, p. 11. Under Proposition 17 passed in 1972, the legislature and the courts could limit the death penalty to only certain offenses, such as the killing of a prison guard or a police officer. Such action would, of course, ease the burden placed upon the governor.

by two agencies—the Adult Authority and the board of trustees of the California Institution for Women—which act in an advisory capacity to the governor. Yet all final decisions are the governor's alone, and not subject to overrule; however, he may not pardon a person twice convicted of felonies without the recommendation of the state supreme court.

RECOMMENDING LEGISLATION   The constitution requires the governor to send a message to the legislature at every session describing the condition of the state and recommending action on specific matters. Like the State of the Union message of the president, the governor's message receives a good deal of public attention and serious consideration by the legislature. The threat of the governor's veto and his ability to call extraordinary sessions give weight to his recommendations.

CEREMONIAL FUNCTIONS   Being "Mr. California" and representing the state at all sorts of public functions demands a great deal of time and effort. The governor must host visiting dignitaries, deliver dedicatory addresses, proclaim a multitude of special "days" and "weeks," cut ribbons upon the opening of new freeways, ride in parades, drink the first glass of orange juice at the Orange Show, and sample the first date at the Date Festival. Though some governors may find, and have found, such activities not unpleasant, these ceremonial functions all too often prevent a chief executive from attending to the pressing business awaiting him on his desk in Sacramento.

The Governor's Office

THE GOVERNOR'S STAFF   To assist him in his many everyday tasks, the governor appoints a staff of assistants. The size and composition of this staff depends upon the governor and the funds at his disposal. The executive department secretariat was approximately the same size under Republican Governor Ronald Reagan as it was under Democratic Governor Edmund Brown. It includes more than a dozen top staff jobs: an executive secretary (the governor's chief adviser), press secretary, legislative secretary, legal affairs secretary, appointments secretary, education secretary, cabinet secretary, program development secretary, community relations secretary, intergovernmental relations secretary, and administrative assistants. The secretariat, of course, also includes clerical, stenographic, and office management help.

THE GOVERNOR'S CABINET   Until recently the governor met about once a month with some twenty-five department heads to discuss the coordination of governmental operations. Within the past few years, as a result of the recommendations of "the Little Hoover Commission," Governor Brown met regularly with a cabinet of nine department heads. Governor Reagan's reorganization plan also consolidated various governmental agencies so that the cabinet consisted of about ten persons.

The governor is also in charge of the large administrative machinery of the state government consisting of more than 200 agencies, boards, and commissions. Under the constitutional revision amendment of 1966, the governor was given the authority to draft and initiate plans for reorganization of the state administration. In turn, the legislature can approve or disapprove, but if it fails to take action within sixty days the governor's program automatically becomes law. (See discussion at the end of this chapter on the organization of the administration of state government.)

Qualifications, Term, Succession, Salary

To be elected governor of California a person must be a voter who has been both a United States citizen and a resident of California for five years preceding his election. He is elected for a term of four years, beginning the first Monday after New Year's Day following his election.

Prior to 1967 the constitution contained a detailed list of succession to the office of governor in case the governor was unable to complete his term. The 1966 constitutional revision provides that the lieutenant governor succeeds to the office but further successors are to be designated by the legislature through statutes.[8] Constitutional revision also

[8] The present order of succession following the lieutenant governor is senate president pro tem, assembly speaker, secretary of state, attorney general, treasurer, and controller.

authorized the California supreme court to determine when the governor is unable to carry out his duties and should be removed from office.

The governor's salary is presently $49,100 a year, which is lower than that of the governor of New York as well as of several California state officials.[9] However, in addition to his salary, the governor receives expenses for his rented home [10] and "contingency" expenses which bring his annual compensation to about $95,000. The governor also has the services of a chauffeured limousine, a jet airplane, and a liberal travel allowance. An expense account is also provided for running the governor's office; in recent years it has totaled more than $2 million.

Who Becomes Governor?

Most of California's governors have been about fifty years old at the time of inauguration and have brought with them previous experience in state government. With the exceptions of Hiram Johnson, a noted criminal lawyer from San Francisco, and Ronald Reagan, a motion picture and television actor, all California's chief executives had already held important public offices in the state. The attorney general's office has become increasingly regarded as a stepping-stone to the governorship (as it indeed served for Earl Warren and Edmund Brown). Lieutenant governors have succeeded to the office of governor in seven instances because of the death or resignation of the incumbent, the most recent being Goodwin Knight's assumption of the office upon

[9] A bill to raise the governor's annual salary to $60,000 was turned down by the 1974 legislature.

[10] In the old-fashioned governor's mansion, the gubernatorial bedchamber was not equipped with a fire escape. So, in 1959, the legislature provided a Rube Goldberg type of rope contraption on which the governor was supposed to slide to safety in case of emergency. So neatly was it hidden behind a large bureau that it was several weeks after Governor Brown moved in that he accidentally discovered it. Governor and Mrs. Reagan moved from the mansion (now a state museum) to another Sacramento home after only a few weeks' occupancy. The state has recently purchased land and plans have been drawn for the construction of a new governor's mansion. However, newly elected Governor Jerry Brown has rented an apartment and has refused to live in the mansion when and if it is completed.

the appointment of Earl Warren to the U.S. Supreme Court in 1953. There is no legal limit to the number of terms a person may serve as governor. Yet, only five California governors have been elected to more than one term—John Bigler in 1854, Hiram Johnson in 1914, Earl Warren in 1946 and 1950, Edmund Brown in 1962, and Ronald Reagan in 1970.

THE LIEUTENANT GOVERNOR

The constitutional status of California's lieutenant governor is much like that of the U.S. vice-president—once described by Benjamin Franklin as "His Most Superfluous Majesty." This does not mean that any occupant of either post is doomed to obscurity and political impotency, but there is a built-in anonymity to the office difficult to overcome. The lieutenant governor is to serve as president of the senate but has only a casting vote (one needed to break a tie). He becomes acting governor for any temporary disability of the governor or upon the governor's absence from the state. He becomes governor when a vacancy occurs in the office of governor.

The spotlight may fall on a lieutenant governor, however, if the person who is then governor has a flair for travel. The lieutenant governor is "acting governor" when the chief executive is out of the state or when physically disabled. And, of course, he is next in line should the office of governor become vacant. Heading the rank of successors as it does, the lieutenant governor's office may become more of a political plum in the future. If there is a high probability that any California governor may become the presidential or vice-presidential candidate of his party, there is also a good chance that any lieutenant governor may succeed to the governorship, since presidential elections come in the middle of gubernatorial terms.

THE ATTORNEY GENERAL

The attorney general is the most important executive officer in the state after the governor. Article V, section 13, of the constitution specifies that among the responsibilities of the attorney general:

. . . It shall be his duty to see that the laws of the State are uniformly and adequately enforced. He shall have direct supervision over such other law. . . . Whenever in the opinion of the Attorney General any law of the State is not being adequately enforced in any county, it shall be the duty of the Attorney General to prosecute any violations of law of which the superior court shall have jurisdiction, and in such cases he shall have all the powers of a district attorney. . . .

Although the attorney general is *constitutionally* subject to the governor in insuring that the laws are faithfully executed, he is in fact the "police chief" for California. This position is of signal importance because in the American federal system the major responsibility for the maintenance of law and order is accorded the states rather than the national government.

The attorney general's responsibility for local law enforcement involves him directly with the state's difficult crime problems, including narcotics, illegal gambling, and juvenile delinquency. He heads the Department of Justice and is legal counsel for the state and most state agencies, rendering them legal advice and representing them in court. It is also his duty to prepare the titles and summaries of all ballot propositions submitted to the voters in state elections.

THE SECRETARY OF STATE

The secretary of state is California's chief clerk, having the responsibility of keeping the official record of the acts of the legislature and the executive departments. He appoints a keeper of the archives who maintains the central records depository in which are kept the enrolled copy of the constitution, all acts and resolutions passed by the legislature, the journals of the senate and the assembly, other official deeds, parchments, maps, papers, and the Great Seal of the state.[11]

An especially important function of the secretary of state is his supervision of elections. He certifies initiative, referendum, and recall petitions and assigns them places on

[11] The Great Seal must be affixed to all documents signed by the governor.

the ballot (see Chapter Six); publishes official and sample ballots and the voters' preelection booklet; certifies and maintains the records of affidavits of candidacy and campaign finances; and certifies and publishes election results. In much of his elections administration responsibilities, he works through and with county election officials.

The secretary of state also processes charters and collects fees for the incorporation of private businesses, counties, and cities.

Up to the present time this office has attracted little interest and its occupants have exercised few discretionary powers. However, when Edmund Brown, Jr., assumed office in 1970 he actively led moves to reform campaign methods and ballot procedures, and this position became a stepping-stone to the governor's office. It is interesting to note that Governor Reagan in his "state of the state" message proposed a constitutional amendment for making the office of secretary of state nonpartisan. He maintained that this officer should be free of conflict of interest in the conduct of elections and in reporting campaign contributions.

THE CONTROLLER

The state's chief accounting and disbursing officer is the controller. He maintains accounts of all state and local government finances, authorizes withdrawals from the state treasury, and audits all financial claims against the state. He also has general responsibility for overseeing the collection of all state taxes, with specific responsibility for the collection of inheritance and gift taxes, the gasoline tax, and the motor vehicle transportation license tax, the insurance company tax, and the petroleum gas tax. (For an explanation of these and other state taxes see Chapter Ten.)

The controller is a member of several boards and commissions, including the state Board of Equalization, the Franchise Tax Board, the state Board of Control, the State Lands Commission, and the Water Resources Control Board. The criticism has been leveled that the controller is a member of too many unrelated boards, and his efforts are spread too thin.

The office of controller has become one of the most important in the state. His staff includes some hundred tax appraisers whom he appoints, thus affording considerable patronage. As the elective state fiscal officer, the controller is a key person in state government. Both Thomas Kuchel and Alan Cranston served in this office prior to their election to the U.S. Senate in 1954 and 1968 respectively. Houston Flournoy, candidate for governor in 1974, was state controller from 1966 to 1974.

THE TREASURER

It is the duty of the state treasurer to provide for the safekeeping of public funds. But he is a custodian only, having no authority to issue payment of moneys except upon authorization of the controller. He is required to report periodically to the legislature on the condition of the state treasury.

Elected for four years, the treasurer is also the chief administrative officer for the sale and redemption of state bonds and the investment of surplus state funds under general authorization of the legislature.

Charles G. Johnson held the office from 1922 until 1956. Ronald Button, appointed to succeed Johnson, after being in office only a short while reported to the governor: "It is my considered opinion that the office of State Treasurer with its *present* duties and responsibilities does not justify independent constitutional status." [12] There seems to be no logical reason for maintaining it as an elective post.

Ivy Baker Priest, elected in 1966, became the first woman to occupy this post. She was formerly treasurer of the national government in the Eisenhower administration.

THE STATE BOARD OF EQUALIZATION

The State Board of Equalization, composed of four members (each elected from one of four districts) and the state controller who serves ex officio, is the state's major tax

---

[12] Ibid. Button, incidentally, ran for reelection anyway, but lost to the Democratic candidate, Bert Betts.

agency. The four members are all elected on a partisan basis in gubernatorial election years for terms of four years.

The board surveys average levels of property tax assessment in the fifty-eight counties with a view to equalizing assessments throughout the state, assesses the property of public utilities for purposes of local taxation, and assists local assessors in their duties.

State taxes administered by the board account for more than half of the state's revenue and include: sales and use tax, cigarette tax, alcoholic beverage tax, motor vehicle fuel license tax, insurance tax, and state-assessed property tax.

THE SUPERINTENDENT OF PUBLIC INSTRUCTION

The position of the superintendent of public instruction in the state executive hierarchy is peculiar. He is the only state executive officer elected on a nonpartisan ballot; and though elected by the voters every four years, he is responsible to the ten-man state board of education appointed by the governor, and serves as secretary and executive officer of the board. He is administrative head of the state Department of Education, and in that capacity is expected to execute board of education policies.

This cumbersome arrangement has been strongly criticized by educators and administrators and prompted the legislature to submit a constitutional amendment to the voters in 1958 to change the superintendent's status. The amendment would have made the superintendent an appointee of the board of education, subject to confirmation by the senate. Although the change was championed by civic organizations like the League of Women Voters and even recommended by the superintendent, Roy Simpson (who had just been elected in the June primary), the voters rejected the amendment in the November 1958 elections by nearly two to one. More recently former Superintendent Rafferty has said he would favor making the superintendency appointive, but only if the board is made elective at the same time. Proposition 1, defeated in the November 1968 election, would have revised Article IX of the California constitution to allow for a change in the method of selection of the superintendent. By a two-thirds vote of both houses of the legislature and approval of the governor, the method of selection of both the superintendent and the board of education could have been changed.

The superintendent is charged with the general responsibility for administering the state laws relating to public schools in California. He appoints the boards and commissions within the Department of Education—two important ones being the curriculum commission and the credentials commission. And he sits as an ex officio member on the Board of Regents of the University of California and the Board of Trustees of the State Colleges and University. The contest for this office in 1970 was one of the most active and publicized in the campaign. The incumbent, Max Rafferty, a very controversial conservative (who was defeated as a candidate for the U.S. Senate in 1968), lost the election to Wilson Riles, one of his associate superintendents. Riles became the first black to occupy this position.

THE ADMINISTRATIVE BRANCH

The work of state government is carried on by the several state agencies, departments, boards, and commissions, most of which are responsible to the governor. However, under the plural executive system in California some functions are allocated to the other elected constitutional officers. And two of these, the attorney general and the superintendent of public instruction, are heads of their own departments.

Under the reorganization plans of Governor Reagan, a good share of the state administration was grouped under four agencies—Business and Transportation, Resources, Health and Welfare, and Agriculture and Services. Each agency is headed by a governor-appointed secretary who is responsible for coordinating the activities of the departments assigned to him and handling communications between the departments and the governor's office.

The very important Department of Finance supervises all financial operations of the administration and recommends fiscal policy to the governor. This department also formulates the state budget. The Department of General Services and the State Personnel Board perform staff func-

CALIFORNIA STATE ADMINISTRATION, 1974

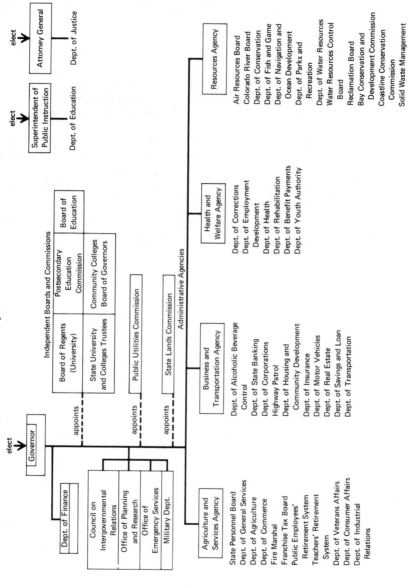

elect → Governor

elect → Superintendent of Public Instruction
Dept. of Education

elect → Attorney General
Dept. of Justice

Dept. of Finance

Council on Intergovernmental Relations
Office of Planning and Research
Office of Emergency Services
Military Dept.

Independent Boards and Commissions

appoints — Board of Regents (University)
State University and Colleges Trustees

Postsecondary Education Commission
Community Colleges Board of Governors

Board of Education

appoints — Public Utilities Commission

appoints — State Lands Commission

Administrative Agencies

Agriculture and Services Agency

State Personnel Board
Dept. of General Services
Dept. of Agriculture
Dept. of Commerce
Fire Marshal
Franchise Tax Board
Public Employees' Retirement System
Teachers' Retirement System
Dept. of Veterans Affairs
Dept. of Consumer Affairs
Dept. of Industrial Relations

Business and Transportation Agency

Dept. of Alcoholic Beverage Control
Dept. of State Banking
Dept. of Corporations
Highway Patrol
Dept. of Housing and Community Development
Dept. of Insurance
Dept. of Motor Vehicles
Dept. of Real Estate
Dept. of Savings and Loan
Dept. of Transportation

Health and Welfare Agency

Dept. of Corrections
Dept. of Employment Development
Dept. of Health
Dept. of Rehabilitation
Dept. of Benefit Payments
Dept. of Youth Authority

Resources Agency

Air Resources Board
Colorado River Board
Dept. of Conservation
Dept. of Fish and Game
Dept. of Navigation and Ocean Development
Dept. of Parks and Recreation
Dept. of Water Resources
Water Resources Control Board
Reclamation Board
Bay Conservation and Development Commission
Coastline Conservation Commission
Solid Waste Management Board

177

tions relating to maintenance of buildings and equipment and personnel for all state agencies.

SELECTED REFERENCES

California Blue Book. Sacramento: State Printing Office, 1968.
"The Governor's Executive Reorganization Authority May End This Year," *California Journal* II, 9 (October 1971): 277–79.
Council of State Governments, *The Governors of the States, 1900–1972.* Chicago: Council of State Governments. Governors' Conference, *Proceedings* (annual).
HARVEY, RICHARD B., *Earl Warren, Governor of California.* New York: Exposition Press, 1969.
MELENDY, H. BRETT, and BENJAMIN F. GILBERT, *The Governors of California, from Peter H. Burnett to Edmund G. Brown.* Georgetown, Calif.: Talisman Press, 1965.

The California
Court System

Our national courts tend to have more prestige than our state courts. The actions of federal judges and juries often receive more space in the media than do those of their state counterparts. Yet the state courts often affect the lives of ordinary California citizens more intimately. Many citizens will never be a party or witness in a federal court case. But there are few who have not paid a traffic ticket to a state court.

Since under the American federal system the state exercises the police power, the criminal jurisdiction of the California courts is extensive, covering violations of state law and municipal ordinances, from murder to parking sixteen minutes in a fifteen-minute zone. The California courts are also responsible for dealing with a variety of controversies arising under the state's civil law: for example, breach of contract proceedings, suits for damages, divorces, annulments, wills, and disputes having to do with real estate.

179

ORGANIZATION AND JURISDICTION

California's court system is organized on four levels: (1) municipal and justice courts (sometimes called "inferior" courts); (2) superior courts; (3) district courts of appeal; and (4) the supreme court.

The Inferior Courts

In each county there is at least one municipal or justice court. Prior to 1950 the "inferior" court system in California constituted a bewildering maze. The courts of lesser jurisdiction had a variety of names and procedures, and often their legal responsibilities conflicted. However, a 1950 constitutional amendment provided for the reorganization of the inferior court system into only two types of courts— municipal and justice. The legislature was directed to establish municipal courts in judicial districts of more than 40,000 people and justice courts in small districts. With the urbanization of the state there has been a gradual decrease in the number of justice courts; about 200 were still in existence in 1975.

MUNICIPAL COURTS   Civil suits for damages of less than $5000 and all nonjuvenile criminal cases of a minor nature (misdemeanors and infractions) carrying penalties not exceeding one year in the county jail or a fine of $1000 are handled by the municipal courts. It is notable that over 90 percent of the criminal cases heard in California's municipal courts concern traffic violations.

The municipal courts also hold preliminary hearings for more serious offenses. When a municipal judge decides there is sufficient evidence to warrant holding him, the accused is bound over to the superior court for trial.

JUSTICE COURTS   The justice courts have a narrower jurisdiction than the municipal courts. They are limited to civil suits of $500 and only the lesser offenses—traffic violations, ordinary drunkenness, vagrancy, infractions of fish and game laws—which carry penalties not exceeding one year in jail or a fine of $1000. The justice courts may also hold preliminary hearings for those accused of felonies.

The Superior Courts

The superior courts are the general trial courts of the state. Each county has one superior court; however, a court may be authorized by the legislature to establish a number of judgeships. The superior court of Los Angeles, for example, has more than 160 judges and Alameda, Orange, Santa Clara, and San Francisco more than 20 each. Each judge conducts his own set of trials in his own courtroom. In the larger counties the superior court judges select one of their number to be the presiding judge, who has the duty of assigning cases to the individual judges. In very large counties the tendency is to assign particular types of cases— juvenile, domestic relations, probate, criminal—to judges in specialized divisions of the court.

The superior courts have *original* jurisdiction over (1) all civil cases where the suit is for at least $5000, and annulment, divorce, and probate of wills cases regardless of the amounts involved; (2) all major criminal cases (felonies) carrying sentences of a year or more in state prison; and (3) all those that involve minors.

Appellate jurisdiction is exercised by the superior courts over all cases originating in the municipal and justice courts. And according to a constitutional amendment passed in 1960, the legislature may specify the circumstances and procedures under which a case originating in the inferior courts can be appealed beyond the superior courts to higher state courts.

The Courts of Appeal

The state courts of appeal are the intermediate layer of tribunals between the superior courts and the supreme court. Three such courts were created by constitutional amendment in 1904, and in 1928 another amendment gave the legislature authority to increase the number of appeals courts as it saw fit. The state is now divided into five districts with one appeals court in each. However, the court of

ORGANIZATION OF THE COURT SYSTEM

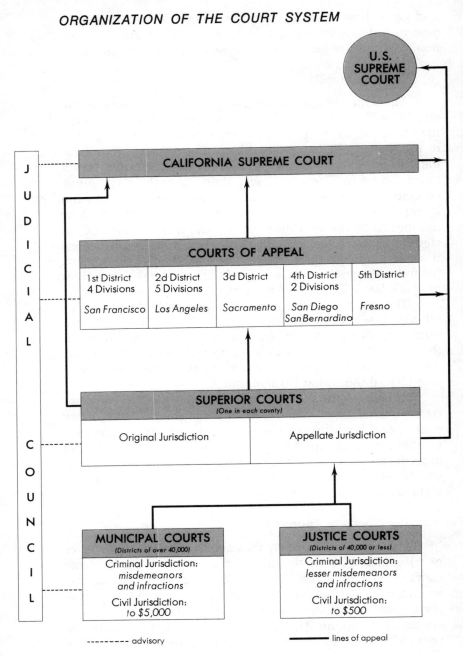

the first district has four divisions, the court of the second district has five, and the court of the fourth district two. A total of fifty-one judges serve in the state courts of appeal; with fourteen in the first district, twenty in the second district, six in the third district, eight in the fourth district, and three in the fifth district.

The jurisdiction of the district courts is strictly appellate. They review cases already tried in the superior courts and are the review courts for appeals from decisions of quasi-judicial agencies, such as the state industrial accident commission. Some cases appealed from the superior courts go directly to the supreme court for review (see below); but many of these wind up on the dockets of a district court of appeal anyway since the high court may delegate any cases it wishes to them. The supreme court also has the right, however, to assume jurisdiction over any case on a district court's calendar.

The State Supreme Court

The supreme court is the top state court. Its decisions are final and cannot be appealed unless the U.S. Supreme Court finds that a decision has violated the federal Constitution.

There are six associate justices on the supreme court and one chief justice. For several years the state constitution had contained a provision for the supreme court to operate in two separate departments as a method of relieving heavy caseloads. With the creation of district courts of appeal in 1928, the department system became obsolete. Under the constitutional revision of 1966 this fact was recognized and the obsolete language was deleted.

The jurisdiction of the supreme court is both appellate and original, but deciding appeals from the lower courts is the bulk of its work. Practically all of the cases reaching the court on appeal originate in a superior court, are then appealed to a district court of appeal, and from there carried to the supreme court. Cases where the death sentence is imposed may be appealed directly from the superior courts to the supreme court. And the supreme court can order certain unique cases transferred to it from the courts of appeal prior to hearing.

The supreme court has original jurisdiction to issue writs of mandamus (to compel a public corporation or officer to act in accord with legal obligations), prohibition (to prevent a lower court from exercising jurisdiction over a suit pending before it), and habeas corpus.

The Judicial Council

California is among the three-fourths of the states that have established a judicial council to oversee the entire state court system. Though not a court, the judicial council is an integral part of the state's judicial organization, with some authority to make rulings on judicial procedure that have the force of law.

The council is composed of the chief justice of the state supreme court and the following judges appointed by him for two-year terms: one associate justice of the supreme court, three justices of the courts of appeal, five judges of the superior courts, three judges of the municipal courts, and two judges of justice courts. In addition, the council consists of four members of the state bar of California appointed for two-year terms by the board of governors of the state bar and one member of each house of the legislature to be chosen by each house.

As chairman of the council, the chief justice is accorded the authority to transfer judicial assignments temporarily within the court system when overcrowded dockets or vacancies create a special need. He may assign a judge to a court of comparable or higher jurisdiction. But only if the consent of the judge involved is obtained can he be assigned to a court of lower jursdiction. A retired judge may be assigned to any court. Upon the request of the chairman of the council, judges are to report the condition of judicial business in their courts.

The main business of the judicial council is to carry on a continuous study of the work of the courts. It publishes biennial reports showing the numbers and kinds of cases handled by the various levels. It recommends and sometimes decrees procedural improvements to the courts. It holds seminars that orient newly appointed judges and keep all judges up-to-date on the law. The judicial council recommends constitutional and statutory changes to the legislature which would improve the administration of justice. And the council has appointed an administrative director to implement its decisions.

JUDICIAL PERSONNEL

Municipal and Justice Court Judges

QUALIFICATIONS   To be eligible for election as a municipal court judge a person must be a registered voter in his own district and must have been a licensed attorney in California for five years. To be eligible for justice court judge (in 1950 the title "justice of the peace" was abolished) a person must be a registered voter of his judicial district and either be a practicing attorney or pass an examination prescribed by the judicial council, unless he was a justice of the peace prior to 1950.

In a unanimous decision the California supreme court in 1974 ruled that, without the defendant's consent, judges who were not lawyers could no longer preside over cases involving possible jail terms. Since this would severely restrict the usefulness of nonattorney justice court judges (there were 127 of them in the state in 1974), the state judicial council recommended the reorganization of justice court districts to make sure that there would be at least one judge in each district who was a lawyer.

ELECTION   Both municipal and justice court judges are chosen for six-year terms by the people of their respective districts through nonpartisan elections. An incumbent judge may be declared automatically elected without his name appearing on the ballot unless a rival candidate files nomination papers or a specified number of voters sign a petition for a write-in campaign against the incumbent. If there is a contest the names of the candidates appear on the ballot. Vacancies on the municipal court bench between elections are filled through appointment by the governor. County boards of supervisors fill between-election vacancies in justice courts.

COMPENSATION   The state legislature sets the salaries for judges of municipal courts. Now all municipal judges receive the same salary, regardless of the size of a court's district. Boards of supervisors in the various counties set salaries for justice courts. In some justice courts judges receive deplorably low wages.

Superior Court Judges

QUALIFICATIONS   To be eligible for a superior court judgeship a person must have been a citizen of the United States for five years, a practicing attorney in California for ten years, and a resident of his county for two.

ELECTION   Superior court judges are elected in nonpartisan primary elections in the same manner as municipal and justice court judges. Most superior court incumbent judges are reelected automatically but occasionally a judge will have a challenger or an incumbent will decide not to run for reelection. The illustration below shows how the ballot appears when there is a contest.

COMPENSATION   The salaries of superior court judges are the same in each county and presently are about $45,000. The state government pays about half toward the salary of each superior court judge, the county making up the remainder. The salaries of the superior court judges are fixed to reflect the change in the cost of living.

Judges of the Supreme Court and the District Courts of Appeal

QUALIFICATIONS   To be eligible for a supreme or appeals court judgeship a person need meet certain minimal requirements—United States citizen, California resident, and practicing attorney in the state for ten years.

ELECTION   Supreme and appeals court judges serve for staggered terms of twelve years. They are elected, but not in the usual kind of election contest. At the end of his twelve-year term a judge of the supreme court or district court of appeals may run for reelection. If he does, only *his* name, without opponents, appears on the ballot for the

PAGE 7		**NONPARTISAN**		
Judge of the Superior Court Office No. 12 **Vote for One**	EDWARD J. O'CONNOR Judge of the Superior Court	115 ➡	○
	EARL J. McDOWELL Attorney at Law	116 ➡	○
Judge of the Superior Court Office No. 18 **Vote for One**	ROBERT W. KENNY Judge of the Superior Court	117 ➡	○
	BELA BOTOS Attorney at Law	118 ➡	○
Judge of the Superior Court Office No. 20 **Vote for One**	JOAN DEMPSEY KLEIN Presiding Municipal Judge	119 ➡	○
	JOHN J. "JACK" LYNCH Judge of the Municipal Court	120 ➡	○
	BONNIE LEE MARTIN Judge, Los Angeles Judicial District	121 ➡	○
	JOSEPH R. RUFFNER Commissioner, Municipal Court	122 ➡	○
	HOWARD J. THELIN Judge of the Municipal Court	123 ➡	○
	DAVID J. AISENSON Judge, Municipal Court, Los Angeles Judicial District	124 ➡	○
	VINCENT N. ERICKSON Judge of the Municipal Court, Los Angeles	125 ➡	○
	JOSEPH R. GRILLO Judge - Los Angeles Municipal Court	126 ➡	○
Judge of the Superior Court Office No. 22 **Vote for One**	ROBERT A. WENKE Judge of the Superior Court	127 ➡	○
Judge of the Superior Court Office No. 41 **Vote for One**	CHARLES H. OLDER Judge of the Superior Court	129 ➡	○
	CHRISTOPHER W. SMITH Deputy Public Defender	130 ➡	○
	ALEX KAHANOWICZ Deputy District Attorney	131 ➡	○

JUDICIAL

judgeship. If the incumbent does not choose to seek another term, the governor, with the consent of the commission on judicial appointments (consisting of the chief justice of the supreme court, the presiding judge of a district court of appeal, and the attorney general), nominates a candidate to appear on the ballot, also without any opponents. The ballot form for supreme and appeals court judges is shown on the following page. If a justice seeking reelection or a guber-

For Associate Justice of the Supreme Court		
Shall MATHEW O. TOBRINER be elected to the office for the term prescribed by law?	YES	
	NO	

For Presiding Justice, District Court of Appeal, Fourth Appellate District, Division One		
Shall GERALD BROWN be elected to the office for the term prescribed by law?	YES	
	NO	

natorial nominee receives more "no" than "yes" votes, the governor, with the approval of the commission on judicial appointments, appoints someone else to serve on the court until the next general election. At the next election, this appointee has the status of an incumbent judge and may appear on the ballot without opposition.

COMPENSATION   The legislature periodically sets the salaries of the high court judges to reflect the cost of living index, and their salaries are now about $55,000, with the chief justice of the supreme court receiving over $60,000 per annum. A judge may retire on half salary at seventy if he has served ten years, or at sixty after twenty years of service. Retirement pensions of judges depend upon length of service, age of retirement, and salary prior to retirement. A 1959 law sought to encourage the older judges to retire in favor of younger men by providing that if a judge retired by a specified deadline he would receive as much as 75 percent of his salary in pension. If he continued to hold office after the deadline he would be entitled to only a 50 percent pension. Thus, the chief justice, Phil S. Gibson, by retiring prior to September 18, 1964, insured for himself an annnal income of $25,500.

Removal of Judges

Public sensitivity to the important role judges play in our society is indicated by the fact that there are several ways a judge may be removed from office in California.

First, he may be recalled by the voters; second, he may be impeached by the assembly and convicted by a two-thirds vote of the senate. Third, if a court finds him guilty of a felony or any crime involving moral turpitude and if the conviction is upheld by a higher court, the supreme court must dismiss him from office. And finally, Article VI of the state constitution declares:

> On recommendation of the Commission on Judicial Qualifications [1] the Supreme Court may (1) retire a judge for disability that seriously interferes with the performance of his duties and is, or is likely to become, permanent, and (2) censure or remove a judge for action occurring not more than six years prior to the commencement of his current term that constitutes willful misconduct in office, willful and persistent failure to perform his duties, habitual intemperance or conduct prejudicial to the administration of justice or that brings the judicial office into disrepute.[2]

THE ADMINISTRATION OF JUSTICE

The law enforceable in the state courts is found in the California constitution and the state's body of statutory law which the legislature has incorporated into a series of codes, such as the *Civil Code, Government Code, Penal Code,* and the *Elections Code.* However, no written law can anticipate every variety of case that may arise. Judges must often rely on English common law precedent to render a decision; and sometimes they have no guide but their own sense of justice. Because of the complexity of the law, its interpretation, and its application to individual cases, detailed rules of procedure are established to protect the citizen against arbitrary handling by the state's legal authorities and to insure each citizen equitable treatment when in court.

[1] The Commission on Judicial Qualifications is made up of the following members: two justices of the district courts of appeal, two superior court judges, one municipal court judge—all appointed by the state supreme court; two members of the state bar appointed by the board of governors; and two citizens who may be neither judges nor members of the state bar selected by the governor with the consent of the state senate. All members serve a term of four years.

[2] Constitution of the State of California, Art. VI, sec. 18c.

Criminal Procedure

A criminal offense is a crime against society. There are three general categories of criminal offense: *felonies*, the most serious crimes such as murder, armed robbery, rape, forgery, and perjury; *misdemeanors*, lesser offenses such as running a stoplight or selling liquor to a minor; and *infractions*, the very least violations, such as illegal parking and operating an automobile without proper equipment. Upon conviction of a felony the judge may impose upon the defendant the sentence of a year or more in state prison or a heavy fine or both. In the case of a misdemeanor the penalty may be a term of not more than one year in the county jail or a fine of not more than $1000 (or both). Those guilty of an infraction suffer only a fine.

The general rights of the accused in criminal cases are outlined in Article I of the state constitution. He is guaranteed a preliminary hearing before a magistrate (if accused of a felony), the right to legal counsel, the right to know the charges against him, the right of trial by jury, the right to confront witnesses against him, and the right to summon witnesses on his own behalf. These provisions have been elaborated by the courts and the legislature to provide for the following procedures.

IN CASES OF FELONY (1) At the time of arrest, the accused must be informed of his rights. He is then "booked" at the police station or sheriff's office, and the section of the law he has allegedly violated is listed against his name. (2) He is taken before a municipal judge or justice court for a preliminary hearing, whereupon the judge informs him of his rights under law. If he pleads guilty he is handed over to the superior court. And if he pleads not guilty, but the judge believes the evidence is strong enough, he is committed to the superior court anyway. Pending further action the accused is held in jail or released on bail. (3) An *information* (accusation) is signed against the accused, usually by the district attorney of the county, or the county's grand jury votes an *indictment*.[3] (4) When the accused

---

[3] Every county has a grand jury consisting of nineteen citizens who serve for an entire year. More important than their indicting duties is their responsibility to study and criticize the general government of their county.

appears in superior court he pleads either guilty or not guilty. If he pleads the former he is sentenced. If he pleads the latter a trial is held. He may waive jury trial, in which case the judge determines his guilt or innocence. If he does not waive trial by jury, a panel of potential jurymen is called up. Prosecuting and defense attorneys may question the prospective jurors and disqualify those whose impartiality is doubted. Ultimately a jury of twelve, satisfactory to both sides, is sworn in. (5) After hearing witnesses and arguments of attorneys, the jury strives for a unanimous verdict of guilty or not guilty. If unanimity cannot be reached within reasonable time, the jury is dismissed and a new trial is ordered. (6) A verdict of not guilty releases the defendant. If guilty, he is sentenced by the judge after an interval of a few days to allow for a probation report. During this period the defendant's attorney may make a motion for a new trial or file notice of appeal.

IN CASES OF MISDEMEANOR   Usually much simpler is the procedure for misdemeanors, a less serious type of crime such as a "moving" traffic violation. But even in the handling of misdemeanors the court procedure will differ with the severity of the offense. In lesser traffic cases, such as making an illegal U turn, the accused generally does not have to appear before the judge but goes to the nearest police station to pay his ticket. (Technically, he is not paying a fine, only posting bail and then automatically pleading guilty, which forfeits his bail.) When accused of a more serious misdemeanor, such as speeding or assault and battery, a person does appear before a judge and frequently pleads guilty. If he does not plead guilty, he may demand a jury trial, or he may waive this privilege in favor of a trial by the judge alone. If found guilty, the defendant may be fined, or sentenced to the county jail, or both.

IN CASES OF INFRACTIONS   The 1968 legislature made provision for a type of criminal offense below the level of a misdemeanor. So far, very few activities fit into this category: illegal parking, driving a motor vehicle which is not properly equipped, "jay-walking," and violations of some regulations dealing with rabies control and dog licensing. Even if the defendant refuses to pay his ticket and demands a court trial, the case will be heard only by a judge and not a jury. Free legal counsel is not guaranteed to the accused, and only fines, not jail sentences, are meted out.

Civil Procedures

California civil law, like all law based on English jurisprudence, is divided into two broad categories—cases *at law* and cases *in equity*. Cases at law generally include all suits brought by one party to collect money from another party for debts owed or for damages already done. Cases in equity are usually to prevent harm, especially irreparable damage. Equity also involves annulments and divorces (where often the harm has already been done), the administration of trusts, cancellation of fraudulent contracts, and various judicial writs and most injunctions.[4] A voter who feels he has been deprived of his rights, for example, files an equity suit against the appropriate elections official.

IN CASES AT LAW   The procedure for cases at law (providing they are for more than $500 in damages) is briefly as follows. (1) The plaintiff (or his attorney) files suit against the defendant stating the amount of money he expects to collect and the reasons for his claim. (2) The defendant, after having been notified of the suit, has any one of three options. He may decide not to contest the suit and allow the plaintiff to win by default; he may seek to settle the dispute with the plaintiff out of court; or he may decide to contest the matter, in which case his attorney files a formal answer to the charges and sometimes a countersuit. (3) Both parties appear in court and decide whether or not to waive a jury trial. If either party wishes a jury trial, members are selected and sworn in (twelve jurors unless both parties agree to less). (4) After witnesses are heard and arguments are given, the jury deliberates. The jury must decide whether the defendant is liable as charged, and also to what amount he is liable (if a jury has been waived the judge makes these decisions). Three-fourths of the jurors must agree in order to deliver a verdict.

---

[4] Another example of an injunction (in equity) is a court's order to a labor union to prevent a strike.

Cases under $500 are classified as *small claims* and are handled by a simplified procedure. There are no attorneys or juries. The plaintiff merely appears at a municipal or justice court (some larger municipal courts have special small claims divisions) and files a complaint with a nominal filing fee. The defendant is summoned to appear, whereupon the judge hears both parties and renders his decision. If the decision is against the plaintiff, there is no further recourse under state law. But if the judge decides against the defendant, he may petition for another hearing in a superior court.

IN CASES OF EQUITY There are no jury trials in cases in equity. All issues of law and fact are determined by the judge. Justice courts have no jurisdiction over equity matters. A few start in municipal courts, but most are handled by superior court judges. When a case involves a highly important matter, for example, the attempt of one local government to compel another local government to fulfill a contract, the state supreme court may assume original jurisdiction.

The basic steps in equity procedure are as follows. (1) The plaintiff or his attorney files a petition to the court requesting a specific action in equity, such as an injunction or a divorce. (2) The defendant is notified of the charges in the petition and is asked to appear in court to show good reason why the petition should not be granted. The defendant or his attorney thereupon files a formal answer. (3) In open court before the judge both sides present their arguments. (4) The judge renders his decision, which may be appealed by either party to a higher court.

IMPROVING THE ADMINISTRATION OF JUSTICE

Eliminating Unnecessary Delays

Although the state constitution guarantees the citizen a speedy public trial, the overcrowded dockets of the courts have tended to make this a hollow promise. There is frequently a delay of twenty to thirty months between the filing of a complaint in a civil suit and the actual trial. In a criminal case four months may elapse between the time a grand jury indicts a defendant and his trial. Various proposals have been made to remedy this deficiency. The legislature is often urged to create more courts and more judgeships. Approximately every two years the number of magistrates in the larger counties is increased. Recently, a strong campaign has supported the enactment of "no fault" automobile insurance that would remove most of the accident injury cases from the courts. Consumers' organizations and many insurance companies have endorsed "no fault"; the trial lawyers have bitterly opposed it.

In view of the fact that a large volume of the cases in the criminal courts deal with narcotic and alcohol addicts whose problems are predominantly medical, it has been suggested that such "victimless crimes" be removed from the ordinary courts to special tribunals.[5]

Obtaining Better Qualified Judges

Although for the most part California citizens have been satisfied with the quality of the state judicial personnel, there has been some criticism of selecting judges on the basis of their political appeal. Some go so far as to criticize the whole system of popular election of judges. It has been suggested that judges be appointed by the governor with the consent of the state senate (similar to the national pattern). Others have proposed that the state supreme court (whether elected by the people or appointed by the governor) should appoint all lower court judges. The judicial council has proposed a "merit plan" of selecting judges, i.e., when the governor appoints a judge to fill any vacancy he selects a name from a list submitted to him by a nominating commission consisting of an equal number of judges, lawyers, and laymen.

Still others maintain that the method of selecting judges is adequate but that some of our most qualified lawyers do not seek judgeships because the salaries are lower than the income they receive from private practice. More security of tenure has also been advocated as a means of attracting better men—the possibility of recall being

[5] "California's Court System," *California Government and Politics Annual, 1972–73* (Sacramento: Consensus Publishers, 1972), p. 51.

cited as a major deterrent (see discussion of the recall in Chapter Six).

Reforming the Jury System

There is no significant movement to do away with the jury system, since it is generally regarded as a deeply rooted and valuable heritage of American jurisprudence. Yet thoughtful observers are aware of its imperfections. A man's peers are not always his best judges, and often not the most objective. Jurors frequently confuse questions of moral right or wrong (which they are not expected to answer) with questions of legal fact. And where penalties are severe they will at times hesitate to convict in the face of overwhelming evidence.

Most suggestions are for improving the system rather than tearing it down. Higher compensation and fewer exemptions from serving for professional men would increase quality. One proposal would reduce the size of juries. In the case of Williams *v.* Florida (1971) the federal Supreme Court held that the United States Constitution permitted a state to decrease the number of jurors to six. California, so far, has not followed through on this possibility. Another proposal would allow conviction in criminal cases by less than a unanimous vote except for offenses carrying a death penalty.

Reducing the High Cost of Justice

The right to a fair trial in court is one of our most treasured civil liberties; but it can be a very expensive privilege. Lawyers' fees are not low, nor is the cost of printing the record for an appeal to a higher court. Consequently, many persons do not have the money to avail themselves of their constitutional rights. Various attempts are being made to correct this inequity. In criminal proceedings, for example, an indigent is furnished the services of the public defender, or of a private attorney assigned to his case by the court. In civil matters, county legal aid societies and the California Rural Legal Assistance agency, financed by the national government, offer assistance to people with low incomes. It has been pointed out that these efforts still are not sufficient; public defenders are often overworked, and the private attorney appointed by the court to represent the poor man often is not as experienced as the high-priced lawyer his rich opponent has hired. There is pressure to increase the appropriations for the public defenders' offices.

Another problem has been that people of low income cannot post bail and must therefore stay in jail awaiting trial. Various experiments are being made in different parts of the state whereby a person without bail money is released on his honor with the understanding that he will appear for trial.

Maintaining Order in the Court

In August 1970, the friends of a prisoner on trial staged the armed invasion of a courtroom in San Rafael, the result being the death of several persons, including the judge and one of the defendants. This tragedy "has focused attention on another problem of administering the court system: that of balancing the inherent right of the court to maintain order and security during trial with the constitutional right of the individual to have a fair and impartial trial." [6]

In their efforts to maintain peaceful courtrooms, judges have recently ordered obstreperous defendants bound and gagged, have had all visitors searched, and have even carried guns themselves. Those concerned with our system of justice are searching for ways of retaining judicial decorum without the trappings of an armed camp.

Abolishing the Death Penalty

In California murder and kidnapping have been considered capital offenses, punishable by the lethal gas chamber. Penal officers, jurists, and criminologists are divided as to its effectiveness as a deterrent to crime. Bills to abolish capital punishment have been introduced into practically every session of the legislature for over a generation, but in every case they have been defeated in committee or on the floor of the senate or assembly.

Early in 1960, worldwide attention was focused on this issue in California because of the controversial Chessman case. Caryl Chessman had been imprisoned and was under

[6] Ibid., p. 53.

death sentence for eleven years on seventeen counts involving sex crimes and kidnapping. This case had been reviewed by the highest state and national courts, on the plea that there had been a miscarriage of justice and that the penalty was too severe. The night before Chessman was scheduled to go to the gas chamber Governor Brown was alone in the gubernatorial mansion, a Victorian relic resembling the abode of the Addams Family of television horror fame. After brooding over the doomed man's fate, Brown issued a sixty-day reprieve and called upon the legislature to enact an eight-year moratorium on executions. His action stirred up a political tempest, advocates of both sides of the controversy besieging the capitol and the governor with testimony, telegrams, and picket lines. Many leaders of the legislature resented this last-minute shift of responsibility from the shoulders of the executive, and the bill was narrowly defeated in committee. Caryl Chessman went to the gas chamber.

Opponents of capital punishment then turned to the courts, the ultimate testing ground of most of the moral and social issues of American society. There they won some victories. In February 1972, the state supreme court in a six-to-one decision outlawed capital punishment in *all cases* on the grounds that it violated Article I of the California constitution, which prohibits "cruel *or* unusual" punishments. California's attorney general, Evelle J. Younger, appealed this ruling to the United States Supreme Court, where the opponents of the death penalty won a qualified victory. Five of the nine justices declared that the death penalty in the United States is unconstitutional, at least as it is now applied. They pointed to the Eighth Amendment to the United States Constitution which forbids "cruel *and* unusual" punishments. But beyond that point the Supreme Court judges differed. Two of the justices held that capital punishment was unconstitutional under *any* circumstances, whereas three declared that the death penalty *might* be constitutional if it were made mandatory for certain offenses. (It might be cruel, but it would no longer be unusual!)

In California, the attorney general with the assistance of various law enforcement groups circulated petitions and qualified an initiative constitutional amendment for the

November ballot (Proposition 17). It won by a two-to-one majority at the polls. It declared that the death penalty was not to be considered as a cruel or unusual punishment and that all laws imposing capital punishment that were on the statute books when the California supreme court made its decision in February were again to be in full effect. But this measure by itself did not relegalize the death penalty. Standing in the way was the United States Supreme Court decision. Therefore, in face of strong resistance from Assembly Speaker Bob Moretti, the California legislature in 1973 passed a measure which sought to conform to the demands of the federal court. It provided a mandatory death penalty for certain types of homicide, such as the murder of a police officer. After the law became effective in January 1974, a number of persons were sentenced to the gas chamber, but their cases were certain to reach the United States Supreme Court, where the justices would face the painful duty of clarifying their ambiguous position.

SELECTED REFERENCES

California Government and Politics Annual, 1974–75. Sacramento: Consensus Publishers, 1974.

California, Judicial Council, *Biennial Reports.* Sacramento: State Printing Office, 1974.

COOK, BEVERLY BLAIR, *The Judicial Process in California.* Belmont, Calif.: Dickenson, 1967.

10
Financing California
Government

A s California is the most populous state in the nation, its government is big business. The 1974–75 state budget authorized expenditures that totaled $10.13 billion—the highest amount ever spent and five times the sum of expenditures ten years ago. It is also the biggest budget of any state in the nation. California's 21 million citizens call upon their government to provide a great number of services and they cost money. With the largest population of any state, the greatest number of automobiles, the highest proportion of young people attending public schools and colleges, and a comprehensive program for social welfare, California must be willing to assume heavy expenditures.

STATE EXPENDITURES: WHERE THE MONEY GOES

As can be noted from the accompanying chart, the largest state expense is for public education, which takes about forty cents out of every expenditure dollar. Health and welfare, the second largest category, amounting to about 25 percent of total state expenditures, includes budget ex-

EXPENDITURE DOLLAR OF THE 1974–1975 FISCAL YEAR

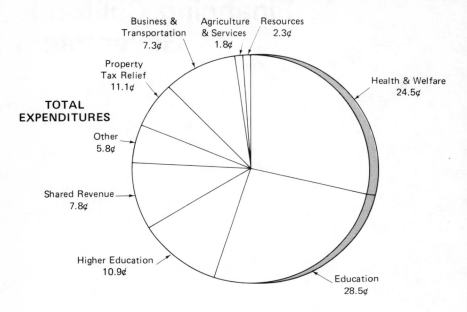

penses for social welfare (programs for the aged, blind, disabled, and needy children), public health, mental hygiene, and corrections. Slightly more than one-tenth of state expenditures for 1974–75 was for property tax relief. This is a recently established budget and is the result of legislation sponsored by Governor Reagan in fulfillment of his campaign promises to reduce property taxes. This program included $668 million for homeowners' tax relief, $261 million for personal property tax relief, and $60 million for senior citizens' property tax assistance.

The remaining segments of state expenditures include shared revenue (with local governments in return for their share of sales taxes, liquor license fees, and motor vehicle taxes which are collected by the state), monies supporting agencies that regulate and control business and transportation, and funds used for agriculture and services and natural resources (parks, conservation, coastal zone regulation, reclamation, and water programs). The day-to-day expenses for the legislature, executive offices and agencies, and a portion of the court system expenses are included in "other."

Funds spent for state operations themselves amount to only one-fourth of the total expenditures budget. Approximately 6 percent goes for the construction of state buildings and facilities. And more than two-thirds of the total state budget is allocated by the state to local governments for designated services. These three general types of budget expenditures are referred to as state operations, capital outlay, and local assistance.

State Operations

The 1974–75 budget included $2.6 billion for expenditures on state operations. One billion was allocated for education, which included $493 million for the University of California and $480 million for the California State Colleges and Universities for general support exclusive of capital outlay funds. About $43 million (a large increase from five years ago) was earmarked for the State Scholarship and Loan Commission to provide scholarships, grants, and loans to worthy students attending private or public universities and colleges in California. (State money for the public school system—kindergarten through community college—is allocated to school districts and is, therefore, put in the local assistance budget.)

Next to education, the state spends most to support its social welfare and health programs; other items of expenditure include property tax relief, highways and vehicle regulation, conservation of natural resources (especially water), corrections, and general state administration.

Capital Outlay

The capital outlay of $581 million in the 1974–75 budget was less than it would have been if a large portion of the state's building and construction had not been financed by bond issues.

About 85 percent of the total capital outlay budget was spent for California's huge highway construction program. Matching federal funds granted to California under the federal interstate and secondary highway improvement program were also added. Other substantial chunks out of the building budget were taken by school and dam construction.

Local Assistance

As already stated, some 68 percent of the total state budget was allocated to local governments—to special districts, cities, and counties. For 1974–75 this amounted to $6.6 billion, with approximately $2.7 billion spent by school districts for elementary, secondary, and community college education. With 4.6 million students enrolled in grades K-12, elementary and secondary education continues to be one of state government's highest priorities. As a result of recent legislation, the dollar amount supplied for each average daily attendance student has risen in the last three years from $366 to $825 for elementary students and from $488 to $1010 for high-school students. The state also provided financial resources to meet special problems—bilingual education, reading, training for handicapped, child care services, and education for the deaf and blind. And state financial assistance for the community colleges has quadrupled since 1966 and now totals $315 million.

About $2 billion of state funds were used for welfare grants to local governments for health and welfare projects. An additional $5 billion was supplied by federal and county governments to provide these basic "people" services for California. Recipients of this aid include the elderly (some 2.7 million residents), low income persons, war veterans, needy children, the unemployed, and the disabled. State monies are also used for treatment of law offenders by the state Youth Authority and the Department of Corrections. A larger proportion of the state's population has been convicted of the more serious crimes of murder, robbery, assault, and rape, and this has increased the state prison population with resultant higher costs.

Additional local assistance funds are used by special districts, cities, and counties for roads, transit plans, airports, navigation and ocean development, parks and recreation, water resources, and damages from storms, earthquakes, and floods.

STATE REVENUE: WHERE THE MONEY COMES FROM

Practically all of the state's income is secured by means of taxes. To meet its expanding government costs, California has moved from its simple two-tax system of 1850 (the

REVENUE DOLLAR OF THE 1974–1975 FISCAL YEAR

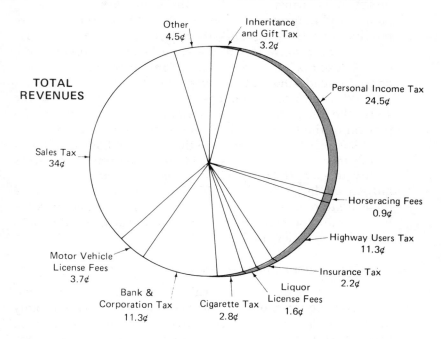

general property tax and the poll tax) to its present multi-tax system, which taps about a dozen different sources of revenue.

Nontax receipts for 1974–75 totaled only 4 percent of the total state income. Such sources of revenue included interest income from investments of state funds, royalties from oil and gas production on state-owned land, medical and board charges to paying patients at state hospitals, traffic penalties, and regulatory charges and special fees for businesses and professions.

The Sales Tax

First used in the days of the Great Depression, when other sources of revenue had dried up, the retail sales tax has become California's largest source of income. A tax of 6 percent [1] on the sales price of all tangible goods except

---

[1] The state collects the tax of 6 percent but retains only 4¾ percent, returning 1¼ percent to the cities and counties. Consumers

food for home consumption; electricity, gas, water, and prescription drugs, and other minor items such as newspapers and magazines is collected by retail merchants from purchasers. The merchants are required to submit quarterly returns and remittances to the state Board of Equalization.

A "use tax" provision levies a similar tax on goods purchased outside the state for use in California.

With practically no cost of collection borne by the state, the retail sales tax has yielded between 28 and 38 percent of the total state revenue since it has been in effect.

The principal objection to the sales tax has been that it is a *regressive* tax—that is, it is not based upon a person's ability to pay. It is argued that the tax places an undue burden on large families with low incomes. An initiative measure to reduce the sales tax by 1 percent and to increase business and personal income taxes was placed on the 1958 ballot but was defeated.

The Personal Income Tax

Like most states, California does not have a high personal income tax though it has been increasing very rapidly in the last five years. This source of revenue is reserved primarily for the national government. In most states, however, income taxes do exist. California's (initiated in 1935) is modeled on the federal income tax, but with much higher exemptions and lower rates. Whereas the national exemption covers only $750 for each individual, the California income tax allows a standard deduction of $1000 for single or $2000 for joint returns. A credit of $25 and $50 for single and joint returns, respectively, plus $8 for each dependent is allowed against the computed tax to derive the taxpayer's actual liability. Like the federal tax, the California income tax is considered *progressive*—that is, rates increase in the higher income brackets. The California rates vary from 1 percent on the first $2000 of taxable income to 11 percent on taxable income over $15,500 (compared with the 17 to 70 percent rates of the federal tax).

In December 1971 a law was passed that initiated a system of witholding for state personal income taxes similar

---

in Alameda, Contra Costa, and San Francisco counties pay an additional ½ percent sales tax which is earmarked for the support of the Bay Area Rapid Transit District.

to that practiced by the federal government. Though Governor Reagan had been adamant in his opposition to this principle in his campaign and first term of office, he finally yielded to the pressure for increased state revenue. It is believed that witholding will prevent some tax dodging, and of course will provide revenue monthly, which will help the cash flow of state finances.

A new law authorized a graduated income tax credit ranging between 20 and 35 percent against 1973 tax liabilities depending upon the adjusted gross income of the taxpayer. It also eliminated any state income tax liability for taxpayers with adjusted gross income less than $4000 (single returns) and $8000 (joint returns). This one-time special rebate was possible due to the fact that the state had a budget surplus for the 1973–74 year. This legislation also had the enthusiastic support of the opponents of the Reagan tax initiative as it preempted a similar rebate provision of that plan.

Taxes on Motorists

It is expensive to provide adequate facilities for California's highly mobile population. The costs to the state of constructing, maintaining, and policing an extensive network of highways generally exceeds $800 million a year. The Californian, as a result, cannot escape paying plenty if he wants to drive to work or take a holiday trip. The variety of special taxes and fees levied on motorists has caused the per capita car cost to zoom to the highest in the nation.

THE MOTOR VEHICLE FUELS TAX   A high-ranking revenue producer for the whole state is the tax on motor vehicle fuels—seven cents per gallon on gasoline and seven cents on diesel fuel. The total yield for 1974–75 was about $702 million. The state constitution provides that this money *must* be spent for activities related to highways, roads, and streets. Much of it is used to construct and maintain the toll-free highways and freeways. About a third is allocated to counties and cities for local streets and roads.

SPECIAL MOTOR VEHICLE TAXES AND FEES   All owners of the 16 million motor vehicles in the state must pay an annual registration fee for each vehicle. Truck and bus

owners pay weight fees in addition. Motorists must also pay
a small fee for their driver's license. All of these fees bring
in about 4 percent of the state's yearly revenue.

Vehicle owners pay another tax that is actually a local
property tax. A motor vehicle is regarded as "real property"
by the state, and owners must pay two dollars for each $100
of assessed value, calculated from the vehicle's original
cost and present age. This tax is collected by the state along
with the registration fee levied when the owner gets his
license plates. They are termed "in lieu" payments and returned by the state to the local governments of origin for
their own use. For 1974–75 this tax amounted to about
$339 million.

Business Taxes

A variety of special taxes are levied on business concerns. Together they account for approximately 11 percent
of the state's revenue. The general tax rate on corporations
is 9 percent on net earnings, while banks pay a 13 percent
rate. In addition, insurance companies pay license fees
and a tax on all premiums collected, with deductions allowed for any real estate taxes already paid to local governments. A special tax is levied on any railroad cars owned by
companies that are not in the railroad business. (Some
concerns own their own oil cars, refrigerator cars, and even
sleeping cars.) These railroad car taxes are collected by
the state in lieu of city and county taxes on such property.

Gift and Inheritance Taxes

Any money inherited upon the death of a relative or
friend is subject to the state inheritance tax, with rates (3
to 24 percent) and exemptions varying according to the
blood relationship involved. Near relatives—wives and children, for example—are taxed less than nephews or third
cousins. Gifts are also subject to similar provisions (or else
a benefactor could avoid inheritance taxes in his waning
years). Life insurance proceeds, however, are exempt from
these taxes, and nonprofit or charitable institutions are not
required to pay taxes on any inheritance or gifts received.

Alcoholic Beverage Taxes and Fees

California levies an excise tax on the manufacturers of all alcoholic beverages and also collects license fees from all retail distributors in the state.[2] The total estimated— $145 million in 1974–75—has been gradually rising along with the state's per capita consumption of alcohol. Excise tax rates range from one cent per gallon on dry wine to $2 per gallon on distilled spirits and have been among the lowest in the nation.

Horse Racing Fees

The state government is always a "winner" at the parimutuel horse races. Revenues from horse racing are derived mainly from a fee of 5½ to 7½ percent on the amount wagered, "breakage" (odd cents on each dollar wagered), unclaimed winning tickets, and license fees, fines, and penalties. About one-sixth of horse racing revenues are earmarked for distribution to fairs and expositions, for wildlife restoration, and for research and improvement in animal husbandry and agriculture conducted primarily by the University of California and some of the state universities. The rest is returned to the general fund.

Cigarette Tax

In 1959 the legislature imposed a tax of three cents per package on the distribution of cigarettes to be prepaid by the distributor through use of stamps or metering machines. This tax was increased to ten cents per pack in 1968. Seven cents of this tax is for the state's general fund, and three cents is for local governments. The cigarette tax is expected to raise about $260 million in 1975.

CALIFORNIA'S FISCAL PROBLEM

In contrast with the national government program of deficit financing, the state fiscal program is conducted on a "pay-as-you-go" basis. Though the state does borrow

[2] Liquor is also subject to the retail sales tax, which brings in more revenue than the alcoholic beverage excise.

through the issuance of bonds, such borrowing may be used only for a portion of the capital outlay obligations, and all bond issues are subject to a vote of the electorate. Thus, the Department of Finance, the governor, and the legislature must propose an annual budget that shows a balance between expenditures and revenues.

In the early 1940's the actual state income not only took care of all budget needs but did permit the establishment of savings reserves. However,when the lean revenue years followed the wartime boom, the legislature declined to vote tax increases, and the "rainy day" fund was siphoned off to meet certain state functions.

When Governor Brown took office in 1958, "the cupboard was bare" and the state government was operating in the red. The legislature then levied a new cigarette tax and increased the tax rates on beer, horse racing, personal incomes, gifts and inheritances, and bank and corporation earnings. Yet, even with these increased taxes the state was faced with a deficit of $500 million when Ronald Reagan became governor in 1966.

The new governor advocated an immediate reduction in state expenditures under his campaign promise of "cut, squeeze, and trim." Upon assuming office, he ordered a decrease of 10 percent in all state budgets across the board and proposed that state employees work on holidays with no extra compensation. Although this program was not fully accomplished, from 1966 to 1972 the administration did carry on a program of drastic curtailment of expenditures, particularly in the areas of education and social welfare.

In the last three years there has been some relaxation in the austerity program. Due to improved business conditions, the state's revenues have increased, with larger income from the retail sales tax, personal income tax, and other business taxes. The 1972–73 budget handed some $700 million back to the taxpayers through tax relief and still ended with a surplus of about $300 million. Though the energy shortage and a cooling off of the economy in 1974 lowered the state's revenues, there was a surplus of about $350 million when the new governor assumed office in 1975.

It can be seen that the state has been on a roller coaster as far as finance is concerned, with some years showing a deficit and other years a surplus. It is difficult to estimate the exact amount of revenues that will result from taxes such as those on retail sales and personal incomes because they are directly related to business conditions, which fluctuate during any given year. A change in the volume of business or a change in price level has an immediate effect upon the amount of taxes collected. A new variable in the state budget has also been introduced by the federal revenue-sharing plan. There is considerable uncertainty as to the amount that will be derived from this source of revenue.

Taxes

There has been considerable controversy surrounding the tax structure in California. While attempting to provide just and equitable taxes, the government is also confronted with the necessity of raising large sums of money to support the ever increasing needs of the people. With the rapid growth in local government services such as education, police and fire protection, sanitation, water, and other people-related services such as welfare, property taxes have been increased to the breaking point. Governor Reagan placed the reduction of property taxes high on his list of priorities. Throughout his administration he sponsored several bills to lower the tax liabilities for property owners. As a culmination of his efforts to reduce government expenditures, Reagan proposed and promoted a constitutional initiative which was placed before the voters in November 1973 (refer to the discussion on Proposition 1 in Chapter Six, pp. 117–18). This new measure provided property tax relief and would allow rebates on 1973 personal income taxes. Though the voters failed to approve this ballot proposition, the provisions relating to tax reductions were included in a tax bill passed by the 1973 legislature.

Much of the controversy concerning California taxes revolves around taxes on property, the personal income tax, and the retail sales tax. Some contend that the retail sales tax is regressive, and that its burden falls upon the poor. It is also believed to be a deterrent to business, because it raises prices and businessmen must serve as tax collectors. On the other hand, a graduated tax on personal incomes is progressive and taxes those who have the ability to pay.

Despite these arguments, the rate of tax on retail sales has continued to increase since the inception of the tax in the mid-1930's, and it is now the major source of state revenue. Certainly, from the standpoint of the government, the tax on retail sales provides large amounts of income with little expense of collection. It also has the ability to keep up with the ever changing business conditions.

Legislators and political leaders are also vitally interested in how the state spends its money, and from time to time Democrats and Republicans alike take strong stands for or against increased expenditures in areas such as education and social welfare. However, it is imperative that, under our present system of state finance of "pay as you go," revenues be sufficient to meet expenditures.

Financing Local Government

Local governments—cities, counties, and special districts—have faced some of the same financial problems as the state. About one-half of the monies spent by counties in California is devoted to social welfare and though some of the funds are supplied by the state and federal governments, local governments must provide a given portion. Other county expenditures are for highways, bridges, flood control, protective services, sanitation, and education.

The largest expenditure of California cities is for police and fire protection, with other large amounts spent for city streets, sanitation, and refuse collection. School districts and other special districts spend funds for education, irrigation, air pollution control, flood control, and other miscellaneous functions.

Local governments receive nearly all of their revenue from two major sources—taxes on property (about 40 percent) and grants and subventions from state and federal governments (about 50 percent). In addition they receive income from charges made for building permits, franchise charges, and refuse collection, and from parking meters, license fees, rental of property, and sales taxes. Some cities charge extra fees for motel rooms, sewer connection, and even a "tippler's tax"—5 percent levied on all drinks sold in a bar.

With the increased urbanization of California's population, the financial demands upon counties, cities, and special districts are considerable. At the same time, property taxes have probably reached their limit, and the income from state and federal government is uncertain. The financial problem, therefore, is a continuous one and presents a real challenge to local governments in California.

SELECTED REFERENCES

California, Governor's Office, *Budget Submitted to the Legislature*. Sacramento: State Printing Office. Published annually.

California, Legislative Analyst, *Analysis of the Budget Bill*. Sacramento: State Printing Office. Published annually.

California, Office of the Controller, *Annual Report of the State Controller*. Sacramento: State Printing Office. Issued annually.

Salzman, Ed, "Inflation's Gift to the New Governor," *California Journal* V, 8 (August 1974): 71.

State of California Budget. Sacramento: State Printing Office. Issued annually.

Local Government in California

A mong the three levels of government in the United States—federal, state, and local—the local governments are the least understood and yet they probably play the most immediate role in the life of the citizen. A wide variety of public services including the protection of life and property, the promotion of health and welfare, the provision of public education, and other essentials of everyday life such as roads and removal of trash are performed for Californians by cities, counties, and special districts. But the voters stay away from local elections in droves. There are approximately 6000 of these local units of government, and most of them are further subdivided into numerous agencies. A substantial part of each Californian's annual tax payment—some of which is collected by the federal government—finds its way back to him in the form of such locally performed services.

RELATION OF THE LOCAL UNITS TO THE STATE GOVERNMENT

All local governments in California, though possessing varying degrees of autonomy, are creatures and agents of

213

the state. Their functions, powers, and structure are determined by the state constitution and by statutes of the state legislature, and they have no authority other than that granted by the state.

Constitutional Provisions

The inherent right of the state legislature to create local governments, define their powers, and prescribe their structure is recognized in Article XI of the state constitution. However, the legislature does not have a free hand in the discharge of these functions. The constitution permits counties and cities to frame their own charters, and outlines in detail what provisions these charters must contain. Important financial relations between local governments and the state are also immune to legislative tampering—the most important being the distribution of motor vehicle tax funds and the apportionment of state money to local school districts. The direct relation between local law enforcement officers and the attorney general also would require constitutional amendment to be altered. Thus, local officers have in many respects no less of a constitutional status than do state agencies and officers. County and city agencies are not necessarily *subordinate* to those of the state.

State-Local Cooperation

Some administrative departments of the state government have established close relations with local government units not so much because of a provision in the state constitution but for the mutual advantages to be gained through practical, day-to-day cooperation. Local sheriffs' offices and police departments, for example, file copies of fingerprints and reports of crimes with the Bureau of Criminal Identification in the state Department of Justice; and the bureau in turn makes available to the local agencies a fund of information and expert analysis possible only in a centralized criminal information agency. The area of social welfare provides another illustration of coordinated effort between levels of government. The state director of social welfare and his staff make rules for the administration and distribution of public assistance monies. However, an individual desiring aid must apply at his county welfare department, and it is the local agency that gives him his check.

THE COUNTY

The entire land area of California is divided into fifty-eight counties varying in size, population and economy.[1] San Bernardino County with 20,131 square miles is larger than any county in the nation; and San Francisco with forty-five square miles is among the smallest. Los Angeles County is the most populous—over 6 million—while Alpine, with slightly less than 500 inhabitants, is one of the least populated.

The county is the local subdivision through which the state performs many of its most important functions: elections administration; public health programs; law enforcement; administration of justice; upkeep of roads; relief administration; and maintenance of vital statistics and property records.

Types of Counties

THE GENERAL LAW COUNTY   Forty-seven of California's counties are organized under general laws enacted by the state legislature. The constitution provides (in Article XI, section b) that:

The Legislature shall provide for county powers and an elected governing body in each county and prescribe compensation for its members. The Legislature or the governing body may provide for other officers whose compensa-

[1] In 1850 the first state legislature created twenty-seven counties, but by 1907 these had been subdivided to make up the present fifty-eight. In 1910 an amendment to the constitution (Art. XI, sec. 3) in effect prevented the legislature from further altering this basic territorial distribution.

tion shall be prescribed by the governing body. The governing body shall provide for the number, compensation, tenure, and appointment of employees.

Successive acts of the legislature have established the present statewide pattern in which the voters in each county elect a board of supervisors, sheriff, district attorney, coroner, assessor, tax collector, treasurer, auditor, county clerk, recorder, public administrator, superintendent of public schools, and judges of the superior, municipal, and justice courts. Needless to say, the voters do not receive a short ballot in county elections. The legislature also requires that the board of supervisors appoint a long list of lesser officers, including a sealer of weights and measures, health officer, civil service commissioner, airport manager, pound master, and many others.

The board of supervisors is the chief legislative and administrative body of the county. It adopts the county budget, sets the county tax rate on general property, enacts special taxes such as the 1 percent sales tax, and in some counties sits as board of equalization to hear complaints against the property valuations set by the county assessor. (A constitutional amendment adopted in 1966 permits a county board of supervisors to create tax assessment appeals boards to perform this function.) The board also has the power to enact civil ordinances—such as prohibitions on gambling—to apply to residents of *un*incorporated areas (not part of cities) within its jurisdiction. It hires and fires county civil service personnel, approves all purchases made by the county, and manages all county property and markets bonds floated by the county and by school districts. In election years the board serves as elections commission. Other ex officio roles of the supervisors are to act as board of directors for the county smog control, flood control, and road districts.

Probably the best known of all elected county officers is the sheriff, whose major responsibility is the apprehension of all alleged offenders against the criminal laws of the state and county within the unincorporated areas of the county. Other important officers concerned with law enforcement are the district attorney, who is the county's prosecuting officer in criminal cases and represents the county in civil cases to which the county is a party; and the coroner, who is responsible for investigating the causes of deaths not attended by a physician, especially those which indicate violence, foul play, or poison.

The most important county officers concerned with finance are the assessor, the tax collector, the auditor, and the treasurer. The assessor, aided by a large staff of deputies, determines the taxable value of real and personal property in the county. The tax collector has that most thankless job—mailing out tax bills to each property owner, deeding to the state property on which tax payments are delinquent, and collecting the various business and license fees. The auditor's (in some counties the controller's) duties are comparable to those of the state controller: authorizing all payments of county funds as provided for in the budget. The treasurer is the custodian of the county funds, depositing them in banks, and making payments only when presented with warrants signed by the auditor.

Another officer with substantial responsibilities is the county clerk. He is the clerk of the superior court, and in most counties the ex officio clerk for the board of supervisors. In many counties he has the weighty duty of managing the official election machinery for state and county elections, which includes handling the filing of candidates' and direct legislation petitions, preparing the ballot, securing the necessary election supplies, and overseeing vote tabulations.

The county superintendent of schools approves the budgets and payrolls, maintains full records, and processes teacher certification for school districts within the county. It is his responsibility to see that the state laws on public education are observed by these districts.

All of these important county officers are elected directly by the people on a nonpartisan ballot, and thus are not subject to central lines of responsibility within the county government, nor are they answerable to political parties. This independence in large part explains why many county officers and agencies seem to the citizen to have an existence of their own, unattached, and almost sovereign in their particular fields of activity.

THE CHARTER COUNTY A state constitutional amendment, adopted in 1911 and revised in 1970, permits a county to frame and adopt its own charter. The charter may be drafted by either the county board of supervisors or by a special charter commission of citizens elected by the voters of the county. After the document is completed it is submitted to the voters in a special election. If a majority votes approval, the new charter is then filed with the California secretary of state and goes into effect.

Large-scale revisions of existing county charters may be drafted either by the board of supervisors or by a charter commission. Individual amendments (or even outright repeal of the whole charter) may be proposed by either the board of supervisors or initiative petition. But all such changes must be ratified by the voters of the county at the polls.

A general law county that has changed over to charter status is not completely exempt from all state laws governing the structure and operation of counties. For example, all charters must provide for an elected board of supervisors.

Flexibility is allowed the charter county in determining the *number* of supervisors (the constitution specifies only that there shall be at least five); deciding whether to make the lesser county officers appointive rather than elective; setting the salary of its own officials; providing, if it wishes, for a county-manager system of centralized administration; and consolidating county offices.

Los Angeles in 1912 was the first county to adopt its own charter. Since then nine other counties have successfully completed all the required steps: San Bernardino, Butte, Tehama, Alameda, Fresno, Sacramento, San Diego, San Mateo, and Santa Clara. (San Francisco is a chartered city-county.)

It is of interest that charters are largely in use in the most populous counties in the state. Though Butte and Tehama are exceptions, the other eight are all heavily populated. And only four general law counties (Contra Costa, Kern, Orange, and Riverside) have a population of more than 250,000.

The Problem of Divided Responsibility

One of the greatest shortcomings of county government is its lack of integrated authority and responsibility. Unlike the national government, the typical county does not have one single elected official who has the major administrative responsibility. And though the state government in California is headed by a plural executive consisting of eleven elected officers, at least the responsibility for general executive policy is centered in one man—the governor. The county not only elects many of its subordinate administrative officers but divides its top executive authority among a five-member board of supervisors. If the voters are dissatisfied with the administration of their county they do not know whom to hold responsible.

Some charter counties in California, taking advantage of the structural flexibility allowed them by the constitution, have made progress toward centering administrative responsibility. In Los Angeles County, for example, all officers except judges, the sheriff, the district attorney, and the assessor are appointive and are directly under the authority of the board of supervisors.

The legislature has tried consolidating county offices in some of the general law counties. In five counties the positions of clerk and auditor have been merged; six counties have combined the duties of the sheriff and coroner into one office. But such consolidations are usually possible only in counties of small population. Thus, even though charter counties are allowed more freedom to consolidate offices, few have done so.

THE COUNTY ADMINISTRATIVE OFFICER   The most effective and widely used means to bring greater integration to county government has been establishment of some kind of appointive chief administrative officer. Over half of California's counties have created such a position. This officer is appointed by and responsible to the elected board of supervisors. Only charter counties may legally establish the position of *county manager,* an official with considerable administrative authority—even the power to appoint and remove the head of some county departments.[2] However, both charter and general law counties may establish the position of chief administrative officer—essentially an agent of the board of supervisors. His principal functions are to implement the decisions of the board and include the preparation

___

[2] In 1970, six counties had executive officers. Only San Mateo County used the title of county manager.

of the county budget. Though there is a legal difference between the *county manager* and the *chief administrative officer*, people generally refer to this official as the "county manager."

Mammoth Los Angeles County has been debating the possibility of creating the office of county executive or county mayor, either to be elected by the voters or to be appointed by the board of supervisors. The proponents of the plan argue that such an official, being granted much greater powers than are now exercised by the county chief administrative officer, would relieve the supervisors of a multitude of administrative details with which they are presently burdened and would allow them to concentrate on matters of general policy.

Though county administration has been somewhat more effectively coordinated by the county administrative officer, as far as the citizen is concerned the county is still an amorphous body speaking with many voices, and therefore able to avoid specific responsibility for its actions.

THE CITY

The California city or municipality is like the county in some respects. Both are creatures and administrative agents of the state, performing in its name certain basic governmental functions such as law enforcement, fire control, and sanitation. But the city is less an arm of the state and more a unit of local self-government than the county. Counties are imposed upon the citizens by the state. A city is created only at the request and consent of the residents in a given area. The city can be defined as a public corporation voluntarily activated by the people living in a local vicinity to perform those mutually desired services where coordination and cooperation are necessary. In theory, cities are agencies rendering needed services which neither private nor state and county agencies are capable or desirous of providing. But in California the practice of city formation has often been less rational. There are many special-interest cities maintained only to provide advantageous tax rates and other privileges to particular industries. Some cities are creatures of retail store owners along main routes and exist only to collect special sales taxes. A few cities contain more livestock than live people. In 1972, California had more than 400 cities, and the number changes every year. Increases occur most frequently in the urban counties. In true California fashion the incorporators of some new municipalities have adopted unorthodox and even exotic names, for example, the City of Industry, the City of Commerce, and the City of Hawaiian Gardens.

Types of Cities

THE GENERAL LAW CITY   The vast majority of California municipalities (over 330 at the start of 1975) are incorporated under uniform state law provisions. The constitution of 1879 specified that the legislature could not enact a *special* law that granted a charter to a particular city; rather the legislature had to pass *general* laws that set the procedure whereby the people of any locality which met the requirements could incorporate themselves into a municipality. The laws made pursuant to this constitutional provision are very specific as to the steps by which incorporation may be accomplished.

Let us assume that some residents of a community known as Smith's Table Top desire to incorporate. They must first make a formal application to the Local Agency Formation Commission of their county. They must convince the commission that their proposed city will include at least 500 inhabitants (in Los Angeles County 500 registered voters), that its boundaries will not overlap those of existing municipalities, and that there is a definite public need for incorporation. If the commission approves, the sponsors of the new city then circulate petitions which must be signed by 25 percent of the property owners—who must also possess at least 25 percent of the real estate value of the area. By this time the proponents have agreed upon a name for the new entity—Mesa Estates. The petitions are submitted to the county board of supervisors who hold a public hearing. Any property owner who objects to being included in the new city may appear before the board. The supervisors may alter the boundaries of the proposed city (with the consent of the Local Agency Formation Commission). However, the new boundaries must still contain the minimum required number of residents or registered voters. A special election is called in which the voters living within the prospective Mesa Estates decide two things: (1) Shall they incorporate as a city? (2) If so, who shall serve on the first city council? If a majority vote "yes" on the first question, the county board of supervisors then declares the city of Mesa Estates in existence and proclaims that the five candidates receiving the most votes are the new city council.

THE CHARTER CITY   Once having become a general law city, a municipality may, like a county, frame a charter of its own and thereby become somewhat more independent of the state legislature. In 1975, there were seventy-seven charter cities in California, the majority in densely populated areas. Practically all cities with over 100,000 inhabitants are charter cities, while only a few charter cities have fewer than 10,000. Thus, while less than a fifth of the total number of cities are chartered, they contain more than half of the state's population.

A city may gain charter status through procedures similar to those available to a county. The document may be drafted either by the city council or a charter commission elected for the purpose. The charter is submitted to the voters of the city and if approved by them it becomes the organic law of the city.

The primary advantage a charter city has over a general law city is greater *flexibility*—in determining structure, such as the number of councilmen, and in determining functions, since it need not wait for legislative authorization to add additional departments and services. The charter city has considerable sovereignty in municipal affairs. Occasionally there have been conflicts with the legislature, however, over the definition of a "municipal" matter. The California courts have grappled with this problem for sixty years and have yet to arrive at a satisfactory answer. Their practice has been to decide each case on its own merits. The salary of a San Francisco policeman, for example, is a "municipal" matter while the license fees set for local liquor dealers is within the jurisdiction of state agencies. And the California supreme court in 1962 declared unconstitutional a Los Angeles ordinance against prostitution on the grounds that it went beyond the provisions of a preexisting state law. Similar problems arose when local authorities sought to prevent card game gambling.

Forms of City Government

California cities illustrate various types of two main forms of city government: (1) the mayor-council and (2) the council-manager. Either plan may be selected by general law and charter cities, but charter cities have a greater range of choice in that more variations of the mayor–council plan are open to them.

THE MAYOR–COUNCIL FORM   The traditional form of American city government is one in which a legislative body (the council) and an executive officer (the mayor) are elected by the voters of the city. In some cities all the councilmen are elected at large (by the entire city); in others the councilmen are each elected from a district of the city. There are many variations in the respective spheres of authority exercised by mayors and councils and many ways of classifying these variations. The most appropriate classification for the purposes of this survey, however, is the distinction between the "strong-mayor" and "weak-mayor" types— terms which have nothing to do with the personality of the mayor but rather the amount of power granted him by his city's charter.

In a *strong-mayor* city the mayor is the principal administrative officer, having the authority to appoint many of the city's officials and, under specified circumstances, to remove them. A strong mayor in some cities has a veto power over the ordinances passed by his council. The relationship between the mayor and council in the cities with strong mayors is similar to the relationship between the governor and the state legislature. Among the few cities in California that have the strong-mayor form of government are the two largest, Los Angeles and San Francisco. In Los Angeles the fifteen members of the city council are elected by districts for staggered terms of four years each. The mayor, elected at large, also for a four-year term, has the power to veto council ordinances; and the budget is prepared under the mayor's authority with the assistance of his appointed city chief administrative officer. The appointive power of the Los Angeles mayor is somewhat limited, however. The city has nearly twenty administrative departments, each supervised by a part-time commission or board of citizens appointed by the mayor with the approval of the city council. But commissioners serve longer terms than the mayor; and no board member may be removed by the mayor without the consent of the council.

In a *weak-mayor* (or strong-council) plan the council has substantial administrative as well as legislative power. This is the basic pattern in most of California's general law cities. The mayor is primarily a ceremonial figurehead, possessing little if any administrative authority. He is merely one of the councilmen, selected by his fellow members to serve as chairman and mayor for a one-year term. The mayor presides over council sessions, digs the first shovelful of dirt for new public buildings, and presents visiting celebrities with keys to the city, but he has no veto or appointing power. The city's administrative jobs are filled either by election or through council appointments. In some of the smaller cities the city clerk is really the chief administrator, coordinating the day-to-day operations of the municipal government. Some general law cities have provided by a vote of the people that the mayor is to be elected independently of the council and at large; however, they have not substantially increased his powers.

THE COUNCIL–MANAGER FORM   The most prevalent type of city government in California is one in which a city manager is appointed by the elected council. California leads all other states in the number of municipalities organized in this manner. Two-thirds of the state's incorporated cities have delegated most administrative functions to a central office, thus bringing about a more complete integration of municipal activities. A city may choose this plan by a vote of the people or through council ordinance. The typical city manager supervises the administration of ordinances passed by the council and has the power to appoint and remove most of the heads of the city's administrative departments. He is selected for an indefinite term and holds office as long as he enjoys the confidence of the majority of the council, whether it be for twenty days or twenty years. This system is quite similar to that of a private corporation—the voters being the stockholders, the council the

FORMS OF LOCAL GOVERNMENT

MAYOR-COUNCIL   COUNCIL-MANAGER

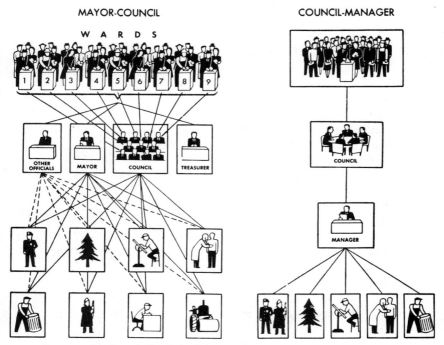

Source: National Municipal League.

board of directors, and the city manager the general manager. The mayor in such a city presides over the council and has ceremonial duties.

Some cities have adopted a modified form of council–manager government in which the council appoints an administrative officer somewhat more restricted in his functions than a city manager. Such an officer does not have appointment or removal power over all administrative officials and is subject to greater control by the council. This type of arrangement is often a step toward the adoption of a true council–manager form of government.

Most authorities in the field of public administration agree that the manager form of government does much to integrate authority and responsibility in government, thereby improving the services of the city to its people. A professionally trained administrator not required to face periodic public elections is better qualified to execute the policies of the city council and to manage the technical and complex business of modern city government.

THE CITY AND COUNTY OF SAN FRANCISCO

San Francisco is one of the very few city-counties in the United States.[3] In 1853, the rural part of old San Francisco County was separated from the urban part and became San Mateo County. Urban San Francisco was organized into a combined city and county by a special act of the legislature in 1856. Its first charter, issued in 1898, was replaced by its present charter in 1932. (A state constitutional amendment passed in 1914 provides that cities and counties may consolidate through the charter process, though none has made use of this particular provision.) The difficulty of making city-county consolidations is often the result of opposition from rural communities within the counties who fear that consolidation would likely bring an increase in taxes.

Rather than maintaining two sets of officers performing overlapping functions in the same metropolitan area, the City and County of San Francisco has one board of supervisors (its ordinance-passing body), one police force, and one set of financial officers. Unlike the citizen of metropolitan Los Angeles who, if involved in an auto accident, might have to determine the side of the street he was on before deciding to call the chief of police or the sheriff, the San Franciscan knows who is responsible for him and to whom he is responsible.[4]

San Francisco's board of supervisors consists of eleven members elected by districts for four-year terms, six and five members respectively coming up for election every two

[3] Denver is also a city-county; but certain cities like Philadelphia, though they have consolidated most city and county functions, still operate with some elected county officials independent of the city government.

[4] There are fine divisions of authority among some San Francisco officials, but these are based upon *function* rather than geography. The sheriff thus acts in civil matters and the police chief in criminal matters. A similar division exists between the city attorney and the district attorney.

years. The mayor is elected at large every four years and is the city's chief administrative and ceremonial officer. He is a "stronger" mayor than the mayor in Los Angeles since, in addition to the veto power and authority over the budget, he also has full appointment power over the police commission, the planning commission, and the civil service commission. The city employs a chief administrative officer (appointed by the mayor upon approval by the board but removable only by a two-thirds vote of the supervisors or by popular recall) who has direct supervision of nine other city departments including finance, purchasing, public works, and public health. As in most California municipalities, the judges, sheriff, district attorney, city attorney, public defender, assessor, and treasurer are elected by the people and conduct their offices somewhat independently of the mayor and the chief administrative officer.

SACRAMENTO

In the 1970's the trend toward consolidation of city and county governments into combined city-counties received new impetus. For two years a commission of forty citizens worked on a charter to merge the Sacramento County government with those of its constituent cities. But it developed that the strongest desire for consolidation came from the city of Sacramento, whereas the other three cities in the county—Folsom, Galt, and Isleton—wanted the chance to decide for themselves whether to merge with the county. Thereupon, the voters of California approved Proposition 8 on the June 1974 ballot, granting those three cities the opportunity of either voting themselves into the new government or retaining their separate identity. Ironically, Sacramento County voters turned down the whole idea of consolidation in a local proposition on the November ballot.

SPECIAL DISTRICTS

The most varied and least known of all units of government in the state are the special districts. They deal with matters such as water supply, irrigation, air pollution, public education, and flood control—problems that extend beyond city and county boundaries. After all, flood waters originate high in the mountains and in their flow to the river or sea cross areas occupied by many cities and sometimes several counties. Forming a third category of local government, special districts are created from time to time as the demand arises and as an alternative to city or county administration.

Special districts are to some degree independent of other local governments. Normally, they have their own elected governing boards, which raise their own funds by a special tax collected from property owners served by the district, and from special fees and service charges.

Number and Types of Special Districts

California has over 5000 special districts whose total annual financial transactions amount to more than those of all cities and counties of the state. In addition, thousands of county and municipal improvement districts are merely agencies through which county boards of supervisors and city councils levy special assessments for improvements such as paved streets, curbs, sidewalks, and ornamental lights. Such local districts, strictly speaking, are not governmental units since they have no legal status of their own.[5]

California's special districts can best be classified according to the function they perform, ranging all the way from public education to cemetery maintenance and mosquito abatement. School districts—elementary, high school, unified, and junior college—account for about one-fourth the total number and three-fourths the total expenditures of all special districts in the state. Most of the remaining are utility districts, irrigation districts, fire protection districts, air pollution districts, sewage and sanitation districts, flood control districts, and hospital districts. Some forty other types relating to bridges, airports, cemeteries, garbage disposal, levees, libraries, mosquito abatement, parkways, and ports and harbors complete California's myriad of local government agencies.

[5] There are at present over 600 such districts in Los Angeles County alone.

Organization of Special Districts

The enabling acts passed by the legislature authorizing special districts are multitudinous and varied. A petition by citizens interested in a new district, followed by favorable action of the board of supervisors, may lead to state action. In other cases a special election may be called to determine the wish of the voters in the area concerned. A public hearing before the board of supervisors must nearly always be held before the state will consider the formation of a new district.

The act of the state legislature outlines the functions and the powers as well as the composition and selection of the governing body. In many districts, such as school districts and the Sacramento Municipal Utility District, the governing board is elected by the voters and serves a definite term. In some districts the county board of supervisors acts as the ex officio board of directors and appoints an administrator and other officials. Examples of this type of organization are the county road districts, the Orange County Flood Control District, and the Los Angeles County Air Pollution Control District. The supervisors appoint governing boards of directors for certain special districts such as parking and cemetery districts.

Much of California's recent population growth has occurred in areas surrounding big cities, creating sprawling metropolitan communities. As a result of the need for new services, large regional metropolitan districts like the San Francisco Bay Area Rapid Transit District (BART), the Golden Gate Bridge and Highway District, the San Francisco Bay Area Air Pollution Control District, and the Metropolitan Water District of Southern California have been established. These agencies are large-scale operations involving several cities and often several counties, and their boards of directors are appointed by the governing bodies of the various cities and counties that make up the district.

While the number of special districts performing functions other than public education has been increasing, the number of school districts has been decreasing. For years educators have been urging the consolidation of the smaller districts into larger units that could maintain a better-rounded educational program for their pupils. Speaker of the Assembly Jess Unruh authored a school finance bill in the 1964 legislature that would have combined the 1500 districts into fewer than 150. The bill, as finally enacted, did not contain this drastic provision, but it did encourage the smaller districts to merge. The one-room "little red schoolhouse" of which so much romantic nonsense has been written and sung is rapidly receding into the past.

REGIONAL GOVERNMENT

Local government in the metropolitan areas of California is a crazy quilt of counties, cities, and special districts, each with its own taxing authority, administration, and rules. This arrangement creates no end of confusion for the citizen. For example, it may be legal to park a pick-up truck on the east side of Citrus Avenue, but not on the west side, since Citrus is the dividing line between two municipalities, the westerly one being very opposed to such plebeian vehicles vulgarizing its patrician curbs. However, the water one drinks, the air one breathes, and the highways one travels cross county, city, and special district lines; and the problems of pollution, traffic, and law enforcement must be handled on the basis of an entire metropolitan region.

Urban atomization is most marked in the two largest metropolitan areas of the state. The San Francisco Bay Area includes about fifty incorporated cities, nine counties, and a host of special districts. Most of the Los Angeles metropolitan area is included within Los Angeles County but that county contains more than seventy-five municipalities, the largest being the City of Los Angeles itself. Some of the other cities, such as San Fernando, are enclaves completely surrounded by the "City of the Angels." A lesser degree of governmental fragmentation is to be found in some of the other metropoli like San Diego and Sacramento.

Many efforts have been made to bring order out of this urban chaos. One result has been the creation of the large regional special districts such as the Bay Area Rapid Transit District, which furnishes public transportation for the people of several counties. But this expedient does not solve the problem. The San Francisco Bay region not only has BART but also has several other regional special districts, e.g., the Golden Gate Bridge and Highway District and the San Francisco Bay Air Pollution District. Each serves a single purpose, each has its own board of directors,

MAP OF THE COUNTY OF LOS ANGELES

Scale in Miles

0 1   6   12

☐ Incorporated Areas

▨ Unincorporated Areas

— Supervisorial District Boundaries

SAN BERNARDINO COUNTY

ORANGE COUNTY

VENTURA COUNTY

Pacific Ocean

Claremont
Pomona
Walnut
West Covina
La Verne
San Dimas
Glendora
Covina
Azusa
Irwindale
Baldwin Park
La Puente
City of Industry
Duarte
Monrovia
Bradbury
Sierra Madre
Arcadia
Temple City
El Monte
S. El Monte
Santa Fe Springs
Whittier
La Mirada
Cerritos
Hawaiian Gardens
Pasadena
San Marino
Alhambra
Monterey Park
Montebello
Pico Rivera
Bell Gardens
Downey
Norwalk
Artesia
Lakewood
Signal Hill
S. Pasadena
Rosemead
City of Commerce
Vernon
Bell
South Gate
Cudahy
Paramount
Glendale
Beverly Hills
Maywood
Huntington Park
Lynwood
Compton
Long Beach
Carson
Burbank
Culver City
Inglewood
Hawthorne
Gardena
Lawndale
Torrance
Lomita
Palos Verde Est.
Rolling Hills
Rolling Hills Estates
San Fernando
Santa Monica
Marina del Rey
El Segundo
Manhattan
Hermosa
Redondo
CITY OF LOS ANGELES
Hidden Hills
Avalon
Santa Catalina Is.
San Clemente Is.

1
2
3
4
5

Lancaster
Palmdale

N

231

each its own source of revenue, each its own bureaucracy, and each guards its own authority jealously. And none can make and enforce a general plan of development that will make the Bay area the beautiful and livable place it can be.

Therefore, the legislature has repeatedly been urged to create multipurpose regional governments for the great metropolitan areas of California. These new entities would have a jurisdiction crossing city and county boundaries, would have the power to tax, and would have authority to deal with the area problems of air pollution, water supply, sewage, transportation, and land use. So far, bills to create such regional governments have been blocked in the legislature in part by city and county officials who fear loss of their independence and by right-wing elements who see regional government as a part of the Communist conspiracy.

A more respectable opposition has arisen from a Task Force on Local Government appointed by Governor Reagan in April 1973. The task force attacked as false many of the commonly held assumptions about local government. Among other things it reported that: (1) local government in California is not unplanned, uncoordinated, inefficient, and uneconomical; (2) special districts are more efficient than other forms of local government; (3) there is a tremendous amount of cooperation among governmental agencies; (4) multipurpose regional governments are not the solution "because air basins run east and west, water runs north and south, transportation routes differ, and there is no logical boundary for such a governmental agency in any of California's urban areas." [6] The task force strongly favored letting people at the lowest level make their own decisions. This objective could be achieved by making it easy for people in a neighborhood to form (and to dissolve) small special districts. So the experts disagree not only on the cure, but on the nature of the ills of local government.

Planning Commissions

Various measures short of regional government have been adopted in order to meet the metropolitan problems.

[6] Ed Salzman, "Reagan Task-Force Surprise: Special District Is the Most Efficient Form of Local Government," *California Journal*, 5, no. 1 (January 1974): 28–31.

A state law of 1953 authorized area planning commissions. One of these was set up in a six-county area around Sacramento. The commission is appointed by the county supervisors and city councils of the region, and it merely makes recommendations to its constituent cities and counties on such matters as land use and zoning.

Proposition 20 adopted by the voters in 1972 created six regional commissions to assist the California Coastal Zone Conservation Commission in regulating the development of the coastal areas of the state. These bodies have legal authority to grant or deny permits for construction work along our beaches.

Councils of Governments

The San Francisco Bay area led the way in another development—the voluntary association of local governments. Availing themselves of a state law passed in 1921, forty-two cities and five counties created the Association of Bay Area Governments (ABAG) in 1961, for the purpose of providing "a forum for discussion and study of metropolitan area problems of mutual interest and concern to the counties and cities of the San Francisco Bay Area and for the development of policy and action recommendations." [7] ABAG was not to take any action binding on its member cities and counties. However, since its inception, ABAG has gained some authority through the fact that it determines how federal funds be distributed for housing, law-enforcement, recreation, and pollution control.

ABAG is directed by a general assembly to which every member city and county appoints one of its elected officials. It also has a permanent staff of administrators and planners in its headquarters in Berkeley. ABAG has led the way in making regional plans for matters such as land use, open space, recreation facilities, transportation, refuse disposal, and shoreline development. However, all efforts in the legislature to give ABAG more authority and make it a genuine regional government have failed. Contrariwise, bills that would set up a rival Conservation and Development Agency

[7] "Regional Government Proponents Seek To Move State Off 'Dead Level Plateau,'" *California Government and Politics Annual, 1972–73* (Sacramento: Consensus Publishers, 1972), p. 91.

whose governing board would be elected directly by the people of the Bay area have also been defeated.

Inspired by ABAG, six counties and about 110 cities in the Los Angeles region chose to join the Southern California Association of Governments (SCAG). The extreme southwestern area of the state came up with the San Diego County Comprehensive Planning Organization. Both councils of governments exercise functions similar to those of ABAG. For example, SCAG, by threatening to cut off federal funds, compelled the Southern California Rapid Transit District to change its master plan for rapid transit so that the proposed lines would connect with those planned by the Orange County Transit District.

Contractual Cooperation

Something less than either city-county consolidation or regional government is the arrangement whereby a city contracts with its county to furnish to the city's residents municipal services such as fire and police protection, street construction and maintenance, assessment and tax collection, election supervision, library services, sewer construction and maintenance, and parks and recreational programs. Los Angeles County has done the most in this field of contractual cooperation (or "functional" consolidation as it is sometimes known). Almost all of the seventy-nine cities in that county have arranged to have the county registrar of voters conduct their municipal elections; all but two have contracted for the county to assess and collect their city taxes. Most spectacular is the "Lakewood Plan." Since its incorporation in 1954, the residential suburb of Lakewood has relied upon Los Angeles County for all its municipal services except playgrounds and recreation. For example, the sheriff of Los Angeles County is Lakewood's chief of police and furnishes the city with as much police protection through his deputies as the city is willing to pay for. Many of the newer cities in the county have followed the Lakewood scheme. In Northern California, San Mateo County furnishes a large number of services to Atherton and Woodside, and Contra Costa County does the same for Pleasant Hill.

CITIZEN PARTICIPATION

Observers of the American political scene have decried the apathy of the average voter toward his local governments; this is most unfortunate since many of the decisions that affect our daily lives are made, not in Washington or Sacramento, but in our city halls, county courthouses, or board of education headquarters. Furthermore, if the citizen bestirs himself, his impact on his local officials is more direct and persuasive than on state and national authorities. A delegation of irate housewives may not be able to affect the course of a bill in Sacramento, but can derail efforts of real estate developers to railroad through the city planning commission a change of zoning that would erect a superfluous service station in the middle of a residential neighborhood.

In local elections a relative handful of dedicated campaign workers can bring victory to a dark-horse candidate. This was illustrated by the recent political history of Berkeley. In the spring of 1971 a number of so-called radical groups formed an alliance called the April Coalition and drew up a slate of candidates for the four seats of the nine-member city council which were open in the election in April. The coalition put on an active registration and get-out-the-vote campaign especially among ethnic minorities and University of California students. When the results were tallied, three of the new council members were candidates of the Coalition and the fourth was a liberal Democrat. In addition, Warren Widener was elected the first black mayor of Berkeley. Two of the holdover councilmen were also liberal Democrats and one of the two Republican members was a maverick who occasionally voted with the radicals. Some changes were made, e.g., a freeze on rents (two-thirds of the Berkeley residents are renters) and adoption of an affirmative program to end discrimination in employment in the city government.

SELECTED REFERENCES

International City Managers' Association, *Municipal Year Book.* Chicago, 1974.

JONES, VICTOR, "The Changing Role of Urban County in Local Government," *Public Affairs Report* (Berkeley: Institute of Governmental Studies), June 1963.

SALZMAN, ED, "Reagan Task-Force Surprise: Special District Is the Most Efficient Form of Local Government," *California Journal* 5, no. 1 (January 1974): 28–31.

SHERWOOD, FRANK P., and RICHARD W. GABLE, *The California System of Governments*. Belmont, Calif.: Dickenson, 1968.

U.S. Bureau of the Census, *County and City Data Book* (A Statistical Abstract Supplement). Washington, D.C.: Government Printing Office, 1972.

Western City. Monthly periodical of the League of California Cities and five other similar far western organizations. Published in Los Angeles.

WILHELM, GARY L., and THOMAS R. HOEBER, *California Government and Politics Annual, 1972–73*. San Ramon, Calif.: Consensus Publishers, 1972.

WOOD, SAMUEL, and ALFRED HELLER, *The Phantom Cities of California*. Sacramento: California Tomorrow, 1964.

12
The Emerging Issues

How well the political and governmental system is functioning in California can be evaluated in terms of the primary tasks of politics and government: peaceful resolution of conflict (public order); equitable distribution of opportunities, benefits, and burdens (social justice); and maintenance of the basic conditions required for the health and well-being of the population (which increasingly involves the need to subject economic growth to quality-of-life considerations). All of these primary tasks are interrelated. All are bound to become more complicated during the last quarter of the twentieth century and severely test the capacity of the system to adapt to changing human needs. California has always been a bellwether of the newest trends in society. How this state responds to the emerging issues is being watched throughout the nation and by other countries for portents of the future of democracy in a postindustrial world.

PUBLIC ORDER AND SOCIAL JUSTICE

The greatest challenges to public order in California in recent years have come in the form of confrontations between groups who believe themselves to be unjustly disadvantaged under existing conditions and groups or institutions associated with the status quo. The confrontations have been most intense where the aggrieved groups felt little hope in getting their demands fairly processed by the established political and governmental institutions, and therefore have "taken to the streets."

Demands of the Blacks: Changes in Substance and Methods

The period from the late 1950's to the mid-1970's has witnessed an impressive growth in the still evolving role of California's black population—from a minority that felt itself essentially a victim of injustice to a highly activated community at the center of the state's political life. This change in political role has been reflected not only in the methods by which the nearly 2 million blacks have pressed their demands on the majority of the population, but also in the responsiveness of California's institutions to these demands.

The Watts riots of 1965 symbolize the most dramatic turning point in both black and white consciousness of the basic problems. Before 1965, black community demands concentrated mainly on integration issues in schools and housing and on basic civil rights such as voting and fair employment practices. The main methods of pursuing social justice were through court litigation and nonviolent demonstrations against local laws and institutions that were seen to perpetuate racial segregation. Most Californians believed that their state had one of the most progressive civil rights records in the country, both in the degree of integration and upward social mobility being achieved; there were more black doctors and lawyers per capita than in other states and also more blacks who owned their own homes. A drive through the tree-lined streets of Watts in south-central Los Angeles, with its pleasant pastel stucco homes and well-kept lawns, seemed to show that "ghetto" was an outdated concept for the sprawling, racially homogeneous clusters radiating from the central core of the California metropolis.

But then suddenly in August 1965, Watts—of all places—exploded in violence, setting a pattern that was followed in subsequent summers in other California communities and in the ghettos of the older Eastern cities. Blacks took to the streets in marauding bands, looting stores, setting fires, exchanging gunfire with policemen, and sniping at firemen.

The shock had a temporary galvanizing effect. Study commissions uncovered the "new" facts about real poverty conditions in California, facts previously hidden behind aggregate statistics. A close look at county welfare budgets showed that millions of dollars were being allocated each month to pockets of jobless persons crowded into Watts and similar areas in San Diego, San Francisco, and Oakland. The fact that the houses were farther apart than the tenements in Harlem often belied the fact that the conditions inside were crowded and impoverished.

Special measures were recommended: new job-creating and skill-expanding programs on the part of both government and private industry to reduce unemployment; more hiring of black teachers in the public schools; greater pressure on labor unions to integrate their memberships; and, in response to minority group charges of police brutality and unfair patterns of selective law enforcement, programs to improve police-community relations. But the massive programs to build needed housing, schools, hospitals, neighborhood centers, and transportation facilities, which had been recommended by prominent black leaders, did not gain sufficient backing; and in 1966 a conservative backlash to the growing militancy of the poor brought to power a governor pledged to reduce public expenditures.

Although in the following years no single outbreak of violence approached the dimensions of the Watts riots, the sense of relative deprivation was mobilized from San Diego to Oakland by a new generation of militant "black power" leaders talking the language of revolution. Although the majority of black Californians still identified with the NAACP and the Urban League philosophies of racial integration, young blacks increasingly looked to self-styled Leninists of the Black Panther party for their heroes.

By the late 1960's the immediate demands had changed from civil rights to economic redistribution—*to* the black community and its own leaders for subsequent allocation among their own people. The long-term goal changed in emphasis from integration to black independence from the larger society and its political system. The preferred tactics changed from litigation and peaceful sit-ins to coercive confrontations against "the system," often involving threats and acts of symbolic violence. The underlying strategy was designed to frighten the dominant white community rather than to appeal to its sense of justice and reason.

The California black community, however, showed itself to be no more capable of unity than other movements in the state. Factionalism was high among the militants—some wanted to pursue a go-it-alone black nationalist policy, others advocated pragmatic "popular front" alignments with other disadvantaged groups. Moreover, the revolutionary pressure from the black "left" had the effect of opening up more opportunities for black moderates to participate in the mainstream of California politics and government—in part, because the conscience of many Californians *was* aroused; in part, because of white fears of a radicalization of the whole black community if greater opportunities for integration and participation were denied them.

The result of this interplay of forces has been a renewed reliance by blacks on the electoral process to obtain positions of power and status and to bring pressure on government programs. The first major statewide breakthrough was the election of Wilson Riles as superintendent of public instruction in 1970. The lieutenant governor's office was captured by a black, Mervyn Dymally, in the 1974 elections. Probably the most impressive gain thus far has been the election of Tom Bradley as mayor of Los Angeles in 1973 (a spectacular comeback after being defeated in his 1969 mayoralty bid). Bradley was able to win in a city with a black population of only 18 percent. After only two years in office he was being touted as a possible gubernatorial or vice-presidential candidate. Other powerful black elected officials include Assemblyman Willie Brown, Jr., and two members of the California congressional delegation: Ron Dellums of Berkeley and Yvonne Brathwaite Burke of Los Angeles.[1]

[1] Even the Black Panthers have been attempting the electoral route to power. Panther leader Bobby Seale lost in the 1973 race for mayor of Oakland, but the Panther organization demonstrated con-

But many antisystem militants remain skeptical of the tangible gains that victories by black politicians will bring to the black community at large. In percentage black unemployment is still higher than white unemployment. There are continuing complaints that the state welfare programs have rules and are administered so as to deny blacks equitable benefits. And there are persistent cries of discrimination at the hands of the institutions of law enforcement and corrections. The Robin Hood aura accorded by many young blacks and whites to recent exploits of the Symbionese Liberation Army (especially their capture of Patricia Hearst in 1974 and their food-for-the-poor ransom demands) is a symptom of the persisting frustrations of the militant activist population. The *SLA* demonstrates the explosive potential of the upwelling of bitterness that results from a conviction that substantial progress is not being made in the alleviation of perceived socioeconomic disadvantages.

Emergence of Chicano Consciousness

Though more numerous than the state's blacks, Californians of Mexican ancestry have, until recently, been more sluggish in their quest for social justice. The "Chicanos" (the name itself expresses their newfound self-image) constitute 14 percent of the population, and are clustered mainly in the farm belt and in East Los Angeles. Their average standard of living is well below that of the whites and somewhat lower than that of the blacks.

The best-known Californian of Mexican ancestry is Cesar Chavez, head of the United Farm Workers (UFW). It would be incorrect to characterize Chavez simply as a Chicano leader. The UFW is a labor union composed of farm workers of various ethnic backgrounds, and Chavez is dedicated to improving the lot of them all. But because a large number of the workers are Mexican-American, the union's activities are of interest to the Chicano community, and

---

siderable skill at the various traditional political tasks of voter registration and mobilization.

Bystanders view the remains of the SLA shoot-out in South Los Angeles in which the leader of this movement was killed. Los Angeles Times *photo.*

Chavez has become a symbol of their rising influence in the politics of California, and in the United States generally.

A firm believer in nonviolence, Chavez has relied on peaceful work stoppages by the union and nationwide boycotts of the locally grown products to gain leverage on the growers to obtain economic gains for the farm workers. The growers' counter strategy has been to break the hold of Chavez and the UFW on the supply of farm labor by refusing to deal with the UFW as the sole bargaining agent. The first round, featuring a five-year nationwide boycott of California-grown grapes, was won by Chavez when the growers in 1970 reluctantly signed agreements with the UFW. Since then, however, the Teamsters, with grower encouragement, have attempted to move in and supplant the UFW as organizers of the farm workers. Struggling to survive, the

UFW in 1973, with AFL-CIO backing, began another nationwide boycott—this time against lettuce, grapes, and
Gallo wines. Anti-UFW moves have also taken the form of
efforts to legislate prohibitions against such "secondary"
boycotts. As of this writing, Chavez's latest confrontation
with the Teamsters and growers is at a stalemate; yet he remains a genuine folk hero and inspiration to the Chicano
community.

Many young Chicanos, however, are more ethnocentric
than Chavez, and through organizations like the Brown
Berets and the La Raza Unida Party are attempting to emu-
late the militant tactics of the various black nationalist
groups. The Chicanos had their own "mini-Watts" in East
Los Angeles in August 1970, in which Ruben Salazar, *Los
Angeles Times* columnist and news director of KMEX-TV,
was killed. Police disruption of a Chicano moratorium
march of 20,000 protesting the Vietnam war led to the violence, which in turn provoked a virtual police occupation of
the area for over a month. Tensions between law enforcement officials and residents still remain high.

Like the blacks, increasing numbers of Chicanos are
now opting for participation in the electoral process. Although the barrier against Mexican-Americans holding major elective office was broken by Edward Roybal's election to
Congress in 1962 from a multiracial district in Central Los
Angeles, some of the more militant Chicano elements
tended to regard this distinguished liberal Democrat as a
sellout to the white establishment. Today, however, the
pendulum seems to be swinging back toward participation
in the system, as militants see the possibilities for winning
more elections in districts with majority Chicano popula-
tions. In 1972 three Mexican-Americans were elected to the
state assembly, bringing their total in that body to five, and
stimulating the formation of the Chicano Caucus headed by
Assemblyman Richard Alatorre. The new Chicano political
muscle is reflected in increasing pressure on the major parties to include Chicanos in their statewide slates. As with
the blacks, the next few years will be a time of testing for
California's Chicanos—testing the system to see if it can be
truly responsive to their rising demands for better treatment.

Cesar Chavez at the signing of a contract that gave farm workers a pay raise and freed most of California table grapes from world-wide boycott. *Wide World Photos.*

Not all Californians with Latin characteristics are of Mexican ancestry—for example, the state's 100,000 Puerto Ricans, and its smaller Filipino community—but they are often lumped by the majority community with the Chicanos, and have suffered similar disadvantages in employment and status. For this reason some leaders of these various communities have suggested joining forces with the Chicanos; but as yet no meaningful all-Latin coalition has emerged.

Other Minorities

Californians of Asian ancestry, numbering some 500,-000, have been systematically denied equality of opportunity at various periods in the state's history—the Chinese in the last decades of the nineteenth century, and the Japanese during World War II. But apart from the sporadic flare-up of youth militancy in these communities, most of the efforts by the oriental ethnic groups to better their conditions thus far have been through highly circumspect civic organizations like the Japanese-American Citizens League.

The original Californians, the Indians, are on most indexes of relative deprivation the most badly treated of the state's minorities. When the Spaniards ruled California the Indians were at least regarded as part of the socioeconomic structure, although their culture was suppressed within the mission system. Under American rule, however, all Indians were deprived of their lands and were forceably confined to reservations where they became wards of the national government. Today California's approximately 90,000 Indians have the highest infant mortality and alcoholism rates, and the lowest average age of death of any ethnic group; and though those who wish to are being encouraged to leave their reservations and become assimilated into the dominant culture, their actual opportunities for full entry into the majority community remain severely limited. Only lately, beginning in the early 1970's, have these "forgotten Americans" begun to seek ways of pressuring the larger society to rectify the historic inequities foisted on them. The Indian symbolic occupation of Alcatraz Island, like the confrontation at Wounded Knee, South Dakota, was an early sign of the inevitable growth of militancy among the Indians.

Age-Group Grievances and Demands

Californians in their late teens and early twenties were perhaps the greatest energizers of what became a worldwide youth movement in the late 1960's, which in turn stimulated a conservative backlash in this state. The elimination of social injustice generally, whatever its specific manifestation, became the overriding cause of activist youth, and "the system" (an amorphous monster appearing in the guise of a university administration here, the Pentagon there), the omnipresent enemy. This turn from cooperation with adults and moderate forces in the civil rights movement to a more totalistic rejection of the values of their parents and the established institutions of society can be traced to the 1964 Free Speech Movement at Berkeley. The ostensible demands of the relatively affluent under-thirty generation of California have been for the betterment of the more disadvantaged groups in society (and in this the youth were undoubtedly sincere), but there were also demands—equally insistent—that the power to make the decisions on who should get what, when, and how should be transferred to these upper-middle-class young people. This characteristic of the youth movement, when combined with a sometimes reckless provocation of law and order elements, tended to generate a standoffishness on the part of various minority groups whose causes the youth wanted to champion. Consequently, their hope of leading a broad-based coalition for social justice fizzled; and by the middle 1970's, in the context of inflation and a tightening job market, the college-age youth appeared to be returning to the more "serious" business of completing their formal schooling and preparing for adult careers in the system.

At the other end of the age spectrum, inflation has intensified demands for greater social justice. Many Californians over sixty are on fixed pensions, and thus particularly vulnerable to steeply rising prices. An elderly couple who have no outside income other than their social security checks live very close to the poverty line—indeed, an estimated 15 percent of the elderly are now below it. In a fashion reminiscent of the Townsend movement of the middle 1930's, California's senior citizens are again becoming more militant, pushing for better medical care, nursing home inspection, better housing, and more public transportation; and a "Grey Panthers" organization has formed in Berkeley. Neither major political party can afford to ignore their demands, for 13 percent of California's population is now over sixty, and longer life expectancy plus the recent slowing of the birthrate points to an even higher percentage of over-sixties by the end of the decade.

Cumulative Implications for Politics and Government

Uncompromising insistence by each particular group that social justice requires that priority be given to the rectification of *its* disadvantages may seriously strain the capacity of the existing system of politics and government. If the preferences and grievances of the various groups, however legitimate, are translated into nonnegotiable ultimatums, with the threat of pulling out of the system or bringing it down if one's demands are not satisfied, then the process of representative democracy cannot function. The process is based on minority rights *and* majority rule, and therefore requires (1) an ability of various groups to compromise with one another in order to achieve an adequate consensus; (2) their willingness to accept some decisions that temporarily go against their preferences in order to achieve the greater and more lasting benefits of constructive participation in the system; and (3) the willingness of majorities to respond to the needs of minorities partly on grounds of social justice, not simply on the basis of the political power of this or that minority group.

Without such mutual restraint and mutual responsiveness between minorities and majorities, the formal system of representative democracy would exist only on paper; and decisions would be made primarily on the basis of who had the most raw power and/or willingness to make things messy for other people. Even if public order were imposed by groups temporarily in control of society, the apparent domestic tranquility would be largely a sham and ultimately very unstable, since it too would rest on raw power rather than on a consensus on the legitimacy of the system.

At the end of the 1960's and in the early 1970's, it appeared as if the conditions of the balance between minorities and majorities in California were being seriously undermined, and an untenable choice was emerging between anarchy and authoritarianism. But the increasing turn toward electoral strategies by the state's minorities in recent years appears to have given the normal processes of politics and government a new lease on life.

PRACTICAL DIFFICULTIES IN ACHIEVING SOCIAL JUSTICE: THE WELFARE PROGRAM

Probably the most important means available to the state for attempting to alleviate the disadvantages suffered by various groups has been the program of welfare relief payments directly to individuals unable to draw an adequate income because of disability, age, the need to care for dependent children, or simply the unavailability of employment. Aid to individuals within clearly specified categories of need, rather than to ethnic groups per se, has seemed the most equitable procedure and the one most likely to avoid intergroup resentments.

Because of the numbers of individuals in need, the program turned out to be very expensive, and many citizens who were required to contribute to the program but were not its direct and immediate beneficiaries began to develop resentments against those whom they felt were taking undue advantage of the opportunities to receive income while not working. At the beginning of the 1970's about 2.25 million Californians were on the state's welfare rolls, with cash grant payments running at $160 million per month.

Governor Reagan was among those who felt the financial costs far outweighed the benefits and led an aggressive move for reform, terming the problem the "welfare monster." He appointed a special task force to find out what was wrong and prescribed tightening eligibility standards, closing possible legal loopholes that might lead to abuse, strengthening family responsibility, requiring "employable" welfare recipients to seek work, increased enrollment in job training, and increased assistance to the truly needy.

The final result of the task force report was the Welfare Reform Act of 1971, which though somewhat modified by legislative action, nevertheless carried out most of the governor's proposals. The key provisions focused on reducing the number of persons on the Aid to Families with Dependent Children (AFDC) and particularly the unemployed father rolls. Previous state eligibility standards for allowances were tightened and the administration was authorized to strengthen employment registration requirements and job search programs. The act authorized the attachment of wages and property liens against absent parents of AFDC children.

Under the terms of the new law, AFDC-unemployed recipients were required to accept employment when offered, to enroll in a job training program, or to take part-time work in a community work force or lose their grants. The most publicized aspect of the program was the Community Work Experience Program, which Governor Reagan termed "a practical and sensible way" to reduce welfare dependency. However, critics have labeled this program as nothing more than slave labor as recipients were paid only the amount of their welfare grant.

The new bill contained procedures for double checking the outside earnings of welfare recipients. A computerized system was set up using social security numbers of registered recipients; with county and state cooperation a search was made for any discrepancies that would result in disqualification for payments. Early test runs showed that many welfare recipients had been receiving outside income beyond limits and should have been removed from the rolls.

The bill also contained provisions designed to help those who were in real need. Appropriations were increased for job opportunity programs in state and local government, child care services, and family planning services.

Considerable savings in the welfare budget were realized in the first two years following the passage of the Welfare Reform Act. Governor Reagan pointed to this reform as one of the major achievements of his administration. The Nixon administration was so impressed that Robert Carleson, the director of California's social welfare program, was employed by the Health, Education, and Welfare Department in Washington to assist other states in the solution of their social welfare problems.

However, there had been considerable controversy over social welfare legislation for many years, and the 1971 act was bound to become the eye of the storm. Some government officials and many of the social-work professionals maintained that the provisions of the bill created undue hardships upon many deserving people. Critics of the program pointed out the alleged budgetary savings to the state would have come about without this new act, as improved business conditions in 1972 and 1973 would have decreased the number of persons on relief anyway. Not surprisingly, there has been difficulty implementing the act of 1971. (Welfare legislation is in any case highly complex and detailed and involves both state and local governments in the administration of financial assistance to several different classes of recipients.)

Additionally, the act came under heavy attack in state and federal courts as to its legality. The first of many law suits was filed within one month after the passage of the bill by the Alameda Legal Aid Society. A whole battery of court challenges were issued charging that the state had not complied with federal regulations. The state supreme court as well as several superior courts issued restraining orders holding up certain actions of the welfare administration. Court suits dealt with matters such as discrimination in payments to working mothers, earnings of stepfathers, payments to the blind and disabled, and unfair penalties for welfare recipients who have been able to find part-time work. The endless numbers of court cases have handicapped the enforcement of the act. In 1974 the state supreme court invalidated two regulations of the Department of Social Welfare which had reduced benefits in the aid-to-needy-children program. This was viewed as a significant setback to the program.

With many of the provisions of the 1971 Welfare Reform Act still subject to court interpretation and with a change in governors, the future effectiveness of California's welfare program as an instrument of social justice remains in doubt.

ECONOMIC GROWTH AND THE QUALITY OF LIFE

Probably the deepest challenges to the state's political and governmental system emanate from the recent collapse of the assumption of abundance, which for over a century underlay "the California phenomenon." There was enough room for everybody and plenty of natural resources just waiting to be exploited, so *everybody come!* The more who came, the more dwellings and roads would be built, the more land would be cultivated, the more local industries would proliferate, the more diversified the economy would become, with a greater number and variety of jobs—a steadily expanding economic pie, and a bigger slice of the good things of life for each person.

In the late 1940's, smog began to cast a pall over this sunny outlook. Large-scale organizational and technical campaigns of smog control were launched, but suggestions that something more fundamental than inefficient fuel consumption was the problem and that some drastic changes

Oil from leak in an off-shore well being corralled by log boom at the entrance to Santa Barbara harbor, February 1969. *Wide World Photos.*

in California life-style might be required were winked at—albeit with a smarting eye—by most people.

In the growth-oriented 1950's and 1960's the Sierra Club tried to alert citizens to the depletion of California's forests and wildlife, and the journal *Cry California* featured articles on the ecological effects of unrestrained land and coastal use, but these remained isolated shouts in the wilderness.

Then, early in 1969, Californians were shocked out of their complacency by an 800-square-mile oil slick caused by a leak in the Union Oil Company's rig in the Santa Barbara Channel. Staring into the ugly blotch of oil despoiling prized beaches from Goleta to Oxnard was like looking at a giant Rorschach test and confronting one's guilt for excessive hedonism. Suddenly the deeper causes of neglect became a popular preoccupation, and politicians tried to top one another in demonstrating concern over "the environment." Bumper stickers began to demand "Support a Lesser Los Angeles." In Palo Alto voters elected a "slow growth" majority to the city council in April 1970. In 1971, a Ralph Nader study group on California charged that public officials were "prostituting" themselves to land developers in overexploiting desert, mountain, and seacoast land.[2] The Nader charges were heatedly denied by state officials; but in March 1972 the state's own official Environmental Quality Study Council warned that population increases were severely taxing California's resources, and predicted that if the existing lack of attention to environmental impacts persisted, "our posterity will inherit a vast wasteland."[3]

On top of this rise in ecological consciousness came the energy "crisis" of 1973–74, calling into question the state's special dependence on the automobile (in California, mobility has been virtually a synonym for development) and further challenging our consumption-oriented way of life.

Today, most Californians grant the truth of the principle that the general welfare requires striking a proper balance between growth and the quality of life. But efforts to elaborate this principle in the form of specific transportation services, air pollution control, and land and coastal use are highly controversial, and are likely to generate deep cleavages in the body politic for years to come.

The Energy-Use Issue

Although suddenly dramatized by the Arab oil embargo in the Arab-Israeli war of 1973 and the associated price hike by OPEC, California local officials, environmentalists, and public utility companies have been aware for years of an impending energy use issue. California alone accounts

[2] Robert C. Fellmeth, *Politics of Land: Ralph Nader's Study Group Report on Land Use in California* (New York: Grossman, 1973).

[3] "Pollution Called California Peril," *New York Times,* March 26, 1972.

for about 4 percent of the world's total energy consumption; transportation by itself takes 36 percent of the state's energy use. The internal combustion engine is only 25 percent efficient, yet Californians continue to be addicted to cars with higher speeds and more air conditioning. Moreover, most of the current air pollution control devices further decrease the efficiency of auto fuel consumption.

Compared with most other states, California relies to a relatively high extent upon oil and gas for residential and industrial use. Other fuel sources such as coal, hydro-electric power, nuclear power, and geothermal energy are presently contributing less than 14 percent of the total supply. Although California is an oil producer, its wells now supply about three-fourths of the oil and only one-fourth of the natural gas required in the state. As demand for energy grows—recent projections indicate a doubling from 1973 to 1985—California will probably have to import as much as 80 percent of its petroleum supply. There is a large supply of oil offshore, but the costs of developing it are very high. Furthermore, the public, remembering the Santa Barbara oil spill, is wary of the threat such development would pose to coastal ecologies. Nor will the Alaskan oil pipeline be of much help, as it will be constructed to deliver oil to the Midwest and the East.

Hydropower now supplies about 9 percent of the state's total primary energy. A substantial increase from this source is doubtful, as there are very few desirable dam sites left and conservationists are opposed to further development of rivers for this purpose. Geothermal energy from steam beneath the earth is now being utilized on a small scale from Sonoma County geysers, but so far utility companies have not considered it an important source of energy and thus development has been slow. Though there are several ways of securing energy directly from sunlight, solar energy has not yet been developed on a large scale. Research is expanding and this source eventually may provide large quantities of energy in a clean and efficient manner. But it appears that solar energy will not become a significant factor in California's supply for at least ten years.

Recently, there has been considerable interest in development of nuclear power. Southern California Edison Company has successfully operated a nuclear power plant for the last several years at San Onofre. This company and other private and public utilities have planned several additional nuclear plants at various locations in the state. However, such programs have been delayed because of the risks in the use of core-cooling systems and the disposition of radioactive nuclear wastes. Ralph Nader and other environmentalists have filed a suit to prevent further operations of nuclear plants until the safety problem is solved. There is also concern that the supply of uranium might be quickly exhausted unless a new type of equipment can be developed. Many believe, however, that these problems will be overcome and that nuclear power will become a major source of power within the next twenty years.

As early as 1965 the state legislature established a Power Plant Siting Committee to locate all new locations for power plants. Several state agencies, including the Public Utilities Commission (which regulates privately owned gas, electric, water, and communications utilities), State Lands Commission, Resource Agency, Division of Oil and Gas, California Coastal Zone Conservation Commission, and Office of Planning and Research, have participated in various studies and actions concerning the energy problem. The Rand Corporation and the Stanford Research Institute each made significant studies in 1972. The Rand report recommended a slowdown in nuclear power expansion and urged steps to develop solar energy and geothermal reserves. In contrast, SRI advocated a rapid expansion of nuclear generation equipment in preference to exploiting solar and geothermal sources. As a result of these efforts, in 1974 the legislature passed and the governor signed the Energy Resources Conservation and Development Act. Perhaps without precedent in the United States, this legislation established a powerful state commission to control the use and development of all existing and potential California energy resources. The five-member commission must certify all new power plant sites, set minimum operating efficiency standards for all appliances, prescribe per unit energy requirement allotments based on square footage of various classes of buildings, and develop plans to deal with future energy shortages. A one-tenth of a mil per kilowatt hour surcharge on all electricity sold in the state (50 cents per household each month) supplies money for the work of this new commission. The new act became operative January 1, 1975.

While California has not yet been subject to a true energy crisis, the state is indeed experiencing an "energy crunch." Faced with a tight supply situation in fuel oil, gasoline, and natural gas, the problem will get worse before it gets better. The real crunch will be felt by public officials. On the one side they will be pressured by utilities confronted with declining supplies, and on the other side by the environmentalists who want to slow nuclear power generation and protect the natural resources of the state. But the utilities and environmentalists alike have come to appreciate the need for *some* conservation of energy. Conservation means reduced consumption by someone, which is unpopular with those asked to sacrifice. Can the democratic process respond to this challenge?

Transportation Issues

Extensive and efficient transportation has been essential to the economic growth of this vast state; at the same time it has been a part of the problem of runaway growth, as manifested in the issues of energy use, air pollution control, and land use.

In the first third of this century, California had a well-developed system of railways. Major cities had extensive streetcar lines. In Northern California the electric trains of the Southern Pacific, the Key System, and the Sacramento Northern Railway connected San Francisco with many communities of the Bay region. In Southern California the Pacific Electric was hailed as the world's largest and best interurban railroad, in 1930 operating 88 trains daily in each direction from downtown Los Angeles to Glendale, 109 to Pasadena. Northern California was connected to Southern California by almost a dozen daily passenger trains on the Southern Pacific and Santa Fe, and the state was tied to the rest of the nation by three transcontinental railways.

At the same time Californians were turning to a more individualized and seemingly convenient method of transit

—the automobile. In 1910 the voters adopted the first of a number of bond issues for a system of paved state highways. In the 1920's the legislature began to levy a tax on gasoline to help pay for the new roads. And in 1938 the people added Article XXVI to the state constitution requiring that all tax revenue from motor fuels be spent only for the building and maintaining of streets and highways.

After World War II, however, public transportation systems were allowed to deteriorate with no effort being made to replace them; service became less and less frequent, while fares increased; line after line was discontinued. By 1963, hardly a single streetcar, except San Francisco's cable cars, was operating in California. Today motor buses are supposed to provide the public with the mobility once gained from streetcars and trains, but the luckless passenger often has to wait an hour in the hot sun on a noisy street corner for his bus; and in many areas there is no public transportation at all.

Nor has the private automobile proved itself the gift of the gods which it appeared to be in the early 1900's. There are some 17 million registered motor vehicles in the state—more than one for every two persons. If these cars were spread out evenly on California's 150,000 miles of streets and roads, a steady flow of traffic might be possible. But the cars, of course, are not evenly distributed at all; they are bunched together in the state's nine metropolitan areas containing 90 percent of the population. Add to this the one million tourist autos pouring in each year, and the severity of California's traffic headache is readily seen. Every public event—football game, parade, department store sale, and even Easter church service—generates an exasperating traffic jam. And during the morning and evening rush hours of working days, whole cities commute by automobile.

POSSIBLE SOLUTIONS   There has been a widespread view that the solution of the traffic problem was simply to build more freeways. Thus, after World War II, the state launched a huge freeway construction program, financed by taxes on motorists. Although a substantial improvement, both in terms of commuter time saved and diminished accident rates (1.22 accidents per million miles on freeways compared with 2.95 on other state highways [4]), the new freeways have provided only a small opening in the traffic bottleneck. Often between the start of construction of a freeway and the cutting of the ribbon at its dedication the increase in the volume of traffic in the locality has made the new facility inadequate. Even the Los Angeles four-level interchange—the most elaborate of its kind—is a victim of its own efficiency. The nearly 350,000 vehicles passing through the interchange every twenty-four hours jam up traffic for two or three miles in several directions many times each day. One prominent commuter, former County Supervisor Warren Dorn of Pasadena, described the Pasadena Freeway as the "world's longest parking lot." [5]

Undaunted, the state Department of Public Works in 1959 recommended a comprehensive system of freeways that by 1980 would connect every section of the state with 12,000 miles of concrete ribbon, touching almost every town with a population of more than 5000. The motorist in a hurry to reach San Francisco from Los Angeles would have his choice of five routes, and the nature lover would be able to cross the Sierra Nevada in about ten different places. The legislature acted to implement this recommendation by passing the Collier Master Plan for Freeways, which established the California freeway and expressway system and incorporated into it practically all of the important state highways then in operation or projected for the next twenty years.

But as the *Los Angeles Times* declared editorially in 1966, "in recent years . . . it finally has become apparent that no amount of new freeways could ever completely solve our overall transportation problem." [6] The energy shortage of 1973–74 further exposed the inanity of bumper-to-bumper rush-hour clogs on the freeways, car after car carrying only one person—the driver. In addition, environmentalists are no longer alone in their complaint that the freeways are turning California into a "concrete desert."

Not surprisingly, demands are rising for a new system

[4] *California Statistical Abstract, 1958* (Sacramento: State Printing Office, 1958), p. 250.
[5] *Los Angeles Times*, January 15, 1959, p. 1.
[6] *Los Angeles Times*, November 9, 1966, Part II, p. 4.

of public mass transportation. This brings forward other issues: What means of transportation should be used— buses? trains on fixed rails? vehicles operated on air cushions? How shall the routes be determined? And above all, who should pay for it—the property owner through higher real estate taxes? the automobile user through higher gasoline taxes or license fees? or the general public through increased sales or income taxes?

In 1970, strong campaigns were mounted to spend some of the federal and state highway funds (raised by taxes on motor fuels) for public transit systems. This proposal aroused powerful opposition by the automobile clubs, oil companies, and highway construction firms. Proposition 18 on the California ballot in November 1970 would have amended the state constitution to permit some of the state gasoline taxes to go to public transportation. The measure was overwhelmingly defeated after a well-financed opposition campaign. However, the energy crisis of 1973–74 apparently convinced many people of the urgency of public transit, as the voters in the June primary of 1974 adopted Proposition 5, permitting diversion of a portion of the motor fuels taxes to mass public transit. Meanwhile, Congress adopted an act allowing some of the federal gasoline tax funds to be spent for the same purpose.

Probably the fastest way of improving public transportation in California cities is to upgrade existing bus lines. In various parts of the state, county boards of supervisors and city councils have voted large subsidies to their local bus systems in order to expand their service and reduce their fares. The Southern California Rapid Transit District (SCRTD), operating the buses in metropolitan Los Angeles, had maintained a complicated and annoying system of zones in setting its fares; in April 1974, a single, uniform rate of twenty-five cents was established. The city of Simi established a five-cent fare. Furthermore, in Los Angeles County federal and state monies were used to build a busway, that is, a lane was added to the San Bernardino Freeway for the exclusive use of buses. To make the busway effective, certain lanes in the streets of downtown Los Angeles have also been reserved for bus traffic.

Proponents of rapid mass transit hold that buses, although very necessary in any comprehensive transportation

A Bay Area Rapid Transit (BART) train zips along an elevated section of tracks in Oakland. *Wide World Photos.*

system, cannot do the job of moving large numbers of people over the long distances of our great metropolitan areas. They argue that only some kind of fixed guideway system—two-rail, monorail, air-cushion, etc.—will meet the need. The San Francisco Bay region has led the way in building such a system. In 1962 the voters in San Francisco, Alameda, and Contra Costa counties created the Bay Area Rapid Transit District (BART) by approving a $792-million bond issue. The directors of BART decided on the traditional system of cars with steel wheels riding on steel rails, but with the cars operated automatically by computers. The entire system was expected to be completed by July 1, 1971, at a cost of $995.9 million, the debt to be paid off by fares and by a special sales tax levied throughout the district.

These targets were missed by a wide margin. The cost has mushroomed to $1.3 billion and it was not until September 1974 that BART trains began to run between Oakland and San Francisco under the Bay (although limited service between Oakland and Fremont began in the fall of 1972). In addition, the computers proved quite fallible, on one occasion allowing a train to run off the track at the end of the line at Fremont, and a few months later stalling a train in the tunnel under San Francisco Bay. Much time and money has been spent in developing a back-up system whereby human motormen can countermand the automatic equipment to prevent similar accidents. However, as Harre W. Demoro points out in the *California Journal:* "Despite the problems, the designers, builders, and administrators of BART have nonetheless produced the first totally new rapid-transit system in the United States since Philadelphia opened its Market Street subway in 1907." Among BART's specific accomplishments, Demoro particularly emphasizes the following:

1. a 3.6-mile underwater tube was laid, without serious trouble, in a trench on the floor of San Francisco Bay;
2. subways were built through the hearts of three cities (where downtown streets were turned into ditches 100 feet deep);
3. thirty-eight stations are either finished or nearing completion, and each has been praised for its design;
4. the rapid-transit cars, in spite of the "bugs," furnish a smooth, fast, comfortable ride;
5. the number of riders for its limited service is about 97 percent of what it is estimated the lines will serve when the system is in full operation.[7]

On the other hand, rapid transit in Southern California is still in the planning stage. The legislature created the Southern California Rapid Transit District in order to build an adequate system for the region. In 1968 the voters of the district rejected a bond issue of $2.5 billion to build an eighty-nine-mile rail system. In 1973 Thomas Bradley was elected mayor of Los Angeles on a platform stressing rapid

[7] "What BART Can Teach Los Angeles," *California Journal* IV, 10 (October 1973): 325–29.

transit. Urged by the mayor and impelled by the energy crisis, the directors of the SCRTD placed on the November 1974 ballot a proposal for a special 1 percent sales tax, one half of the money to go for immediate expansion of the bus system and the other half to go into a fund to build 145 miles of high-speed transit lines. In addition, the SCRTD expected to receive several billion dollars of subsidies from the state and federal governments. Mayor Bradley appointed Thorton Bradshaw, president of Atlantic Richfield Oil Company, as chairman of a citizens' committee in support of the bond issue, which symbolized an about-face of the oil industry after 1970.

In an effort to pass Proposition A the SCRTD distributed attractive brochures and promised to establish new bus lines and furnish commuter service on the existing railroad lines while building the rapid transit system. However, it was to no avail. On November 5, 1974, the voters of the district defeated Proposition A, resistance to additional taxation during a period of economic "stagflation" being a primary cause of the negative vote. On the same day the Orange County Transit District was denied a 1 cent sales tax revenue to build a fifty-five-mile rapid transit system, the Orange county voters being more emphatic in their rejection than the inhabitants of the SCRTD. Transit leaders in Southern California then pinned their hopes on securing more funds from the state and federal gasoline taxes.

Finally, there is an attempt to rehabilitate passenger rail service between major California cities. By the early 1960's, regular passenger train service on such railroads as the Southern Pacific and Santa Fe had dwindled, the Southern Pacific running only one train daily between Los Angeles and San Francisco and that without a dining car. Air travel, although rapid, was reaching a saturation point, with airport facilities crowded and with many people finding that it took longer to drive from their homes to the airport than it did to fly between airports. Recently Congress, in an attempt to rehabilitate passenger train service, created a government corporation known as AMTRAK to operate all the passenger trains in the United States. Under AMTRAK a strenuous effort has been made to improve service and make train travel once again attractive. Though plagued with equipment problems, AMTRAK has gained much popularity, especially because of the energy crunch. The Daylight running between San Diego and Portland offers a beautiful ride along large sections of the California coast, and train service has been resumed through the San Joaquin Valley.

The Air Pollution Issue

That there might be a cruel tradeoff between industrialization and the enjoyment of clean and healthy air has expanded from a preoccupation of Los Angelenos to a statewide and now a national and worldwide concern. But even in Southern California, where the problem is three decades old, there is a reluctance to swallow the medicine of adequate control, which might mean substantial changes in life-style—particularly the automobile culture. Prior to 1970, California led the nation in attempts to clean up the air, but with the passage of amendments to the federal Clean Air Act in that year (the Muskie bill), the federal standards have become tougher, and there is much local balking at their implementation.[8] Thus a 1974 task force to Governor Reagan warned that the Los Angeles region would face "economic and social paralysis" if it implemented the transportation control plan proposed by the federal Environmental Protection Agency.[9]

EARLY ATTEMPTS AT CONTROL   In 1948, the Los Angeles County Air Pollution Control District (LACAPCD) adopted a rule that any industry setting up equipment that could emit air contaminants must first get authority from the APCD to install such equipment and must have a permit to continue to operate it. Such permits are granted only when devices for reducing the amount of pollutants emitted into the atmosphere are attached to the equipment. Under this program over 7000 kinds of devices for controlling air pollution have been installed in industrial establishments in Los Angeles County, ranging from steel mills and oil refineries to meat smokehouses.

In 1956, the Los Angeles County Board of Supervisors

[8] See Bob Simmons, "State Lags in Clearing the Air," *California Journal* IV, 10 (October 1973): 330–32.
[9] *Los Angeles Times* editorial of September 22, 1974.

Los Angeles
on a clear
day (top), on
a smoggy
day at 8 A.M.
(center), and
at 10 A.M.
(bottom).
*County of
Los Angeles
Air Pollution
Control
District*

established an "alert" system. When a concentration of pollutants reached a prescribed level, industries and citizens were notified to reduce the burning of fuel or refuse. The Air Pollution Control District was authorized to close industrial establishments if necessary, and to halt motor traffic upon a disaster-area proclamation by the governor. In 1957, Los Angeles County banned all refuse-burning in backyard incinerators and recommended a collection system instead. And the county Board of Supervisors voted in 1958 to ban the burning of fuel oils in industry for several months of the year. At present, local industries must burn only natural gas from April 15 to November 15 and at other times when adequate supplies of natural gas are available. The APCD has recently been issuing alerts to school authorities in the Los Angeles region to restrict playground activities of their pupils during periods of heavy smog concentration. Other regions of the state have set up their local authorities to combat smog, the most notable being the San Francisco Bay Area Air Pollution Control District (SFBAAPCD), which covers several counties. The SFBAAPCD has launched some of the same attacks on the murk as has the LACAPCD, and in both cases the *stationary* sources of smog have been curbed. However, many air pollution experts insist that the principal producer of smog is the motor vehicle. The automotive industry has spent millions of dollars for research on the problem, but Californians have wheezed that the efforts of Detroit have been too little and too late.

Two principal sources of automotive air pollution are (1) the "blow-by" gases coming out of the crankcase and (2) the emissions of the exhaust pipe. To reduce both big leaks the 1960 extraordinary session of the California legislature passed the Motor Vehicle Pollution Control Act. This measure created a motor vehicle pollution control board within the state Department of Public Health. The board's main function was to determine whether "suitable" devices were available for controlling the emission of air contaminants from trucks and automobiles and to order their installation on new cars sold in the state and even on some used vehicles.

Pursuant to this authority, the board directed that all new motor vehicles sold in California after April 1963 must have an approved device for reducing crankcase emissions. After 1965, all used cars had to have such an apparatus installed if and when they changed ownership.

In 1965 the federal government took increased interest in the problem of atmospheric purity, as indicated by the passage of the Federal Clean Air Act. When the law was revised in 1967, California won a victory over the automobile makers in the adoption of the "Murphy amendment," which gave the state authority to set more stringent standards for automotive emissions than prevailed in the nation as a whole.

California then moved to take advantage of this dispensation. The 1967 state legislature created the California Air Resources Board (CARB) and transferred to it the functions of the former motor vehicle pollution control board. The CARB then obtained the variance from the secretary of HEW to impose its own air purity standards in California. The 1968 legislature passed the Foran Act, which brought smog control legislation up to date and provided very stringent emission standards for all new motor vehicles, beginning in 1970.

RECENT ATTEMPTS AT CONTROL   Federal legislation enacted in 1970 requires that the automobile industry perfect a dependably smog-free engine by 1975. An expert in California's Department of Health, doubting Detroit's ability or willingness to comply with the law, proposed that gasoline-powered motors be outlawed in California. Some authorities urge the development of electric automobiles, or those driven by steam. Two gas companies have produced autos powered by natural gas.

A campaign to reduce the lead content of gasoline has had considerable success nationally as well as in the state. In 1970, the legislature required that all new 1972 car models must be able to run on fuel of ninety-one octanes or less, which means low lead or no lead gasoline could be used in all such autos.

Meanwhile, the pollution from aircraft has not been forgotten. Effective January 1, 1971, the legislature ordered all airlines to install devices on their jet planes that would reduce the vaporous rubbish spewed into the atmosphere. Under the Muskie bill, however, the federal government immediately preempted control over this matter and little has been done since.

The People's Lobby, impatient with the slow pace of the legislature, placed an initiative statute, the Clean Environment Act, Proposition 9, on the state primary ballot in June 1972. Among many other things it would have established rigid standards for the amount of lead in gasoline and stringent controls on industrial polluters. A vigorous campaign was launched against the proposition by automobile companies and oil producers, and it went down to defeat by almost a two-to-one margin.

The federal Clean Air Act sets 1977 as the deadline for local areas to achieve air quality standards. And the Environmental Protection Agency, charged with the national responsibility of implementing the Clean Air Act, has suggested that gasoline rationing be imposed on six Southern California counties during the smoggy months of May to October and that this be done as early as 1975. EPA studies have concluded that there are thirty-eight cities in the country, with Los Angeles the worst of the lot, where only severe measures to reduce auto use will be consistent with public health. EPA has called for an 80 percent reduction in vehicle miles driven in Los Angeles, and suggests that in order to accomplish this the metropolitan area impose heavy parking surcharges and major incentives to use public transportation. But the trouble with this plan, editorializes the *Los Angeles Times*, "is that Los Angeles does not yet have any significant way for people to get to work or anywhere else other than by the use of private cars." [10] The *Times* goes on to recommend a grace period, perhaps of ten years, within which Los Angeles should build a comprehensive mass public transportation system.

Land Use and Coastal Zone Issues

The growing realization that unbridled economic growth may be wasting the state's resources and degrading the quality of life translates itself most directly, and controversially, into efforts to put substantial controls on the free market in real estate, and on the utilization of land and

[10] *Los Angeles Times,* September 24, 1974.

Only God can make a tree . . . .

. . . But only man can make a buck.

Renault in the Sacramento Bee, *July 12, 1974.*
Reprinted by permission.

coastal areas. Stricter rules and property tax changes to inhibit urban sprawl, to contain industrial facilities within specially demarcated zones, to preserve various types of agricultural areas, to prevent soil erosion and other geological and ecological harms, to conserve particular types of flora and fauna, and to maintain park and recreational areas have become the order of the day. The pressures for greater control cut across the free enterprise philosophy that the operation of supply and demand, with minimum governmental intervention, will result in the most social utility. These pressures also incur the determined opposition of the state's most powerful landholders—particularly the Southern Pacific, Newhall Land and Farming Company, Shasta Forest Company, Tenneco, Inc., Tejon Ranch Company, and Standard Oil of California, who own more than 11 percent of all private landholdings in California.

Actually, nearly half of California's total land area of 100,185,000 acres is publicly owned. The federal government owns 44,394,000 acres (44.4 percent). The state owns 2,310,000 acres, and local governments 2,050,000. The huge federal holdings are mostly desert or mountainous forest areas in northern and eastern California. The 51.2 million acres that are privately owned, however, include most of the state's 1100-mile-long coastal belt and nearly all of its rich agricultural valleys.[11]

With about 85 percent of the state's population living within thirty miles of the coast, it is hardly surprising that use of the coastal zone has become such a highly-charged political matter. The issues are well illustrated by the controversies surrounding Proposition 20, the 1972 coastal zone initiative measure. Approved in the 1972 general election by 55 percent of the voters, Proposition 20 mandated a California Coastal Zone Commission to prepare an ecology plan for the California coastal zone (extending seaward for three miles and inland for five miles) to be submitted to the legislature by December 1975. While the master plan was being drawn up, anyone wishing to undertake development in the zone was required to obtain a permit from the appropriate regional commission, and permits were not to be issued unless the commission found that development "will not have any substantial adverse environmental or ecological effect."

Proposition 20 was supported by various environmental groups who formed the California Coastal Alliance, by the Sierra Club, by Senators Tunney and Cranston, and by the League of Women Voters and the Congress of California

---

[11] Fellmeth, *Politics of Land*, pp. 3–25.

PTAs, among others. But it was opposed by the California Real Estate Association, the California Chamber of Commerce, the California Manufacturers Association, the Teamsters Union, and the Building and Construction Trades Council of California. Opponents were particularly adamant against the permit system, seeing in it a moratorium on recreational development for a four-year period, and arguing that this would cause a severe economic depression in coastal counties.

In fact, however, since passage of Proposition 20 a good share of the development applications brought before the coastal zone commissions have been approved.[12] Subjected to intense political pressure, the commissions thus far appear to be acting as symbols of environmental concern rather than as real regulators of coastal zone use. It remains to be seen how forthrightly the state commission will fulfill its mandate to develop a meaningful master plan.

Prognosis

The fact that local coalitions for restrictions on economic growth lose a battle here and win a battle there should not obscure the magnitude of the change taking place in the socioeconomic climate of the state. Restricted growth has become a central issue, if not *the* central issue, in California—a development that challenges the inherited assumptions and processes of politics and government in ways only beginning to become evident.

One of the most portentous signs is the breakdown of any neat division between so-called eco-freaks and the rest

---

[12] The most controversial approval involved the proposed expansion of a nuclear power plant at San Onofre, south of San Clemente. Southern California Edison and the San Diego Gas Company wanted more reactors, and had obtained the approval of the U.S. Atomic Energy Commission, the federal Environmental Protection Agency, and the California Public Utilities Commission. The environmentalists presented their case to the coastal zone commission during the gas crisis winter of 1973–74, and—surprisingly—won out against the utilities. But, in response to subsequent protests from legislators, the press, interest groups, and irate citizens, the commission reversed itself, albeit with some stipulations to be followed by Edison and the gas company. (See Rosa Gustaitis, "The Fight Over 'Improving' the California Coastline," *Washington Post*, August 18, 1974.)

of the population. As detailed in a recent article in the *California Journal,* "The drive to limit growth and development draws at least equal force from local taxpayers more worried about the costs to them of unbridled development in their own communities than what it will do to the environment." [13]

The prospects are now large enough that the last quarter of the century will feature the dominance of a "slow growth" majority. In contrast to past eras, when politicians and public officials vied for popular approval on the basis of their ability to stimulate the expansion of the state's economy and population, the new quality-of-life goals may turn out to be the orienting philosophy of mainstream California. If so, the state could make another of its historic contributions to the substance and style of America—this time, showing the way to adapt to the stresses and strains of postindustrialism.

SELECTED REFERENCES

BARBA, SUZANNE, "The Awakening of Another Political Giant," *California Journal,* October 1974, pp. 344, 345.

California Journal, June 1973, pp. 184–208 (special report on the energy crisis).

FELLMETH, ROBERT C., *Politics of Land.* New York: Grossman Publishers, 1973.

FORBES, JACK D., "The Native American: Low Man on the Totem Pole," *California Journal,* June 1974, pp. 180–85.

HARRIS, TOM, "Californians Are Saying 'No' to Growth in a Spreading Revolt That Makes Strange Allies," *California Journal,* July 1973, pp. 224–29.

LENHART, MARIA, "All Quiet on the Campus Front," *California Journal,* October 1974, pp. 337–39.

LOFTIS, ANNE, *California, Where the Twain Did Meet.* New York: Macmillan Publishing Co., 1973.

Rand Corporation, *California's Electricity Quandary,* Santa Monica, Calif., 1972.

ZUMBURN, R., R. MOMBOISSE, and JOHN FINDLEY, "Welfare Reform: California Meets the Challenge," *Pacific Law Journal* 4, no. 2 (July 1973).

[13] Tom Harris, "Californians Are Saying 'No' to Growth in a Spreading Revolt That Makes Strange Allies," *California Journal* IV, 7 (July 1973): 224.

Index